The Taxonomy of Metacognition

Metacognition is a complex construct which is fundamental to learning. Its complex, fuzzy and multifaceted nature has often led to its colloquial application in research, resulting in studies that fail to identify its theoretical foundation or elements. In response to this, the research community continues to call for a comprehensive understanding of the construct of metacognition. This book is a response to this call for clarity.

Pina Tarricone provides a theoretical study of the construct of metacognition in terms of psychological theory. The first part of the book analyses the relationship between reflection and metacognition, and the second part goes on to analyse the construct of metamemory as the foundation of metacognition. The third and final part of the book analyses the construct of metacognition to present the final conceptual framework of metacognition and the taxonomy of metacognition. This framework builds a picture and a nexus of the construct through visual links to the related concepts that contribute to what is known as metacognition.

The Taxonomy of Metacognition provides a comprehensive representation and categorisation of all of the terms, concepts, categories, supercategories, subcategories and elements of metacognition. It clarifies the construct so that researchers and teachers can develop a better understanding of it. This important and broad ranging contribution can be applied to many related areas, by researchers, psychologists, teachers and any profession interested in psychological learning processes.

Pina Tarricone completed her Doctor of Philosophy in Educational Psychology at Edith Cowan University, Australia. Her thesis was awarded the 2007 University Research Medal, the 2007 Faculty of Education and Arts Research Medal, and the Western Australian Institute of Educational Research Postgraduate Award. She is now completing a Master of Education in Assessment, Measurement and Evaluation with the aim of utilising her theoretical work. She works as an educational consultant for government agencies, universities and industry.

The Taxonomy of Metacognition

Pina Tarricone

Ψ Psychology Press
Taylor & Francis Group
HOVE AND NEW YORK

Published in 2011
by Psychology Press
27 Church Road, Hove, East Sussex BN3 2FA

Simultaneously published in the USA and Canada
by Psychology Press
270 Madison Avenue, New York, NY 10016

*Psychology Press is an imprint of the Taylor & Francis Group, an
Informa business*

© 2011 Psychology Press

Typeset in Times by Garfield Morgan, Swansea, West Glamorgan
Printed and bound in Great Britain by TJ International Ltd, Padstow,
Cornwall
Cover design by Design Deluxe
Cover illustration © Bruce Rolff

This publication has been produced with paper manufactured to strict
environmental standards and with pulp derived from sustainable
forests.

British Library Cataloguing in Publication Data
A catalogue record for this book is available from the British Library

Library of Congress Cataloging-in-Publication Data
Tarricone, Pina.
  The taxonomy of metacognition / Pina Tarricone.
     p. cm.
  Includes bibliographical references and index.
  ISBN 978-1-84169-869-4 (hb)
  1. Metacognition. I. Title.
  BF311.T27 2011
  153–dc22

                                          2010035311

ISBN: 978-1-84169-869-4 (hbk)

Dedication

I dedicate this book to my dear parents, my father Vincenzo and my mother Tindara.

Contents

List of tables   x

List of figures   xi

Foreword   xiv

Preface   xvi

Acknowledgements   xix

1   Introduction   1

Metacognition: The first operational definition   1

*The intricate web of metacognition: Obscurity, fuzziness and
     frustration   3*

The conceptual framework of metacognition   6

The taxonomy of metacognition   7

Conclusion   9

PART I
Reflection: The quintessence of metacognition   11

2   Reflection and metacognition: Historical dialectic   13

The historical foundations of reflection   13

Dewey, reflection and problem solving   15

The synchronic interaction of reflection and reasoning   16

*Piaget's contribution to reflective thinking: Higher-order
     reasoning   17*

Piaget's theory of axiomatisation and formalisation   20

The reflective activity of reasoning and inference   21

Reflection: A dialectical process – Vygotsky and metacognition   23

*Habermas' theory of self-reflection in socially mediated
     contexts   24*

Conclusion   26

3 **Critical reflection and critical thinking: Facilitators of metacognition**   28

Critical reflection: Beyond reflection 28
Critical thinking as skilful thinking 30
Conclusion 41

4 **Reflection and metacognition: Affirming the connection**   43

Self-knowledge: Uniting reflection and metacognition 43
Conclusion 52
Conclusion to Part I 55

PART II
Metamemory: The foundational construct   57

5 **Memory monitoring and metamemory**   59

Metamemory: Early contributions and memory
monitoring 59
Conclusion 79

6 **The foundation of metamemory**   82

The foundation of metamemory: Brown, and Flavell and
Wellman 82
Conclusion 89

7 **Metamemory and its components: The basis of metacognition**   93

Categories of metamemory: Knowledge of memory and
regulation of memory 93
Conclusion 118
Conclusion to Part II 123

PART III
Metacognition: The taxonomy   125

8 **Models of metacognition**   127

Conceptual contributions to metacognition theory 127
Conclusion 152

9 **The categorisation of the taxonomy of metacognition**   155

Knowledge of cognition or metacognitive knowledge: Declarative,
procedural and conditional knowledge 155
Regulation of cognition, metacognitive skills or metacognitive
regulation 166

Other metacognition: Metacognition and affective beliefs *176*
Conclusion *181*

10 The taxonomy of metacognition   182
Analysis of higher-order assertions *182*
Conceptual framework of metacognition *187*
Taxonomy of metacognition *187*
Conclusion *214*

11 Future directions in research and conclusion   215
Research possibilities *215*
Other areas of research *218*
Conclusion *219*

References   221
Index   251

Tables

2.1   Blasi and Hoeffel's interpretation of Inhelder and Piaget's
        discussion of reflection in formal operations   18
3.1   Interpretation of Kuhn's elements of meta-knowing and
        relationship to the development of critical thinking   37
4.1   Cornoldi's components of metacognitive reflection   48
6.1   Flavell and Wellman's four broad categories of memory
        phenomena matched with Brown's taxonomy of memory   86
6.2   Flavell and Wellman's facets or varieties of metamemory
        as a foundation for the taxonomy of metacognition   87–88
7.1   Declarative metamemory in person, task and strategy
        variables   97
7.2   Procedural metamemory in task and strategy variables   101
10.1   Taxonomy of metacognition (see Tables 10.1.1–10.1.7
        for elaborations)   194–196
10.1.1 Taxonomy of metacognition: 1. Knowledge of
        cognition   197
10.1.2 Taxonomy of metacognition: 1.1 Declarative
        metacognitive knowledge   198–202
10.1.3 Taxonomy of metacognition: 1.2 Procedural
        metacognitive knowledge   203–205
10.1.4 Taxonomy of metacognition: 1.3 Conditional
        metacognitive knowledge   206
10.1.5 Taxonomy of metacognition: 2. Regulation of
        cognition   207
10.1.6 Taxonomy of metacognition: 2.1 Regulation of
        cognition and Executive functioning   208–210
10.1.7 Taxonomy of metacognition: 2.2 Metacognitive
        experiences   211–213
11.1   Metacognition and reflection research possibilities   216
11.2   Metamemory research possibilities   217
11.3   Metacognition research possibilities   219

Figures

1.1   Foundation of the conceptual framework of metacognition   7
2.1   Amplification of reasoning in the conceptual framework of
      metacognition   17
2.2   Amplification of higher-order reasoning processes in the
      conceptual framework of metacognition   20
2.3   Amplification of inferences and reasoning in the conceptual
      framework of metacognition   22
2.4   Amplification of verbalisation in the conceptual framework
      of metacognition   25
3.1   Amplification of critical reflection in the conceptual
      framework of metacognition   31
3.2   Amplification of critical thinking in the conceptual
      framework of metacognition   36
4.1   Amplification of the relationship between self-knowledge,
      consciousness and introspection in the conceptual
      framework of metacognition   46
4.2   Amplification of major contributions to metacognition in
      the conceptual framework of metacognition   49
5.1   Amplification of Corsini's cognitive operative system in the
      conceptual framework of metacognition   62
5.2   Amplification of the relationship between successful
      performance on memory tasks and memory development
      in the conceptual framework of metacognition   62
5.3   Amplification of knowledge of memory processes in the
      conceptual framework of metacognition   65
5.4   Amplification of the memory–metamemory connection in
      the conceptual framework of metacognition   70
5.5   Amplification of the metamemory and metamemory judgments
      connection in the conceptual framework of metacognition   77
6.1   Amplification of Brown's theories of knowing in the
      conceptual framework of metacognition   85
6.2   Amplification of Flavell and Wellman's metamemory taxonomy
      as interpreted in the conceptual framework of metacognition   90

7.1 Amplification of declarative metamemory in the conceptual
    framework of metacognition   99
7.2 Amplification of procedural metamemory in the conceptual
    framework of metacognition   103
7.3 Amplification diagram of the connections between
    declarative and procedural metamemory from Figure 7.1
    and Figure 7.2.   104
7.4 Nelson and Narens' model depicting the flow of information
    between the meta-level and the object-level   106
7.5 Nelson and Narens' theoretical metamemory framework   108
7.6 Amplification of regulation of memory in the conceptual
    framework of metacognition   110
7.7 Amplification of the relationship between executive
    functioning and self-awareness in the conceptual framework
    of metacognition   112
7.8 Amplification of the relationship between monitoring and
    mnemonic strategies in the conceptual framework of
    metacognition   113
7.9 Amplification of the relationship between memory
    self-efficacy and beliefs in the conceptual framework of
    metacognition   115
8.1 A model of cognitive monitoring as depicted by Flavell   131
8.2 A model of cognitive monitoring incorporating the
    additional elements of the model as suggested but not
    depicted by Flavell   132
8.3 Amplification of cognitive monitoring in the conceptual
    framework of metacognition   135
8.4 Amplification of Brown's knowledge of cognition in the
    conceptual framework of metacognition   139
8.5 Amplification of Brown's regulation of cognition in the
    conceptual framework of metacognition   143
8.6 Amplification of Borkowski and colleagues' model in the
    conceptual framework of metacognition (Part I)   148
8.7 Amplification of Borkowski and colleagues' model in the
    conceptual framework of metacognition (Part II)   149
8.8 Amplification of Kuhn's theory of meta-knowing in the
    conceptual framework of metacognition   153
9.1 Amplification of knowledge of cognition in the conceptual
    framework of metacognition   157
9.2 Amplification of declarative knowledge in the conceptual
    framework of metacognition   161
9.3 Amplification of procedural knowledge in the conceptual
    framework of metacognition   164
9.4 Amplification of conditional knowledge in the conceptual
    framework of metacognition   167

9.5   Amplification of regulation of cognition, including
      self-regulation, in the conceptual framework of
      metacognition   171
9.6   Amplification of metacognitive experiences in the conceptual
      framework of metacognition   177
9.7   Amplification of metacognitive experiences, including
      metacognitive feelings, in the conceptual framework of
      metacognition   178
9.8   Amplification of metacognitive experiences, including
      metacognitive judgments, in the conceptual framework of
      metacognition   179
10.1 The conceptual framework of metacognition – reflecting
      declarative knowledge in the final taxonomy of
      metacognition (Table 10.1)   188
10.2 The conceptual framework of metacognition – reflecting
      procedural knowledge in the final taxonomy of
      metacognition (Table 10.1)   189
10.3 The conceptual framework of metacognition – reflecting
      conditional knowledge in the final taxonomy of
      metacognition (Table 10.1)   190
10.4 The conceptual framework of metacognition – reflecting
      regulation of cognition and executive functioning in the
      final taxonomy of metacognition (Table 10.1)   191
10.5 The conceptual framework of metacognition – reflecting
      metacognitive experiences in the final taxonomy of
      metacognition (Table 10.1)   192

Foreword

On April 15, 2003, I found among my email messages one from Edith Cowan University in Australia headed 'Proposed reconceptualisation of metacognition'. One of their doctoral students was 'planning to construct a clearer conceptualisation of metacognition', which would involve a taxonomy and a conceptual framework. Good luck with that, I thought, marvelling at the audacity of the project, but I agreed to review and provide feedback on the proposal as part of ECU's formal process.

I subsequently heard from the student, whose name turned out to be Pina Tarricone, and received a copy of her proposal for a dissertation entitled 'Demystification and reconceptualisation of the intricate web of metacognition'. On May 2, prior to her defence of the proposal, I provided my evaluation:

> My main reaction is that Pina has an exceptional grasp of the enormous and heterogeneous literatures in metacognition and related areas, including an integrative framework for relating these to each other in meaningful and insightful ways. I have no doubt that she is capable of producing an excellent dissertation and should be authorised to proceed.

I did warn, however, that 'the scope of this project seems to me more like a lifetime plan than a dissertation.' I suggested that 'some portion of this project' might suffice for a dissertation. Pina thanked me graciously and profusely, multiple times, but seems to have ignored this advice. After I later agreed to serve as an outside examiner of the final dissertation, I began my March 2007 report:

> This is the most comprehensive and systematic overview of the literature on metacognition and related concepts that I have ever seen. The coverage is simply awesome. I can't think of any major theorist or topic that has been overlooked. The treatment of diverse topics and theorists, moreover, is consistently fair and accurate, and often insightful.

I didn't just recommend a doctoral degree; I recommended finding a publisher, and I'm delighted that Psychology Press is making this unique work available to students and scholars of metacognition. It will stand for years, I expect, as an unrivalled overview of the concept of metacognition, and will remain thereafter the definitive record of how psychologists thought about metacognition in the opening decade of the twenty-first century.

David Moshman
Professor of Educational Psychology,
University of Nebraska-Lincoln
June 2010

Preface

This book, *The Taxonomy of Metacognition*, is an analysis and theoretical study of the construct of metacognition in terms of psychological theory. My fascination with metacognition developed from a keen interest in understanding how people learn, know and apply their knowledge. This book is the outcome of my PhD research. When I began I planned to investigate self-system effects on metacognition during the solving of complex problems. I quickly realised, however, that my naive view of metacognition needed to be rectified if I were to knowledgeably and accurately make connections between metacognition and complex problem solving to provide a framework for an empirical study. I also realised that the fuzziness, expansiveness and complexity of metacognition limited the depth of understanding of the construct to the experts in the field. As a result, the focus changed from an empirical study to a theoretical study with the aim of clarifying the construct to provide frameworks for researchers and educators to use. This book is, therefore, a theoretical analysis of the construct of metacognition. Arguments and discussions are drawn from substantial works, whole lines of inquiry such as those of Flavell and Brown, and many other significant contributors to the theoretical development of the construct of metacognition.

The contributions this book makes rely upon extensive reading and analysis to identify the categorisations of metacognition. The expansive literature and different theoretical contributions to the construct made the task of determining what metacognition is and its processes creative and exciting, but also demanding. The process involved identifying and analysing significant contributions to the construct to determine the categories, supercategories, subcategories and elements of metacognition. This involved conscious consideration and critical reviews of theoretical frameworks, conceptual reasoning and connections. The book does not aim to provide a meta-analysis of research findings on metacognition, but an in-depth analysis and unification of the conceptual contributions to metacognition, clarifying the construct so that researchers and teachers can develop a better understanding of it. This has important implications for teaching, learning and specific research on metacognition. The book provides usable frameworks, including the *taxonomy of metacognition*, and *conceptual framework of metacognition*, which can be used by researchers, psychologists, teachers and any profession interested in psychological learning processes, especially metacognition. They provide references for researchers to obtain a better understanding of the construct, enhancing future research by distinctly identifying the categories and related concepts being investigated, including the relationship between these concepts. The work can be drawn upon and applied in any related context as its contribution is broad-ranging for it has not been written in a particular context, e.g. teacher education.

Purpose

The overall purpose is to:

- Identify the issues relating to existing theories about metacognition and identify gaps and problems and how these impact on research.
- Identify where relevant research literature has made a contribution to the development of the construct of metacognition.
- Identify where the research and theoretical literature do not reflect each other and explain why there is a need for a developed theory of metacognition.
- Apply high levels of abstraction, analysis and theory building to conceptualise the various theoretical stances of metacognition to critically describe associations and relationships between theories on metacognition.
- Develop theoretical connections presented as assertions to inform the development of the *taxonomy of metacognition*, and *conceptual framework of metacognition*.
- Develop a *taxonomy of metacognition* which is informed by the *conceptual framework of metacognition* amplification and complex diagrams.

Organisation

The book contains three main parts: Part I, Reflection: The quintessence of metacognition; Part II, Metamemory: The foundational construct; and Part III, Metacognition: The taxonomy.

Part I contains three chapters which discuss the relationship between reflection and metacognition. Part II contains three chapters which discuss the construct of metamemory as the foundation of metacognition. Part III contains four chapters which analyse the construct of metacognition to present the *taxonomy of metacognition* and the *conceptual framework of metacognition*, identifies future research possibilities, and presents the final conclusion to the book.

Analysis and assertions

Critical analyses are represented throughout the book by means of assertions. These can be described as declarations, statements, claims, affirmations, advancements or arguments which represent the analysis of the conceptual relationships made through theorisation. Within each chapter they are presented at the end of sections and subsections using Arabic numerals beginning with the relevant chapter number and increasing incrementally with each assertion, e.g. 3.1, 3.2 or 4.1, 4.2. These assertions were used as the basis for the development of the *conceptual framework of metacognition* and the *taxonomy of metacognition*.

At the end of each chapter, higher-order assertions (HOA) are identified. These represent higher-level theorising demonstrating the further conceptual analysis presented in preceding sections and subsections. The conclusion to each part provides further analysis and discussion of all the HOA in each chapter that have contributed to the development of the *taxonomy of metacognition*.

Outcomes

The book achieves the following outcomes:

- Identifies the elements, key elements, subcategories, supercategories and categories of metacognition and develops the *conceptual framework of metacognition* and *taxonomy of metacognition*.
- Identifies the relationships between metacognition and other related constructs to develop the *conceptual framework of metacognition* and the *taxonomy of metacognition*.
- Analyses the contributions to the construct of metacognition including significant theoretical contributions and relevant empirical research papers.

Acknowledgements

I am duly grateful to many who have supported this book based on my PhD thesis which aims to contribute to a better understanding of cognitive, developmental and educational psychology.

A special thank you is owed to the reviewers Professor Alison Garton, Professor David Moshman, Professor Bennett Schwartz and an anonymous reviewer for their helpful comments. I also thank Professor Anastasia Efklides, who reviewed the book proposal. I wish to express my sincere thanks to Professor David Moshman, Professor Anastasia Efklides, and Professor Peter Afflerbach for their time in expertly examining my thesis. I also thank my PhD supervisors Professor Mark Hackling and Professor Alison Garton for their feedback.

I am honoured that Professor David Moshman agreed to write a foreword to my book. He is a theorist and a significant contributor to the theoretical basis of the construct of metacognition. I believe that he is the foremost expert on epistemic cognition and its development. I look forward to his future research in this field.

Thank you to my dear friend Ken Whitbread BA(Hons)Lon who proofread my manuscript and to the editorial team at Psychology Press who were responsive to all correspondence and always very helpful.

1   Introduction

This chapter introduces the construct of metacognition and discusses the major issues surrounding it.

Metacognition: The first operational definition

'Meta' is a Greek word meaning after, behind or beyond (Zechmeister and Nyberg, 1982). Why is 'meta' added to terms such as metamemory, metacomprehension and metacognition? This has been done to signify a change in emphasis to 'knowledge about one's own cognition rather than the cognitions themselves' (Brown, 1978, p. 79). Nelson and Narens (1990) cite Carnap (1934), who used the term 'metalanguage', and Hilbert (1927), who used 'metamathematics', as examples of the early use of this term 'meta'. It also occurs in metacomprehension, metaattention, metalearning, metacommunication, metacomponents and metamemory to name a few (Biggs, 1985; Flavell, 1976; Flavell, Miller and Miller, 1993; Schraw, 2009; Sternberg, 1979). In relation to the term metamemory, Zechmeister and Nyberg (1982) explain that Flavell 'wanted to draw attention to an aspect of memory not directly related to the specific process of encoding, storage and retrieval' (p. 229).

The problem with the term is that it is difficult to distinguish clearly between what is meta and what is cognition (Baker, 1991; Brown *et al.*, 1983; Cheng, 1999). Generally, the main distinction between the two is that cognition is a 'constant flow of information' (Langford, 1986) and metacognition is knowledge and awareness of processes and the monitoring and control of such knowledge and processes (Butterfield, 1994; Efklides, 2001; Flavell, 1977; Flavell *et al.*, 1993; Langford, 1986; Schraw, 2001; Schwebel, 1986; Slife, Weiss and Bell, 1985). The main distinction between cognition and metacognition is that metacognition is considered to be 'second-order cognitions' (Kuhn, 2000a; Weinert, 1987). It is not the focus of this book, however, to delve deeply into this distinction.

The first definition of metacognition can be found in Flavell (1976). He identifies what metacognition means and then provides an example of a metacognitive process.

'Metacognition' refers to one's knowledge concerning one's own cognitive processes and products or anything related to them, e.g. the learning-relevant properties of information or data. . . . . Metacognition refers, among other things, to the active monitoring and consequent regulation and orchestration of these processes in relation to the cognitive objects or data on which they bear, usually in the service of some concrete goal or objective.

For example, I am engaging in metacognition (metamemory, meta-learning, metattention, metalanguage, or whatever) if I notice that I am having more trouble learning *A* than *B*; if it strikes me that I should double-check *C* before accepting it as a fact; if it occurs to me that I had better scrutinize each and every alternative in any multiple-choice type task situation before deciding which is the best one; if I become aware that I had better make a note of *D* because I may forget it; if I think to ask someone about *E* to see if I have it right. Such examples could be multiplied endlessly. In any kind of cognitive transaction with the human or nonhuman environment, a variety of information processing activities may go on.

(Flavell, 1976, p. 232)

In Flavell's subsequent publications (1978, 1979, 1981a, 1987), he defines and refines his definition of metacognition and supports his discussion with a model of cognitive monitoring (Flavell, 1979, 1981a). This model builds upon Flavell and Wellman's (1977) metamemory taxonomy.

Brown (1987) defines metacognition and identifies the main problems with the term:

Metacognition refers loosely to one's knowledge and control of one's own cognitive system. Two primary problems with the term are: it is difficult to distinguish between what is meta and what is cognitive; and there are many different historical roots from which this area of inquiry developed. The confusion that follows the use of a single term for a multifaceted problem is the inevitable outcome of mixing metaphors.

(p. 66)

Both Flavell's and Brown's definitions provide a foundation for identifying knowledge of cognition and regulation of cognition as the two main categories of the construct. Although there is some disagreement and confusion as to whether executive functioning and control processes should be considered to be metacognition (see Cavanaugh and Perlmutter, 1982), this categorisation is accepted and supported by other theorists (e.g. Efklides, 2008; Kluwe and Friedrichsen, 1985; Schraw, 1998; Schraw and Moshman, 1995; Tobias and Everson, 2009). This is mainly related to the difficulty in clearly distinguishing between the two components (Brown,

1981, 1987). In addition, there have been concerns that it would be difficult to distinguish clearly between the two components and that it would lead to an oversimplification of their differences. Even so there is agreement that this categorisation is necessary for clarity of the construct and for future research (Brown, 1981, 1987; Brown and Palincsar, 1982; Weinert, 1987).

The intricate web of metacognition: Obscurity, fuzziness and frustration

Metacognition is considered in the literature as a somewhat perplexing, mystifying and complex construct, one that has intrigued cognitive psychologists and educational researchers for decades (e.g. Brown, 1987; Brown *et al.*, 1983; Efklides, 2008; Flavell *et al.*, 1993; Flavell, Miller and Miller, 2002; Schraw and Moshman, 1995; Veenman *et al.*, 2006; Wellman, 1983; Yussen, 1985). The difficulty of the construct lies in its many facets and its rich conceptual history (Brown, 1987; Brown *et al.*, 1983). Brown (1987) explains that 'metacognitive-like concepts are fraught with some of the most difficult and enduring epistemological problems of psychology' (p. 66). Metacognition has been labelled as 'a buzzword', 'ill-defined', 'obscure', 'fuzzy', 'vague', 'faddish', 'messy', 'a many headed monster' and an 'epiphenomenon' but also a conceptually significant phenomenon in cognitive psychology and educational research (Baker and Brown, 1984b; Brown, 1978, 1987; Brown *et al.*, 1983; Brown and Campione, 1981; Efklides, 2008; Flavell, 1981a; Flavell *et al.*, 1993; Kitchener, 1983; Schoenfeld, 1987; Wellman, 1983). Its fuzziness is due to the multiplicity of influences and connections that constitute the construct. Wellman likens metacognition to a 'family of conceptual bedfellows' comprising 'partially synonymous constructs' (Wellman, 1983, p. 35). There is also a fuzziness and blurring of the terms metacognition and metamemory as occasionally they are used interchangeably for metamemory is used to describe aspects of metacognition and vice versa (e.g. Flavell, 1981a; Hacker, 1998; Nelson and Narens, 1990; Schneider and Lockl, 2002; Weinert, 1988; Wellman, 1983). Issues of obscurity and fuzziness surrounding metacognition have filtered through from metamemory theory. This is because the development of the construct of metacognition is based upon metamemory theory. These problems include the question of whether executive memory processes are part of metamemory, as well as knowledge of memory and secondly what roles these executive processes play in memory performance, how they interact with knowledge of memory (Cavanaugh and Perlmutter, 1982; Schneider, 1985) and whether these processes are implicit or explicit or a combination (Flavell, 1977; Kelley and Jacoby, 1996).

Researchers have commented on metacognition's multiple perspectives and understandings resulting in its complexity and variability in theory and research outcomes (Brown, 1987; Brown *et al.*, 1983; Dinsmore *et al.*, 2008; Schraw and Moshman, 1995; Schunk, 2008; Yussen, 1985). Although there have been significant attempts to clarify it and its historical roots (see Brown, 1987; Cavanaugh and Perlmutter, 1982; Flavell, 1987; Fox and Riconscente, 2008; Hacker, 1998; Langrehr and Palmer, 1998; Metcalfe, 2008; Wellman, 1983; Wellman, 1985b), the academic community continues to call for further clarification of the construct (e.g. Borkowski *et al.*, 2000; Efklides, 2001; Schraw, 2000; Schunk, 2008). This is not to say that metacognitive theory is so underdeveloped that it does not have a strong and well developed conceptual foundation. The problem lies in its different theoretical contributions, its complexity, multifacetedness and lack of a clear definition (Borkowski *et al.*, 2000; Dunlosky, 1998; Efklides, 2008; Nelson, 1998; Schraw, 2000; Tobias and Everson, 2009; Veenman *et al.*, 2006).

Defining metacognition is a 'thorny issue' and that any cognition related to knowledge and thinking could be identified as metacognition makes it difficult to provide an inclusive definition of the construct and to identify, define and isolate adequately all the specific constructs that relate and contribute to it (Flavell, 1977, 1993; Garner, 1987; Paris and Winograd, 1990). Many researchers 'eschew [the] rigid or operational definitions' that are available and prefer to refer to metacognition as 'thinking-about-thinking' and 'cognitive judgments about . . . cognitive states and abilities' (Paris and Winograd, 1990, p. 16). Other simplistic descriptions include 'mental mirroring' (Antaki and Lewis, 1986; Langford, 1986); 'thoughts about cognition' (Yussen, 1985); 'thinking your own thinking'; 'reflections on cognition' (Schoenfeld, 1987); 'thinking about thinking' (Babbs and Moe, 1983; Yussen, 1985) and 'cognition about cognition' (Georghiades, 2004; Kluwe, 1982; Wellman, 1985a). Its attractiveness and its obscurity have led to colloquial, hackneyed and often misuse of the term, resulting in studies that fail to identify clearly specific elements of metacognition, or which theoretical position they are based upon (Brown *et al.*, 1983; Cavanaugh and Perlmutter, 1982; Dinsmore *et al.*, 2008; Efklides, 2001; Schraw, 2000; Schunk, 2008). This continues to occur because researchers are not clear as to which 'head of the beast they are attacking or defending' (Brown, 1987, p. 106) and 'researchers bemoan the imprecision of the term and attribute to it those things that they feel are important about thinking and learning' (Paris and Winograd, 1990, p. 19). Examples of studies and discussion papers such as Babkie and Provost (2002), Boylor (2002), Maule (2001), Samuels and Betts (2007), and Abell (2009) do not provide the reader with any clear definition or theoretical position, such as that espoused by Flavell or Brown, in their discussion of metacognition. Many authors, such as Phillips (2003), assume that the reader has a good and shared understanding of the construct including the element(s) researched. Some authors, such as Grimes (2002), assume without thorough theoretical research that a particular element or category they have identified can easily be squeezed into the fuzzy boundaries of metacognition.

The importance of a clear theoretical framework as a foundation for research on the construct of metacognition is emphasised in the papers by Dinsmore *et al.* (2008) and Schunk (2008). Dinsmore *et al.* (2008) conducted an extensive investigation of the use of the terms metacognition, self-regulation and self-regulated learning in empirical papers and they stress how important it is for researchers to 'monitor their choice of terminology [and] control the manner in which their constructs are conceptually and operationally defined' (p. 407). Similarly, Schunk (2008) emphasises that one of the major consequences of a lack of a clear theoretical foundation is that the research is disconnected from the specific theory and from other research in the field and therefore contributes little to educational outcomes.

The fuzziness and generalisation of the construct is fuelled by the lack of theoretical models which make connections between metacognitive categories and processes. This lack is related to problems of different theoretical stances and terminology for similar metacognitive processes. Both these issues affect the identification of research categories of metacognition and the consistency between metacognitive theory and methodologies to measure and investigate metacognition (Borkowski, 1996; Efklides, 2008; Schraw, 2000, 2009). On a positive note, its fuzziness has some advantages as it still allows for and may even spur the formation of derivative theoretical constructs of increased precision.

Considering these problems, the literature and research community called for 'an integrated conceptualization' (Efklides, 2001, p. 298) of metacognition, and emphasised 'the need for a comprehensive, unified theory of metacognition' (Schraw, 2000, p. 298). Years earlier Flavell (1987) was also calling for 'deeply insightful, detailed proposals about what metacognition is, how it operates and how it develops' (p. 28). Wellman (1985b) also asked, 'What, exactly, is metacognition?' (p. 1). This book addresses this call for an illumination and in-depth discussion of the construct by providing a significant conceptual step towards the demystification and reconceptualisation of metacognition.

Klausmeier (1990) contends that 'fuzzy concepts', in this case metacognition, have multiple attributes, an ill-constructed category system and limited widespread shared knowledge of their attributes. He explains that to 'defuzz' these concepts they must go through a process of theory conceptualisation.

Brown *et al.* (1983) identified a three-stage process of scientific theorising which outlines the stages of a construct's development. They discuss this specifically in terms of metacognition. Stage one involves applying and operationalising the new theory and stage two develops and refines the elements, categories and subcategories for efficient functioning. Stage three involves 'the theorist step[ping] back and consider[ing] the entire problem space and systemiz[ing] it or reorganiz[ing] it into a cohesive whole' (p. 125). They considered that metacognition had passed the initial stage and at that time was progressing through the second stage of 'theory building' (Brown *et al.*, 1983, p. 125; Miles and Huberman, 1994, p. 18; Ryle, 1949, p. 286) or 'theory construction' (Richards and Richards, 1994). Importantly, and especially in terms of this book, referring to the third stage, Brown *et al.* (1983) believed that once the 'main subsystems were better understood, metaprocedural reorganization may be possible and a full understanding of the domain of metacognition will be attained' (p. 125). Brown *et al.* had doubts whether metacognition, because of its complexity and multifaceted nature, could be fully understood or proceed through stage three (Brown, 1987; Brown *et al.*, 1983).

Metacognition is at the third stage of theorisation as it has been through a process of rich conceptual development having moved through the first and second stages. However, there are doubts as to the tractability of the construct and the tackling of stage three (Brown *et al.*, 1983). The aim of this book has been to move metacognition into the third stage. As suggested by Brown *et al.* (1983), and later by Brown (1987), the process of metaprocedural reorganisation is a process which has been applied and has facilitated this third stage of theory building. The outcomes of the third stage of theory building include the *conceptual framework of metacognition*, and the *taxonomy of metacognition*.

The conceptual framework of metacognition

> Concept maps assist us in transforming linear material into more holistic visual imagery and therefore help us to evaluate, synthesize, and perceive in new ways.
>
> (Deshler, 1990, p. 338)

A conceptual framework is defined as 'the main things to be studied – the key factors, constructs or variables – and the presumed relationships among them' (Miles and Huberman, 1994, p. 18). The *conceptual framework of metacognition* is a depiction of the relationship between the elements of metacognition based upon an in-depth critical analysis and critical reflection of the literature (Brookfield, 1990; Deshler, 1990). Derived from theoretical contributions to metacognitive theory, the *conceptual framework of meta-cognition* builds a picture and a nexus of metacognition through visual links to the related concepts that contribute to what is known as metacognition. The *conceptual framework of metacognition* is informed by the related amplification diagrams. These diagrams use a combination of symbols such as pointed arrows and rectangles to present a picture of the interrelationship between concepts. The amplification diagrams provide an intricate depiction of some of the concepts which form part of the *taxonomy of metacognition*. The *conceptual framework of metacognition* informs and is informed by the *taxonomy of metacognition* and is therefore reflective of the taxonomy (Huberman and Miles, 1998; Miles and Huberman, 1994). The development of the *conceptual framework of metacognition* is based upon research and theoretical discussion of the use of concept maps as a metacognitive tool (Novak, 1990). Figure 1.1 presents the foundation of the *conceptual framework of metacognition*.

Figure 1.1 Foundation of the conceptual framework of metacognition

The scope of this book does not allow for an in-depth analysis of epistemic cognition theory; the intention is, however, to provide an overview of the links between metacognition, reflection, and epistemic cognition. Moshman (2009b, 2011) provides a detailed theoretical review of epistemic cognition, epistemic development and their relationship to metacognition. The *conceptual framework of metacognition* provides a solid foundation for future research into the relationship(s) between epistemic cognition and reflection.

The taxonomy of metacognition

> Taxonomy is the theoretical study of classification, including its bases, principles, procedures, and rules.
>
> (Simpson, 1961, p. 11)

The *taxonomy of metacognition* provides a detailed and comprehensive representation and categorisation of all of the terms, concepts, categories, supercategories, subcategories and elements of metacognition. It is developed from the assertions made throughout each chapter which are analysed to identify the elements, subcategories and categories of metacognition reflected in the *taxonomy of metacognition*.

Taxonomy is a Greek word meaning classification or arrangement (taxis) and law (nomos). Taxonomies usually comprise groups or units which are also labelled as taxa (singular = taxon), frequently but not necessarily hierarchical in structure. The *taxonomy of metacognition* is not intended to be a hierarchical framework of the construct, but represents a classification or nomenclature of metacognition. Classifications can be subdivided into 'subtypes or subtaxa or subclasses' (Bailey, 1994, p. 9; Moseley *et al.*, 2005).

The focus of many educational taxonomies and the *taxonomy of metacognition* are different. Educational taxonomies such as Bloom's (1956) taxonomy of educational objectives and its revision by Anderson and Krathwohl (2001), Gagné's (1977) taxonomy of learning outcomes, and Jonassen and Tessmer's (1996/1997) outcomes-based taxonomy, to name a few, have traditionally had a strong teaching, learning and instructional design focus. The *taxonomy of metacognition* intends to meet the needs of the academic research community by providing a comprehensive view of metacognition, reflective of the literature. Jonassen and Tessmer (1996/1997) contend that 'a taxonomy should be a comprehensive research and development system' (p. 23). This is reflected in the process and outcome of categorising, organising and identifying the characteristics of each specific category, supercategory, subcategory and element of metacognition into a 'special kind of framework' and 'continuum' which are considered to be characteristics of a taxonomy (Anderson and Krathwohl, 2001). It is intended that the *taxonomy of metacognition* will be used as a guide for future metacognitive research and provide the academic research community with a complex and inclusive, but not prescriptive, view of metacognition. Metacognition, like many other theoretical constructs, is evolving and the future may bring new and exciting contributions to the theory and therefore to the taxonomy. Its detail is necessary to reflect the breadth and depth of the considerable theoretical and conceptual literature on metacognition. Congruence, complexity, inclusivity and depth are essential characteristics of any educational taxonomy (Martin and Briggs, 1986), but at the forefront of this book is useability and practicality, and therefore the former characteristics do not detract from this taxonomy. It is envisaged that the academic research community will find this taxonomy an understandable, readable and applicable framework that will be used to conceptualise future metacognitive research studies. It may also provide teachers with a foundation for understanding what metacognition is and what processes they could integrate into learning and problem solving situations.

The book presents a coalescing of the different theoretical stances of metacognition into categories, supercategories, subcategories and elements of the construct represented in a *taxonomy of metacognition*, supported by a *conceptual framework of metacognition* which depicts the interrelationships between metacognition and related concepts. It does not answer complex questions regarding the measurement of metacognition, but contributes by clarifying metacognitive theory to enable better research to be conducted on the specific categories, supercategories, subcategories and elements of metacognition. It does not aim to provide a distinct, precise definition of metacognition as this could diminish and trivialise the construct and would possibly be a fruitless exercise (Flavell *et al.*, 1993, 2002). It is, however, a comprehensive representation of the state of metacognition as it stands today, increasing the construct's clarity and future availability to researchers and ensuring its continued integrity, status and importance in what Flavell describes as metacognition's 'psychological space' (Flavell, 1987). Its contribution enhances the applicability of the construct, supporting researchers and teachers in their understanding of it, lessening its generalisation and therefore contributing to improving the reliability and validity of future empirical studies.

Conclusion

This book is not only a dialectic and a focus on the multiplicity of meta-cognition's perspectives, but also an investigation into the interrelationship between the categories which contribute to its complexity. This illumination process entailed the identification of the key conceptual contributors to the construct through an extensive critical analysis of the literature, delving deeply into the theoretical core of the development of metacognition, as a theory, including interrelationships with other concepts.

Part I

Reflection: The quintessence of metacognition

Part I establishes that reflection is the quintessence of metacognition. It provides an in-depth discussion of the historical foundations of reflection, making the connection between these historical contributions, from philosophers such as Socrates, Plato, Aristotle, Saint Augustine, Spinoza and Descartes, and psychologists such as Dewey and James. This historical discussion portrays the relationship between reflection and metacognition as having a rich and descriptive past and demonstrates the complexity of the two constructs, their interaction and their importance in problem solving. It is argued that conceptual contributions from Vygotsky, Piaget, Habermas, Moshman, Kuhn and Ennis, to name a few, provide additional connections between reflection and metacognition. These contributions include internal verbalisation, higher-order reasoning, critical thinking, and critical reflection. A specific focus on theoretical and empirical contributions is also made to identify and support the connection between metacognition and reflection. The development of the *conceptual framework of metacognition* and the *taxonomy of metacognition* begin in Part I.

Part I comprises three chapters: Chapter 2 Reflection and metacognition: Historical dialectic; Chapter 3 Critical reflection and critical thinking: Facilitators of metacognition; and Chapter 4 Reflection and metacognition: Affirming the connection.

Part 1

Reflections: The quintessence of deliberations

2 Reflection and metacognition: Historical dialectic

Life without enquiry is not worth living
(Socrates [469–399 BC] as quoted by Plato [427–347 BC]
in *Great Dialogues of Plato* [Plato, 1984, p. 443])

The historical foundations of reflection

At his trial in 399 BC at the age of 70, Socrates made the above statement regarding the importance of reflection in all aspects of life. This was recounted by McCracken (1950) as 'an unreflective life is not worth living' (p. iii).

Philosophers such as Socrates, Plato, Descartes, Spinoza, and Locke (1947), who first published his *Essay of Human Understanding* in 1690, Baldwin (1909), Dewey (1933), and Spearman (1923) are all considered to have contributed to the conceptualisation of metacognition through their theories about reflection (Brown, 1987; Cavanaugh and Perlmutter, 1982; Metcalfe, 1996, 2008). Binet (1903, 1910) also contributed to metacognition through discovering that auto criticism, or the self-regulation aspect of reflection, is essential to metacognition (Brown, 1987; Brown *et al.*, 1986; Cavanaugh and Perlmutter, 1982). Cavanaugh and Perlmutter consider that Ach (1905) and Kuhlmann (1907) both investigated 'self-awareness of problem solving strategies' (p. 11). Essentially, self-awareness or autonoetic awareness is developed and instigated by reflection and prompted by problem solving contexts. The following discussion draws from some of these historical contributions to provide a foundation for cementing the interrelationship between metacognition and reflection.

Historical contributions from Aristotle and Augustine provide evidence that acts of remembering and memory generally involve processes of reflection. These include introspection, mental imagery, contemplation, reviewing and reflecting on prior experiences. Aristotle (384–322 BC) considered that memory is the connection between 'perception' and 'conception' (Sorabji, 1972) and involves, as Sorabji interprets Aristotle, cognising through mental imagery. Although Aristotle did not use the term reflection in his description of memory processes, there is a connection between mental imagery or mental representation, reflection and metacognition. This could be akin to the reflective processes imbued in and essential to metacognitive problem solving. Discussions and research into memory are the foundation upon which current conceptualisations of metamemory and metacognition were built.

Centuries later, Augustine's (AD 354–430) work *De Trinitate* (The Trinity), written between AD 399 and 421, also described reflective processes, and the role of memory in these reflective processes. He contended that the mind always knows itself through the process of continually searching to know itself (Augustine, 1991; Pak, 2003) and essentially considered that the mind knowing itself is developed through self-knowledge, based upon self-reflexivity. It is this striving to know oneself that leads to the development of self-knowledge (Moran, 1999). Augustine thus provides a historical link between reflection and metacognition through his decree of 'know thyself'.

Similarly, Descartes (1596–1650) also considered reflection to be the essence of self, which he expressed in his theory of doubt through the 'indubitable proposition . . . I am thinking, therefore I exist' (Urmson, 1960, p. 93) most notably posited as 'cogito, ergo sum' – I think, therefore I am. His quest to find verifiable knowledge depended upon arriving at an indubitable position, and at that point he would accept his beliefs or illusions as real, through the process of thinking, reflecting, introspecting and reasoning (Descartes, 1986). Both Augustine and Descartes provide important introductions to discussions of reflection, self-knowledge and introspection (Lyons, 1986). Essentially, Aristotle, Descartes and Augustine's contributions provide a historical framework for discussing the development of self-knowledge, which is fundamental to metacognition.

Philosophers such as Spinoza (1632–1677) identified links between reflection and metacognitive processes. Spinoza's discussion of reflection encompasses the idea that to be reflective also incorporates an understanding and awareness of one's own learning processes. In addition to Augustine and Descartes, he also considered self-knowledge as being essential to learning. Spinoza (1930) used the terms 'method . . . [and] . . . rules as aids' in explaining that to reflect on an idea it is necessary to apply processes, strategies, aids and methods; which are fundamentally metacognitive processes. However, he emphasised that the methods may not be 'identical with reasoning in the search for causes' (p. 13), which indicates that he sees reflection as part of the methods or metacognitive processes used in problem solving – although he emphasised that reasoning is not identical with methods and processes. Spinoza identified reasoning as an advanced level of reflection, beyond rules and methods reliant upon self-knowledge. He considered that reflection is not a totally specified, iterative process, but one which is inert and based upon thoughts, knowledge and beliefs.

These historical contributions form the foundation for the second section of this chapter where it is argued that self-knowledge is an essential link between reflection and introspection. Self-knowledge is essential for meta-cognitive processes, and also for later development of epistemic cognition. Clearly, these historical contributions intimate the connection between reflection, metacognition and problem solving.

Dewey, reflection and problem solving

Spinoza referred to reflection in problem solving, as did Dewey (1859–1952), but Dewey (1933) built a picture of the function and specific reflective processes that are involved in learning and problem solving. There are many instances in Dewey's work which identify reflective thinking as part of cognitive processes such as awareness, monitoring and regulation. As such, he is touted as one of the first educational researchers to investigate, discuss and present thinking and reflection as important aspects of learning (see Baker and Brown, 1984a; Boud *et al.*, 1985b; Brown, 1981, 1987; Brown *et al.*, 1986; Langrehr and Palmer, 1998; Lipman, 2003; McAlpine *et al.*, 1999; Mezirow, 1990, 1991; Moon, 1999).

Dewey (1933) explained that thinking is a part of the problem solving or inquiry process requiring reflection upon prior knowledge, understandings and processes. He described this metacognitive process, even though he did not use this term, as phases of reflective thinking. The first phase occurs as 'a state of doubt, perplexion and hesitation' when challenged to think about and reflect on a problem or an issue. This mental activity leads to the second phase, which involves the 'act of searching, hunting, inquiring, to find material that will resolve the doubt, settle and dispose of the perplexity' (p. 12). Reflective thinking is the basis upon which these other processes evolve and becomes part of the problem solving process.

Dewey overlooked the possible negative or positive influences of experience, feelings, and beliefs on reflection and problem solving processes and did not specifically refer to the role that beliefs and reflection play and how they impact on problem solving strategies (Boud *et al.*, 1985a; Mezirow, 1991). However, he intimates that some beliefs spur the questioning or purposeful thought that is reflective thinking. The beliefs which Dewey refers to are about the world around us, which are challenged and become doubtful. Doubt about a situation stimulates a reflective, internal dialectic which leads to judgments and decision making. This is all imbued in the process of problem solving. King and Kitchener (1994) argue that these reflective processes or 'reflective judgments' occur during the solving of complex tasks. Dewey's work is the main conceptual basis for the development of their reflective judgment model. It will be argued later that beliefs and feelings do impact on metacognitive processes.

Dewey highlighted the relationship between the problem, reflection, awareness and self-regulation in stating that, 'The nature of the problem fixes the end of thought, and the end controls the process of thinking' (Dewey, 1933, p. 15). This statement focuses on the relationship between the context, problem, problem solving processes, and strategies applied to solve the problem. Reflection, monitoring and control are relied upon until a solution is found or determined. Dewey's descriptions of cognitive processing referring to reflection and his inferring that self-monitoring – and specifically 'regulation' – are integral aspects of problem solving provide an early basis for the conceptual development of metacognition.

The synchronic interaction of reflection and reasoning

Early conceptions of learning processes, intelligence, perceptual awareness, and reasoning and reflection were promoted by Aristotle, James, and Dewey, whose discussions of reasoning are founded upon the processes of cognising and that reflective thought relies upon reasoning and is imbued in the problem solving process. James' (1890a, 1890b) discussion relates to problem solving and the understanding of phenomena through 'analysis and abstraction'; whereas Aristotle referred to reasoning as a process of recollecting, understanding, and using mental imagery and mnemonic strategies. Aristotle considered that reasoning impacted on reflection at a contemplative level rather than at a critically reflective level in problem solving contexts (see Kemmis, 1985). Dewey stated that reasoning prompts idea creation and aids the contribution of thoughts. It facilitates the identification of terms and theories, which initially seemed confusing. This perplexion or puzzling effect is stimulated by and during problem solving, and connections are formed out of the conflict of elements due to reasoning and inferences made.

Listed below are assertions connecting reasoning, reflective thinking, metacognitive processes and problem solving. The following conceptions draw together Dewey, James, Augustine and Aristotle's historical contributions to reflection, problem solving and metacognition and are represented in Figure 2.1.

2.1   Self-knowledge and self-awareness develop through reflection and introspection, and are essential to facilitate metacognition.

2.2   Reflective thinking is the foundation for the development of problem solving strategies which are integral to metacognition and essential in complex contexts.

2.3   Judgments, self-monitoring and self-regulation are reflective processes imbued in problem solving.

2.4   Challenges to beliefs and doubt stimulate reflection and instigate problem solving strategies.

2.5   Reasoning relies upon reflection, mental imagery, mnemonic strategies, analysis and abstraction, and is essential for complex problem solving.

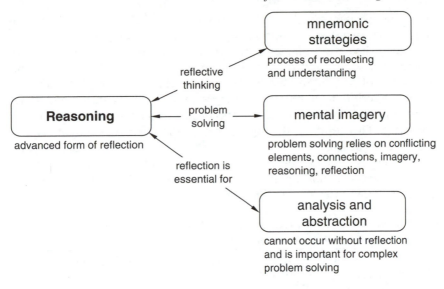

Figure 2.1 Amplification of reasoning in the conceptual framework of metacognition

It has been argued that reasoning is an essential element of reflection and necessary for problem solving. The following section provides further support for this argument and outlines Piaget's contribution to reflection through his theories on higher-order reasoning. It is not the intention, however, to discuss these in detail.

Piaget's contribution to reflective thinking: Higher-order reasoning

There is substantial, expert literature for and against Piaget's stages of cognitive development. This book will not delve into this debate, the specific cognitive developments at each stage, or the issues regarding the development of the postformal stage (see Commons *et al.*, 1984; Efklides *et al.*, 1994; Flavell, 1963, 1971b, 1977; Flavell *et al.*, 1993, 2002; Gage and Berliner, 1984; Inhelder and Piaget, 1958; Moshman, 2011; Piaget, 1970; Plucker, 1998; Sinnott, 1984). Essentially, this section discusses Piaget's higher-order reasoning and its connections with metacognition and reflective processes.

Reflective thinking is clearly part of the development of abstract thinking in adolescence, the formal operations stage and beyond, and an integral element in logic, reasoning, and abstract thought processes (Blasi, 1983; Blasi and Hoeffel, 1974; Inhelder and Piaget, 1958). Blasi and Hoeffel (1974) have identified, in Inhelder and Piaget's (1958) work, three senses of reflectivity. These are knowledge of self, self-control, and self-correction, and are processes essential to a higher sense(s) of reflectivity. Although their discussion specifically refers to the development of self-reflection, and the levels of self-reflection in formal operations, they do not use the term reasoning. Their work alludes to reflection as fundamental to higher-order reasoning processes and the development of knowledge of the world and knowledge of self in the world. Also their elucidation of Inhelder and Piaget's description of reflective thought implies the existence and functioning of metacognitive processes, specifically in senses two and three (see Table 2.1). This supports the argument that the reflective thought, awareness, and purposeful thinking of the formal operations stage and beyond can be seen as contributing to the application and development of metacognition, and is reliant upon self-knowledge. Table 2.1 outlines Blasi and Hoeffel's three senses of reflection.

Table 2.1 Blasi and Hoeffel's interpretation of Inhelder and Piaget's discussion of reflection in formal operations

Three senses or levels of reflection	Description of senses or levels of reflection
Reflection based upon *spatial relations*	Reflection as second-degree operations, using, integrating and building upon lower level thought processes Depending upon self-control and self-correction Relies on spatial relations and metaphors to understand thinking
Reflection as *knowledge of an act of thinking*	Knowledge of the world and knowledge of oneself This sense of reflection is considered to be metacognitive which 'implies a stronger, psychological sense of reflection' (p. 355) Knowledge of oneself as directly impacting on reflection Knowledge of operations which are of the self
Reflection as *knowledge of self*	Knowledge of the world and knowledge of oneself Knowledge and recognition of internal processes as self processes, self being the source Knowledge of operations as *being of* the self, ability to grasp oneself, more abstractly, as the source of operations Lived unity of the self becomes the focus of attention and interest

Sources: Adapted from Blasi and Hoeffel (1974, pp. 355–356) and Piaget (1958).

Beyond doubt, many complex reasoning processes develop during adolescence and adulthood. Most agree that the initial development of higher-order reasoning is the main differentiator between concrete and formal 'stages' of cognitive development (e.g. Commons *et al.*, 1984; Flavell *et al.*, 2002; Inhelder and Piaget, 1958; Moshman, 2009a, 2011; Sinnott, 1984; Sternberg, 1984). Higher-order reasoning encompasses a number of processes such as 'problem solving, decision making, [and] argumentation', signifying the complexity of this level of reasoning (Moshman, 1994, p. 135). Referring to Inhelder and Piaget's (1958) work, both Flavell (1977) and Moshman (2011) consider that formal operations represent a form of 'metathinking' or metacognition.

Piaget's discussions regarding the formal operational stage – adolescence and beyond – incorporate higher-order learning processes reliant upon reflection and metacognition. These processes include the ability to analyse logically, deal with hypotheses, reflect, and apply 'hypothetico-deductive' and 'propositional reasoning' (Flavell, 1963, 1977; Flavell *et al.*, 2002; Hacker, 1998; Moshman, 2009a, 2011; Piaget, 1970). Flavell and Piaget consider that the formal reasoning stage involves abstract thinking about propositions regarded as second-degree operations (Flavell, 1963), and described as reliant upon metacognitive processes (Flavell, 1977). Moshman (2009a, 2011) explains that the formal reasoning stage involves the creation of new possibilities and the assessment of the applicability of those possibilities through reasoning, logic and argumentation. The formal reasoning stage engages hypothetico-deductive reasoning. This form of reasoning involves the creation of new possibilities or hypothetical assertions that are either true or false and applying reasoning processes to explore their applicability. Propositional reasoning involves connections and associations such as 'implication, conjunction, identity, [and] disjunction' (Flavell, 1963, p. 205). These reasoning processes, reliant upon reflection and metacognition, stimulate connections between prior knowledge and experiences in similar problem solving situations, and help to instigate new learning and problem solving processes in novel, complex problems.

Mindful, conscious reflection affects and facilitates the development of propositional reasoning ability in early adulthood and late adolescence. Although metacognition impacts on propositional reasoning in the formal operations stage, it is 'not due to explicit, reflective monitoring but to changes in cognitive functioning and monitoring based on metacognitive experiences only' (Efklides *et al.*, 1994, p. 169). This brings into question the level of metacognitive development in formal operations. Furthermore, Efklides *et al.* refer to a number of studies which provide evidence that it should not be assumed that propositional reasoning only develops in formal operations and postformal reasoning stages of development. This again questions Piaget's stage theory of cognitive development and the level of reflective thinking that develops and occurs at the formal operations stage.

The postformal stage of relativistic operations or dialectical thinking sees the development of third-order reasoning, considered necessary for complex reasoning, and an extension of second-order reasoning, necessary to arrive at solutions for real-world problem solving (Bakracevic Vukman, 2005; Linn and Siegel, 1984; Sinnott, 1984; Sternberg, 1984). These are essentially metacognitive and reflective processes, and are integral to higher-order reasoning processes applied during the solving of complex problems. Figure 2.2 amplifies the elements related to the development of higher-order reasoning.

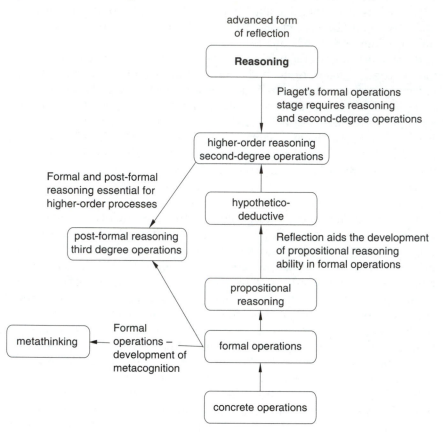

Figure 2.2 Amplification of higher-order reasoning processes in the conceptual framework of metacognition

Piaget's theory of axiomatisation and formalisation

Piaget's (1970) discussions of purposeful, guided, reflective, formalised thinking can be considered early conceptualisations of metacognitive, reflective processes. Higher-order reasoning also involves Piaget's conceptions of axiomatisation and formalisation which contribute to current theories of metacognition and reflection. They are based on processes of reflective abstraction, involving logic and thought processes, essential to fostering reflection.

Formalisation is retrospective thinking guided by logic, purposeful thinking, inference and reason making. It involves reviewing processes, including the situation, and its influencing and impending elements. This retrospection involves reflection on prior experiences, knowledge and processes. Axiomatisation is used to describe the reflective process of reducing axioms, it involves logic, and the processes involved in the formalisation of thought. Reflective abstraction, formalisation and retrospection on past knowledge and experiences facilitate decision making and problem solving in current situations. Axiomatisation and formalisation are processes involved in reflective abstraction. Moshman (1990) considers that reflective abstraction is a 'very powerful form of metacognition that doesn't just . . . direct the execution of cognitive processes but actively reconstructs cognition at a higher level of abstraction or . . . deeper level of understanding' (p. 348). Reflective abstraction is a form of metacognition labelled by Moshman (1982) as endogenous construction of knowledge. These can all be considered to be early conceptualisations of metacognitive, reflective processes.

Referring to Piaget's theories, listed below are assertions connecting reflective thinking, higher-order reasoning, axiomatisation, formalisation, reflective abstraction, and metacognition.

2.6 Reflection enables the development of higher-order reasoning processes and therefore the development of metacognition or metathinking in adolescents.
2.7 Knowledge of self, self-control and self-correction is essential for higher levels of reflectivity and metacognitive functioning.
2.8 Reflection aids the development of propositional reasoning ability in early adulthood and late adolescence.
2.9 Reflective processes are integral to higher-order reasoning processes applied during the solving of complex problems.
2.10 Axiomatisation and formalisation are guided by logic and purposeful thinking, are based on processes of reflective abstraction and are metacognitive, reflective processes.

The following section makes a case for the connection between inferences and reasoning as elements of reflective processes which impact on metacognition and are influenced and guided by reflection.

The reflective activity of reasoning and inference

Kant (1933) and Dewey (1933) implied that reasoning is influenced by inference through reflection on these inferences, especially in problem-solving contexts. Kant considered that reasoning is based upon inferences made in the process of problem solving and decision making. Similarly, Dewey described the role that inferences play in connecting what is known and what is not known, and in instigating thoughtful, purposeful action aiding complex problem solving. Knowledge is the basis for making these connections and involves both inference and reasoning processes. Both

Kant and Dewey consider that reasoning involves inferences governed by prior knowledge and understandings, which inform judgments made during problem solving.

Dewey emphasised the spontaneity of inferences, but also alluded to the need for reflection in their control. This is a metacognitive process, although inferences alone are not metacognitive in nature (Moshman, 2004, 2009b). The ability to have knowledge of, and control of, inferences or meta-cognition begins to develop in later childhood and adolescence (Moshman, 2004, 2009a, 2009b, 2011). Control of inferences relates to Moshman's (1995) description of a 'self-imposed rationality' as a process of applying constraints through reasoning by way of identifying the applicability of particular inferences (p. 54). Therefore, reasoning is used to determine the applicability of inferences to facilitate the achievement of a particular goal. This may be to facilitate the process of problem solving and the attainment of a solution through the use of reflective processes.

If reflection is integral to the control of inferences enabling metacognition, then an internal dialectic may also be engaged. This would most likely occur in decision making and in challenging problem-solving situations. Complex, abstract situations prompt the need for higher-order reasoning relying upon inferences and the control of inferences to support problem solving. If inferences occur during problem solving and involve judgments, beliefs and understandings, it would be logical to consider that an internal and external dialectic would be involved. Figure 2.3 is an amplification of the interaction between inferences and reasoning reliant upon reflection.

The following assertions are derived from the discussion of the reflective activity of reasoning and inference:

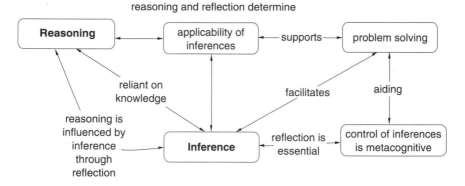

Figure 2.3 Amplification of inferences and reasoning in the conceptual framework of metacognition

2.11 Reasoning and reflective processes are used to determine the applicability of inferences facilitating problem-solving strategies and the solution.

2.12 Reasoning relies upon knowledge and inferences to move from one understanding, intimation, judgment or belief to another to reach a conclusion or solution to a problem.

2.13 Reflection is essential to metacognitive processes, controlling inferences and reasoning and to promoting new knowledge development and problem solving.

The following section specifically reviews Vygotsky's contribution to the theory of verbalisation. It discusses the relationship between verbalisation and reflective processes involved in metacognition.

Reflection: A dialectical process – Vygotsky and metacognition

Vygotsky (1896–1934) focused on the social construction of knowledge contrasted with the essentially individual process of knowledge construction as outlined by Dewey. Dewey viewed reflection as an important element of the problem-solving process and Vygotsky specifically discussed verbalisation and internal verbalisation as important supports during the learning process.

Vygotsky's (1978, 1981, 1986, 1987/1934) conceptions of the zone of proximal development and internal verbalisation are imbued in problem solving and are integral aspects of metacognition (Bruner, 1985). During problem solving, verbalisation and internal verbalisation promote the creation of the 'zone of proximal development'. Vygotsky describes this process as one which moves from an individual to a social cognitive process. Through social cognitive interaction, the zone of proximal development is created by determining the space between the level of 'actual development' and the level of 'potential development'. This social cognitive interaction stimulates the ongoing development of internalised cognitive processes, which are essentially metacognitive processes. Vygotsky emphasises the role of supports or scaffolding, although he did not specifically coin the term (see Wood *et al.*, 1976, p. 90), as integral to facilitating movement through the zone of proximal development to the level of potential development. Jerome Bruner and his colleagues identify scaffolding as integral to supporting problem solving (Callison, 2001; Gaskins *et al.*, 1997; Goos *et al.*, 2002; Roehler and Cantlon, 1997).

The use of inner speech promotes higher-order reasoning about the relationships between the problem, the problem-solving process, and the solution. The internalisation of these processes can be synonymous with reflective thinking. In problem-solving contexts, the zone of proximal development can be established dynamically through dialogue, social interaction, argumentation, collaboration and cooperation (see Braten, 1991a; Brown, 1987, 1997; Brown and Campione, 1996; Brown *et al.*, 1998; Brown and Palincsar, 1989; Bruner, 1985; Duffy and Cunningham, 1996; Palincsar and Brown, 1984; Rogoff and Wertsch, 1984; Wertsch, 1985a, 1985b). In many collaborative problem-solving situations, especially involving real-world problems, individuals employ an internal dialectic instigated by social interaction. Part of social problem solving, especially complex problem solving, involves some level of argumentation, an important higher-order reasoning process, involving verbalisation and reflection (Bryson and Scardamalia, 1996; Cho and Jonassen, 2002; Kuhn, 1991; Tan *et al.*, 2001).

The learning process moves from a predominately social cognitive process to a metacognitive process. Mediation through scaffolding facilitates the movement from interpsychological to intrapsychological functioning, where internalisation is an integral aspect of the intrapsychological state (Jacob, 1992; Schwebel, 1986; Vygotsky, 1978; Wertsch, 1985a). Intrapsychological functioning can be considered to be metacognitive. In this state, learners are reliant upon their own metacognitive processes, enabling them to achieve their learning goals. For example, planning, monitoring and strategy identification and application in a specific problem-solving context rely upon the internalisation of speech, or internal dialogue. The importance of internalisation or intrapsychological functioning in problem-solving situations is directly supported by Vygotsky (1978) who stated that 'voluntary self-regulation of behaviour arise[s] as an internal function' (p. 90). This use of internalisation, or use of inner speech or inner voice, supports the application of volitional control strategies, regarded as essential metacognitive processes (e.g. Braten, 1991a, 1991b, 1992; Brown, 1987; Brown and Palincsar, 1989; Bruner, 1985; Dominowski, 1998; Kuhn, 2000a; Langrehr and Palmer, 1998; Tsai, 2001; Vygotsky, 1978; Wertsch, 1985a).

Figure 2.4 is an amplification of the interaction between internal and external verbalisation and reflection. It demonstrates the movement from an interpsychological state to an intrapsychological state as dependent upon reflection and verbalisation and highlights the relationship between metacognition and verbalisation through the cognitive monitoring of learning.

The following section provides additional support to the argument that metacognitive reflective processes are imbued in individual and social problem-solving situations.

Habermas' theory of self-reflection in socially mediated contexts

> The power of self-reflection, knowledge and interest are one.
>
> (Habermas, 1987, p. 314)

Habermas contributes to understandings of reflection through his theories of social cognitive emancipation and individual and social reflection in real-world contexts. He considers that an individual's development, self-knowledge and reflective processes are influenced by historical, and social contexts (see Greene, 1990; Habermas, 1987; Kemmis, 1985; Moon, 1999;

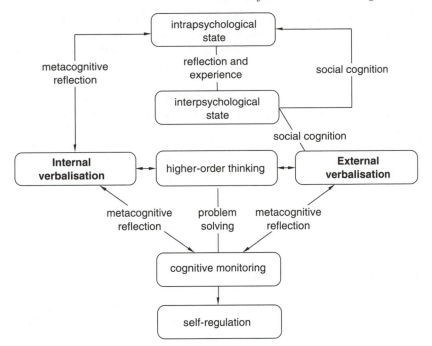

Figure 2.4 Amplification of verbalisation in the conceptual framework of metacognition

Moshman, 2011; Pearson and Smith, 1985; Swindal, 1999). In essence, the above quote highlights the connection between self-reflection and knowledge, both essential elements for engagement in metacognitive processes.

Habermas' work is compared to Dewey's theories on reflection in that they both discuss critical reflection processes in the context of real complex problems (e.g. Moon, 1999; Swindal, 1999). In addition to Dewey, his theory of cognitive emancipation and reflection in complex problem solving is considered to have contributed to the development of King and Kitchener's (1994, 2002; Kitchener and King, 1981, 1990a, 1990b) reflective judgment model (see Moon, 1999).

Although the literature posits a strong link between Habermas and Dewey's theories on reflection, Dewey focuses on individual reflection in problem contexts, whereas Habermas places a stronger emphasis on reflection in social problem-solving contexts. Habermas' theories have a stronger link with Vygotsky's theories of verbalisation and the zone of proximal development, involving reflection, specifically in collaborative problem-solving situations.

Conceptions based upon discussions of Vygotsky's theory of verbalisation and Habermas' theory of self-reflection in socially mediated contexts provided the following assertions:

2.14 Transition from interpsychological functioning to intrapsychological states is a mediational process reliant upon reflection.

2.15 Learning moves from a predominately social cognitive process to a metacognitive process supported by critical reflection and facilitating problem solving.

2.16 Metacognitive processes require inner speech to occur, supporting planning, strategy identification and application in problem-solving contexts.

2.17 Internal verbalisation and verbalisation support metacognitive processes such as planning, strategy identification and application, and the monitoring and control of cognitive processes in problem-solving contexts.

2.18 Argumentation is a form of reasoning, imbued in the process of verbalisation, and important for complex problem solving.

Conclusion

Essentially it has been argued that although the contributions of Aristotle, Augustine, Dewey, James, Kant, Piaget, Vygotsky and Habermas do not use the term metacognition, they have contributed to understanding the connection between reflection, metacognition and problem solving.

Reflexivity is the basis for developing strategies in problem-solving situations. These strategies can be considered metacognitive, involving judgments, monitoring and regulation of these strategies, which are essential in complex problem-solving contexts. Reflective processes are imbued in problem solving and are integral to metacognition. The development of self-knowledge and self-awareness is supported by reflective and introspective processes, all fundamental to the development and application of meta-cognitive processes. Complex problem contexts challenge and stimulate self-doubt. Doubt about knowledge and the efficacy of strategies stimulates reflection. This instigates the search for and development of effective problem-solving strategies.

Reasoning is imbued in reflective processes, especially in problem-solving contexts, and requires a 'higher level' of metacognition. Fundamentally, reasoning relies upon reflection, mental imagery, mnemonic strategies, analysis and abstraction, and is essential for complex problem solving. Piaget's higher-order reasoning is essentially an element of metacognitive thinking or metathinking, as described by Flavell. During adolescence and early adulthood, the development of higher-order and propositional reasoning processes is reliant upon reflectivity. These processes are essential to the solving of complex problems and can only develop through self-knowledge. Therefore, knowledge of self is essential for metacognitive processes relying upon self-control and self-correction to occur. Advanced reflective, purposeful thinking involves processes identified by Piaget as axiomatisation and formalisation. These processes are guided by logic and are infused in metacognitive reflexivity such as reflective abstraction.

Reasoning involves reflection on the applicability of inferences. Reflection is also involved in controlling inferences and reasoning. The control of inferences through reasoning and reflection is based upon metacognitive processes (see Moshman, 2004, 2009b, 2011). Reasoning relies upon knowledge and inferences to assist reflective processes, advance understandings and question beliefs. This process is fundamentally metacognitive, supporting the facilitation of problem-solving strategies and the formulation of a solution.

Based upon Vygotsky and Habermas' social constructivist theories, it has been argued that reflection is a socially mediated, dialectical process relying upon verbalisation, both internal and external. Internal verbalisation and verbalisation are reflective, metacognitive processes aiding planning, and strategy identification and application. It also supports the monitoring and control of cognitive processes, referring to the self-regulatory processes of metacognition. Critical reflection facilitates the movement from a social learning context to an individual metacognitive process. Argumentation is also imbued in the process of verbalisation and reflection, and supports complex problem solving.

The following higher-order assertions (e.g. HOA.1) are drawn from the above discussion.

2.19 Reflection including verbalisation is essential for the development of metacognitive strategies and the monitoring and regulation of these strategies, especially in complex problem-solving contexts (HOA.1).
2.20 Reflection and introspection facilitate the development of self-knowledge and self-awareness, which are fundamental to metacognition (HOA.2).

Relationships between critical reflection, critical thinking and metacognition are identified and discussed in Chapter 3.

3 Critical reflection and critical thinking: Facilitators of metacognition

Many discussions of reflection refer to the term critical reflection or critical knowing. Although in some cases the literature uses the terms reflection, critical reflection or critical knowing and critical thinking interchangeably, there is a significant difference in their meanings. This chapter outlines the essential aspects of each of these forms of reflection and identifies their connection(s) with metacognition. It comprises two main sections: Critical reflection: Beyond reflection; and Critical thinking as skilful thinking.

Critical reflection: Beyond reflection

Critical reflection is an inductive process based upon presuppositions, beliefs and experiences, involving critical assessment and evaluation of understandings, knowledge and assumptions which form the basis of these beliefs. As beliefs are considered to influence critical reflection, prior knowledge and internal dialectics also make an impact. Critical reflection is reliant upon self-awareness or consciousness and dependent upon verbalisation or an internal dialectic. This reflective dialectic attempts to discover how prior knowledge and understandings were developed and their effect on current practice. This provides a foundation for the development of new knowledge, dependent upon critical reflection of new and prior knowledge (Bowne, 1897; Kemmis, 1985; Mezirow, 1991, 1997; Pearson and Smith, 1985; Swindal, 1999).

Critical knowing is a way of knowing, 'knowing about ourselves'. It involves critical self-knowledge and understandings of how our beliefs, feelings, knowledge and strategies affect our current actions, and influence changes in future actions (Pearson and Smith, 1985, p. 74). Critical reflection interacts with self-knowledge to develop critical knowledge. Critical knowledge is a form of metacognition as it represents prior knowledge and the development of new knowledge as reliant upon reflective processes. This would involve knowing about ourselves as learners; knowledge of our cognition and knowledge of the strategies that we use for learning. These are fundamental elements of metacognition. Self-knowledge is the essence of critical knowing and critical reflection. Reflection facilitates the development of self-knowledge and self-knowledge is not necessarily essential for reflection but it is essential for critical reflection or critical knowing.

Critical reflection or critical knowing is essentially active in problem-solving situations, the implications of which are discussed in the following section.

Critical reflection in problem solving

Critical reflection generally occurs during challenging, demanding, stimulating and engaging situations, which draw in and depend upon higher-order, inductive processes affected by beliefs, values, judgments, reasoning and inferences. This inductive process involves challenging one's own thinking, especially in problem-solving situations.

Collaborative problem-solving situations promote critical reflection where group contemplation and discussion foster the advent of reflective judgment through the assessment of beliefs, values, assumptions, feelings, prior knowledge, understandings and construction of experience. The problems engage communicative learning involving creative, interpretive, meaning-making, reflective judgment, and analysis involved in complex problem-solving situations. These critical reflective processes transform learning (Mezirow, 1990, 1991, 1997).

The challenging nature of complex problems instigates critical reflection and creativity, facilitating the identification or development of new strategies to deal effectively with the problem representation and its elements. Reflective interpretation, an element of critical reflection, describes the creative process of strategy identification and application in reassessing and rectifying preconceptions, misinterpretations and biases (Mezirow, 1990). It could be considered a form of metacognition. The interaction between metacognition and critical reflection supports the reflective interpretation process by drawing from knowledge to select appropriate and effective strategies for specific problem-solving contexts. This instigates the need for active, self-regulated critical reflection which depends upon and requires self-knowledge, self-awareness, self-discovery and self-understanding. It will be argued later that self-knowledge is an essential connecting element between metacognition and reflection. Overall, the literature proposes that knowledge is essential to reflection and reflection is the basis of metacognitive processes, and critical reflection has been identified as necessary for the solving of complex problems (e.g. Iran-Nejad and Gregg, 2001; Mezirow, 1990).

The assertions identify that critical reflection contributes to the relationship between metacognition and reflection in the following ways:

3.1 Critical reflection is an inductive process based upon beliefs and experiences, involving critical assessment and evaluation of understandings, knowledge and assumptions which form the basis of these beliefs.

3.2   Critical reflection is promoted in collaborative, challenging problem-solving situations instigating reflective judgments of beliefs, values, assumptions, knowledge, inferences, understandings and experience.

3.3   Critical reflection instigates transformative learning and is reliant upon an internal dialectic aiding our understandings of new knowledge and critiquing prior knowledge.

3.4   Critical reflection is active, mind-regulated and dependent upon and requiring self-knowledge, self-awareness, self-discovery and self-understanding.

3.5   Critical knowing is a way of knowing, forming an understanding and awareness of oneself, identifying processes or strategies to be applied in problem-solving situations.

3.6   Critical reflection is essential to facilitate metacognitive processes in complex problem-solving contexts, assisting the review, monitoring and control of strategies and processes.

Figure 3.1 demonstrates not only the core elements which interact with critical reflection, such as reflective judgment, transformative learning, self-reflection, self-knowledge and critical knowing, but also sub-elements of these processes and conceptions and their interrelationships.

The following section identifies critical thinking as higher-order reasoning and reflective processes, which are essential for complex problem solving.

Critical thinking as skilful thinking

There have been significant contributions in defining and determining the elements of critical thinking (e.g. Brookfield, 1987; Ennis, 1987; Lipman, 1988, 2003; Siegel, 1980). However, there is little consensus regarding a common definition, or specific elements which comprise it. Added to this, the interrelationships between these elements are ambiguous (Brookfield, 1987; Wood, 1997). The literature identifies skilful thinking as a foundational process of critical thinking (e.g. Lipman, 1988; Paul, 1992; Paul and Elder, 2002). It involves skilful thinking instigating judgment, self-correction, self-regulatory and monitoring processes, influenced by context. Lipman explains that critical thinking is 'reliable thinking' relying upon a criterion as an 'instrument' which provides guidance and a means of evaluation. Criteria are reliable reasons which facilitate judgments and promote critical thinking and the relationship between criteria, judgment and critical thinking is based upon interdependency (Lipman, 1988, 2003; Paul and Elder, 2002).

Critical thinking can then be characterised by processes such as reflecting, judging and identifying data as well as contemplating and determining solutions, positions and conclusions based on data. This process can be affected by beliefs, especially in complex, challenging problem-solving situations. Awareness of beliefs about the world, ourselves, and the underlying

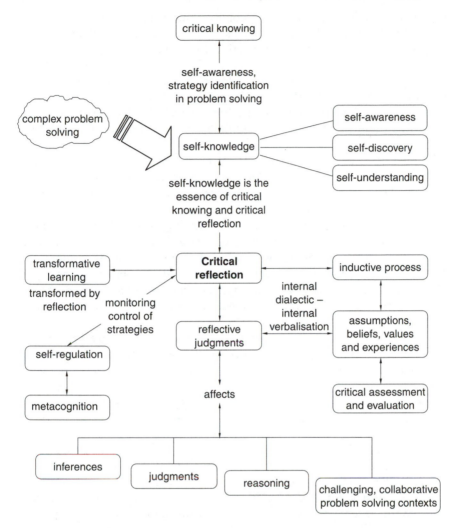

Figure 3.1 Amplification of critical reflection in the conceptual framework of metacognition

assumptions which form the basis of these beliefs can influence critical thinking. Recognition and knowledge of our own and others' beliefs enable justifications of ideas, and judgments of the rationality of justifications (Brookfield, 1987; Ennis, 1987, 1993). Importantly, Brookfield's views of critical thinking represent a connection to previous discussion of critical reflection, where assumptions and beliefs impact on judgments, incorporate self-knowledge, and instigate metacognitive processes.

He endeavours to identify three main contributing concepts which amplify the meaning of critical thinking, including, firstly, Habermas' theory of emancipatory learning, secondly, dialectical thinking, and thirdly, reflection. Similarly, Ennis (1987) uses two core terms, dialogical and suppositional thinking, to describe critical thinking processes. He explains that these terms relate to being open to views other than one's own and using reasoning and judgment to help solve the problem. Both of these terms coincide with Brookfield's concepts, which to some extent characterise critical thinking. Additionally, Ennis considers that critical thinking involves a number of abilities, including '*clarity, basis, inference,* and *interaction*' (ibid., p. 16).

Combining aspects of Brookfield and Ennis' work, various components and facilitators of critical thinking are identified for effective problem solving. These include creative, unexpected, unplanned critical insight; reasoning and inferences, analysing arguments, judging credibility of information, open-mindedness, sensitivity, identifying and challenging assumptions; awareness of the effect of emotions, and beliefs, on critical thinking; and reflection on prior knowledge, understandings, and assumptions. The facilitators involve motivation which is needed to promote task completion and negate doubt and anxiety, especially with complex problems. Collaboration and cooperation provide support and interaction in such contexts.

The key points here for metacognition and reflection are that critical thinking depends upon reflective processes that are more sophisticated than just 'thinking about thinking'. It involves reasoning, judgments, analytical reflective processes that draw and depend upon self-knowledge, prior knowledge, understandings, and beliefs. Both Brookfield's and Ennis' views of critical thinking include both thinking skills and processes impacted by reasoning and judgments, instigated and challenged by complex problem-solving situations. Critical thinking processes can be considered to be metacognitive strategies which can be applied to support complex problem solving. The relationship between critical thinking and metacognition is discussed further in the section titled Critical thinking and metacognition.

From this discussion, the following assertions about critical thinking can be made:

3.7   Critical thinking is affected by decision making, criteria, and complex problem solving. It is reliant upon skilful thinking and good judgment, is self-correcting and considers context.

3.8   Critical thinking involves identifying and challenging assumptions which underlie beliefs, justifying ideas and actions, judging the rationality of these justifications, and analysing of arguments.

The following section describes in more detail the relationship between critical thinking and reflection, especially reflective judgment and its relationship to problem solving.

Critical thinking as reflective judgment: The reflective thinking connection

Lack of critical ability [is the] cause of failure to solve problems.

(Boraas, 1924, p. 147)

Boraas makes this statement in the context of solving real, everyday problems. It is argued that reflection is essential for developing critical ability, and therefore necessary for critical thinking.

The literature identifies a strong link between critical thinking and reflective thinking (e.g. Brookfield, 1987; Bruning *et al.*, 1999; Dewey, 1933; Elder and Paul, 2001; Ennis, 1987, 1993; King and Kitchener, 1994; Kuhn, 1999a; Mezirow, 1990; Pithers and Soden, 2000). Ennis (1987) refers to critical thinking as focused reflective thinking, and Dewey viewed critical thinking as essential to reflective thinking. Dewey used the terms interchangeably, and considered that thinking is not necessarily reflective unless one is critically thinking about the problem or the situation. Reflective or critical thinking about a real problem is influenced by attitudes, beliefs, evaluation of beliefs in light of the problem, information or data, personal experiences and interpretations of available information. Critical thinking involves reflective thinking if engaged in reflective judgments. Reflective judgments promote the development of reflective thinking, but rely upon critical thinking to instigate these reflective processes (see Dewey, 1933; King and Kitchener, 1994; Mezirow, 1990).

Reflective judgments and critical thinking do not occur in isolation from a complex problem, but are connected with finding the solution to the problem. Reflective judgments should be relevant to the issue and be based upon weighing up the facts and elements of the problem and the interaction with the problem solver (Dewey, 1933). Reflective thinking requires an evaluation of conjecture, beliefs and hypotheses against data, knowledge, research findings and interpretations. Judgments are made as a result of identifying and weighing up various views and understandings of the issue. Reflective judgments involve purposeful contemplation, and deliberation on the knowable elements of the problem and its possible solutions. Self-correction, an element of critical thinking, is involved in making reflective judgments (King and Kitchener, 1994; Lipman, 1988, 2003).

Critical thinking refers specifically to skills, rules and methods applied to problem solving in well structured tasks (King and Kitchener, 1994). This is reflected in many of the views on critical thinking (e.g. Brookfield, 1987; Ennis, 1987; Lipman, 1988; Siegel, 1980). Some points raised by these theorists, especially Ennis and Brookfield, acknowledge that assumptions, understandings, judgments and justifications of these judgments are essential to critical thinking and complex problem solving. For example, Ennis' critical thinking abilities and Brookfield's dialectical thinking – which is a process of formulating judgments, determining rules inherent in these judgments, and reviewing judgments in regard to these rules – are especially relevant for complex problem solving. These abilities are processes which entail, and rely upon, reflection in formulating, determining and reviewing judgments (Brookfield, 1987). These points could be considered to be related to King and Kitchener's (1994) view of reflective thinking and reflective judgments. Although their views of reflective thinking, incorporating critical thinking, also take into consideration epistemic assumptions, beliefs and the impact of beliefs on problems solving, their views may lend themselves towards combining theories on critical reflection and critical thinking. This discussion supports the strong relationship between critical thinking, reflection and judgment, specifically reflective judgment, and its necessity in the solving of complex problems.

Extensive research by King and Kitchener (see King, 1986, 1992; King and Kitchener, 1994, 2002; Kitchener and King, 1981, 1990a, 1990b) has identified a fundamental difference in the problem-solving processes children and adults apply. Adults hold epistemic assumptions that directly influence their problem solving, allowing for reflection and reflexive processes. Adults employ critical self-reflective processes, drawing from assumptions, during learning experiences and problem solving, processes which involve post-formal operations (Brookfield, 1998; Fischer and Pruyne, 2002; Mezirow, 1990). Theories of critical thinking which focus on skills neglect to identify the epistemic assumptions or epistemological judgments or commitments or assumptions about knowledge which are involved in reflective thinking and reflective judgments. These assumptions or judgments are applied to evaluate critically the value of particular knowledge and its verity, actuality and applicability in a complex problem (King and Kitchener, 1994; Lipman, 1988; Tsai, 2001; Wood, 1997).

Links are also identified between judgment and critical thinking or critical judgment, and judgment and creative judgment (Lipman, 1991, 2003). The relationship between these types of judgments and their application in complex problem solving would provide rich areas of potential research. This may link to research into the development of metacognition and epistemic cognition, and their importance in complex problem solving.

When critical thinking involves reflective judgments, it is beyond just process or a set of skills and knowledge needed to solve a problem. The following assertions argue that reflective judgment is central to critical thinking:

3.9   Reflective judgment enables purposeful contemplation, deliberation and processes such as analysis, identification, self-correction and elaboration of all the knowable elements of the problem and its possible solutions.

3.10 Reflective judgment involves reflective thinking, such as epistemic assumptions or epistemological judgments and their impact on problem solving.

Figure 3.2 (see p. 36) is an amplification of the contributions to critical thinking drawn from the above discussion. It demonstrates the core elements which interact with critical thinking, such as reflective judgment, self-correction and dialectical and dialogical thinking. It also identifies the effect complex problem solving has on these elements.

The following section identifies the key relationships between critical thinking and metacognition. The literatur, which discusses both critical thinking and metacognition, provides an insight into the convergence of these concepts.

Critical thinking and metacognition

> Critical thinking only makes sense as a construct if we believe humans have some ability to bring established modes or methods of thought to bear in approaching new situations.
>
> (Kuhn, 1999a, p. 24)

There is a scarcity of literature discussing the interrelationship between metacognition or 'meta-knowing' (Kuhn, 1999a) and critical thinking, although this is shown as zeitgeist in recent literature (e.g. Kuhn, 1999a; Olson and Astington, 1993; Pithers and Soden, 2000). Other literature has identified the connection, but has not detailed the specific relationship between metacognition and critical thinking (e.g. Tama, 1989a, 1989b). There is also an emphasis on the need for critical thinking to be taught within a real or relevant context, immersed in the content of the subject domain (see Hartman, 2001b; Kuhn, 1999a; Paul and Elder, 2002; Perkins and Salomon, 1989; Pithers and Soden, 2000; Tama, 1989a, 1989b; Wilen and Phillips, 1995). For this to occur, it is necessary that scaffolding is used to enhance critical thinking processes, supported by effective metacognitive and self-regulatory processes (Pithers and Soden, 2000).

Critical thinking incorporates metacognitive processes such as knowledge of cognition and reflection, referring to the ability and skill to think effectively (Kuhn, 1999a; Kuhn and Dean, 2004; Mezirow, 1990; Olson and Astington, 1993). Lipman (1988; 1991; 2003) and Tsai (2001) consider that critical thinking can only be metacognitive when it is an evaluative, reflective process incorporating self-regulatory processes, based upon specific criteria. It cannot be assumed that critical thinking is fundamentally metacognitive, unless it relies upon specific metacognitive processes that go beyond just 'thinking about thinking' and rely upon self-corrective, purposeful reflection. This type of thinking incorporates a level of reflection on practices, processes and the world around us which depends on a higher level of metacognition that Lipman labels 'complex thinking'. Complex thinking relies upon an advanced level of awareness of 'assumptions . . . reasons . . . [and] . . . evidence' that contribute to determining an appropriate solution or conclusion (Lipman, 1991, p. 25). It also relies upon the development of

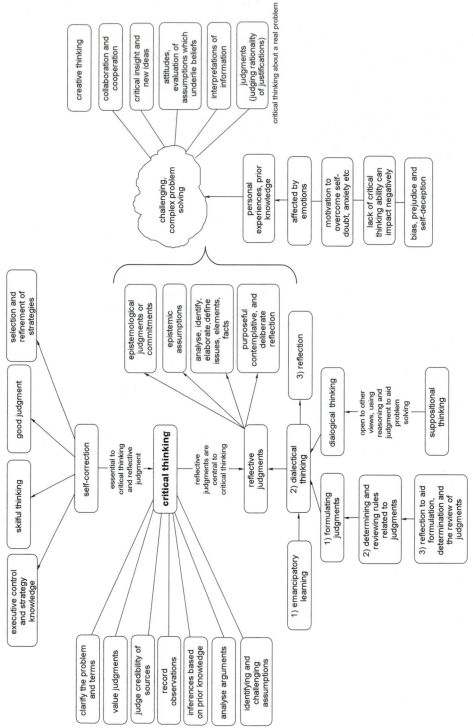

Figure 3.2 Amplification of critical thinking in the conceptual framework of metacognition

processes and methods – dependent upon one's reflection of these processes and knowledge affected by beliefs and prejudices.

Kuhn (1999a) contributes a detailed theory connecting critical thinking and metacognition. She names three main categories or elements of meta-knowing or metacognition connected with critical thinking, 'meta-knowing . . . metacognitive, metastrategic, and epistemological' (p. 23). Similarly, Bruning *et al.* (1999) identify knowledge, inferences and evaluative processes as central to metacognition and critical thinking. This conception of knowledge, evaluation and strategic processes as essential to critical thinking reflects elements of Kuhn's view of critical thinking and metacognition.

Table 3.1 outlines Kuhn's (1999a) theories on meta-knowing and critical thinking. Drawing from the epistemological theories of Perry (1970) and Hofer and Pintrich (1997), Kuhn considers that epistemological understandings have a significant impact on critical thinking and on metacognitive processes.

Table 3.1 Interpretation of Kuhn's (1999a) elements of meta-knowing and relationship to the development of critical thinking

Element of meta-knowing or metacognition	*Relationship to critical thinking*
Metacognitive (Knowing/ Understanding and Skills) ✦ essential to critical thinking	Metacognitive knowing involves reflection on prior and new knowledge Metacognitive skills involves conscious control of beliefs including knowledge of and justification of beliefs, evaluation of assertions
Metastrategic (Skill) ✦ essential to critical thinking	Metastrategic skill ensures consistent evaluation of criterion, including favoured assertions with the same criterion in various contexts Considers all variables in the wider context rather than a limited singular context
Epistemological (Knowing/Understanding) ✦ fundamental to, and underpins critical thinking	Epistemological knowing involves broader understanding of knowing and knowledge Epistemological knowing influences both metastrategic and metacognitive elements Epistemological knowing assertions are judgments and incorporate evaluation of judgments and arguments

Source: Adapted from Kuhn (1999a).

Reasoning is the 'educational cognate' of critical thinking. The ability to be self-reflexive about one's critical thinking processes embraces rationality or reasoning. Siegel believes that learners need to be 'critical about critical thinking itself' (Siegel, 1989, p. 1). This alludes to the reflectivity involved in supporting effective critical thinking. These reflective processes would rely upon both knowledge of cognition and regulation of cognition. Critical thinking is also affected by beliefs, values and the attitude towards thinking effectively (Kuhn, 1999a; Tsai, 2001). Tsai considers that there is a reciprocal interaction between metacognitive processes, critical thinking and epistemological commitments. Each in turn influences the other.

The BACEIS (Behaviour, Attitudes, Cognition, Environment seen as Interacting Systems) model (see Hartman, 2001a, 2001c; Hartman and Sternberg, 1993) identifies the link between critical thinking, and metacognitive knowledge and skills, specifically strategy knowledge and executive control. These metacognitive processes are essential for the development, and application, of critical thinking. Critical thinking interacts with these metacognitive processes to refine and determine appropriate actions and decisions, identify related beliefs, and reflect on these during problem solving. Metacognitive processes are identified as essential to creativity, learning strategies and critical thinking. Metacognition would be a foundation for both critical thinking and creative thinking. Central to the model is the interaction between cognitive and metacognitive, and affective elements. It identifies the influence affective elements have on metacognitive processes; this would be especially evident in solving complex problems.

Both Kuhn's theories and Hartman and Sternberg's BACEIS model reflect Lipman's view of the interaction between critical and complex thinking. He may, in some sense, be alluding to a higher level of metacognition involving higher-order thinking in referring to complex thinking. This book will not investigate the theoretical underpinnings of higher-order thinking as the term is considered to be inherently ambiguous (see Lipman, 1991, 2003), including its relationship to metacognition, although the literature does recognise and establish, to some extent, this relationship (e.g. Resnick, 1987; Vockell and van Deusen, 1989). Future theoretical analysis of this relationship would be a contribution to the literature in this field, including its relationship to complex problem solving.

The following assertions posit the connection between critical thinking and metacognition:

3.11 Knowledge of cognition and reflection and knowledge of regulatory processes of cognition are elements of metacognition in critical thinking.

3.12 Knowledge, selection and refinement of strategies, and the monitoring and control of inferences through reasoning, are metacognition elements identified in critical thinking.

3.13 Evaluative, reflective reasoning, self-correction and self-regulatory processes based upon specific criteria and context are supported by scaffolding, especially in complex problems.

3.14 During problem solving, purposeful reflection involves complex higher-order thinking entailing the identification of beliefs, bias, prejudice, assumptions, epistemological commitments and reflection.

A number of empirical studies provide evidence to support the relationship between metacognition and critical thinking. Although there are numerous studies on critical thinking, only a few examine the interaction between critical thinking and metacognition and fewer still provide a strong conceptual basis for their study and subsequent findings. It is highlighted in these studies that many do not draw from the conceptual links between critical thinking and metacognition. However, these studies do recognise the significance of reflection as an integral element that links critical thinking and metacognition, and some do provide their own descriptions of the concepts.

A study by Hanley (1995) reviewed critical thinking and metacognition in 65 undergraduate students. Two components were identified as necessary to improve critical thinking: metacognitive skills, including strategies involved in monitoring and controlling knowledge; and the development of expert knowledge and skills as important metacognitive processes. Students were asked to: (a) define and identify a problem which they had to solve; (b) review and evaluate the strategies and processes they used to solve it; and (c) provide an overall impression of any improvement in their critical thinking skills. Data were collected with the use of a critical thinking journal. Information was also collected about students' problem-solving activities. The findings demonstrated that students needed to be aware of their problems before they could effectively apply 'critical analysis' skills to develop a problem solution. The findings also highlighted that what students believed they actually learned was not reflected in their grades. Most importantly, Hanley found that the development of expert, critical thinking skills relied upon students' knowledge and application of the correct processes and strategies needed in solving specific problems. This entailed their skills of awareness in identifying problems, not avoiding problems if they are aware of them, and pursuing the successful solving of problems. Hanley found that focusing on increasing expert thinking, knowledge and skills improved critical thinking. Overall, this study supports the relationship between metacognitive processes and critical thinking skills, and the view that both are needed for successful problem solving.

Research by Vojnovich (1998) also established the interrelationship between critical thinking, metacognition and the use of reflective journals. Adolescents who lacked motivation did not participate and were disengaged from learning, especially in traditional, content-orientated classes, and those with underdeveloped skills were identified by their teachers and included in the study. These students also did not use identifiable critical thinking processes in problem solving. The study implemented a number of strategies, including specifically focusing on introducing problems to develop critical thinking; cooperative learning environments; and the completion of a reflective journal focusing on developing metacognitive processes. The results demonstrated that students increased their levels of reflection, critical thinking and metacognition in problem-solving contexts with the support of reflective journal writing.

Another example of research which investigated the connection between critical thinking and metacognition can be found in the work of Hine *et al.*

(2001). They completed three separate studies investigating the use of self-reflection strategies by secondary school students, and first- and second-year university students. Comparing their results, the studies identified that the interrelationship between critical thinking, self-reflection and metacognition could be supported and enhanced by the use of three main strategies.

The first strategy – structured questioning to develop affective thinking – was used with a secondary school history class to prompt students to connect with their own thoughts and feelings and critically self-reflect on them, building empathy and understanding of the past and of situations. The second strategy – student-generated questions within a journalising process – was tested with first-year education students, encouraging them to reflect on their knowledge through self and higher-order questioning of concepts, ideas, and challenges. They were encouraged to share and answer questions in collaborative situations, prompting group discussions, contemplation and further reflection. Challenging, probing questions were used by the lecturer to encourage and stimulate further discussion and reflection. The third strategy – metacognitive questions as a scaffold for reflective learning in a collaborative context – was applied with first- and second-year education and developmental psychology students through the use of concept mapping. The researchers found that concept mapping promotes and enables self-reflection and metacognitive awareness through the critical evaluation of the connections between concepts. Overall, these studies found that the three strategies, with teacher support, increased students' self-reflection and understanding of concepts and processes covered in their courses.

Prompted by the belief that 'underdeveloped metacognitive critical thinking skills impact health care with poor clinical judgments and professional dissatisfaction', Kuiper (2002, p. 78) decided to investigate the critical thinking skills and abilities of 32 newly graduated nurses. The participants completed a reflective journal over an eight-week period. Although her study investigated students' metacognitive critical thinking strategies, she did not provide a description of the term. However, she did base the study on theories of self-regulation, and referred to metacognitive processes in this sense. Analysis of the reflective journals found that graduate nurses reflected on their conceptual and strategy knowledge, made judgments about their capability and work environment, were self-corrective, used inferences, reasoning and monitoring, and interpreted and evaluated their experiences. The study found that strategic self-regulation depended upon critical thinking skills and ability, and the use of reflective journals prompted the development and application of self-regulatory strategies. The study surmised that the development of critical thinking through the use of reflective journals would support the transferability of metacognitive strategies.

To date, there appears to be limited research into the specific connections between critical thinking and metacognition. The studies identified here assume this connection, but do not draw from conceptual foundations of both constructs. Although their findings support many of the conceptual views which contribute to the connection between the constructs, the studies have not drawn on the specific literature. All have relied upon the reflective processes of their participants to identify and justify connections between critical thinking and metacognition.

Overall, the assertions reaffirm the connections identified in the studies between critical thinking and metacognition:

3.15 Awareness and identification of beliefs, values and attitudes impact on critical thinking and metacognitive processes in problem-solving environments.

3.16 Underdeveloped critical thinking and metacognitive skills impact negatively on successful problem solving.

3.17 Critical thinking is enhanced by metacognitive knowledge and regulation of cognition.

3.18 Scaffolding in problem-solving situations supports the development of critical thinking, metacognitive knowledge and skills, executive control and strategy knowledge.

Conclusion

Clearly, in many ways the two concepts of critical reflection and critical thinking overlap, although the discussion highlights that each construct has different significant contributors. Their relationship to reflection and meta-cognition is fundamental as reflection can not be metacognitive unless it goes beyond just 'thinking about thinking' to a higher level of focused, deliberate, purposeful reflection in the form of critical reflection and critical thinking. Both are essential for problem solving in complex contexts and both rely upon reflective judgments to enable this level of reflection, decision making, problem solving, creativity, and judgment. Judgments are fundamental to both critical thinking and critical reflection. Both rely upon the self, but refer to self with varying foci.

Critical reflection specifically refers to self in terms of self-knowledge, and fundamental to self-knowledge is the development of self-awareness, self-discovery and self-understanding. This level of self-knowledge enables strategy selection and application in complex problem-solving situations. Critical thinking has a greater focus on processes applied during problem solving, such as skilful thinking, self-correction, analysing and judging sources of information. Critical reflection relies upon a high level of critical knowing based upon a well developed knowledge of self. This knowledge of self is the essence of critical knowing and critical reflection. Both critical thinking and critical reflection can occur in collaborative, cooperative problem-solving situations.

The connection between metacognition, critical reflection and critical thinking is essentially based upon personal understanding and knowledge.

This includes knowledge of oneself as a learner, prior knowledge, and knowledge and assessment of beliefs and attitudes. This knowledge is especially necessary for complex problem solving. The problem-solving process draws from this knowledge and instigates the selection, monitoring and control of strategies which are applied to facilitate solutions to these types of problems. Higher levels of reflection, such as critical reflection and critical thinking, are essential to facilitate metacognitive processes in problem solving through the review of the appropriateness of strategies, and monitoring and control of these strategies and processes. This level of monitoring and regulation in critical reflection is dependent upon self-knowledge and self-awareness.

Metacognition relies on critical thinking which involves monitoring and the control of inferences through reasoning, and knowledge of cognition and regulation of cognition. It is important to note that critical thinking may not always be metacognitive; to be metacognitive, it must be purposeful and deliberate reflection. Both metacognition and critical thinking rely upon an internal dialectic for the critiquing of prior knowledge and the understanding of new knowledge. Internal dialectic or internal verbalisation is stimulated in collaborative situations where beliefs, judgments, prior knowledge and understandings, and the interpretation of new information are challenged and supported. This occurs in complex problem solving and relies upon a higher level of reflection which brings into play advanced understanding of self.

This purposeful, critical thinking becomes complex thinking, or higher-order thinking, which involves a focus on awareness of issues such as self-deception, bias and prejudice which can affect problem solving. Higher-order thinking is a combination of critical and creative thinking and is considered to be complex thinking. Critical thinking involves epistemic assumptions, epistemological judgments and an understanding of their impact on problem solving.

The higher-order assertions generated in this section are listed as follows:

3.19   Critical reflection and critical thinking operate on a higher level of focused, purposeful reflection relying upon reflective judgment and involve decision making, problem solving and creativity (HOA.3).

3.20   Critical reflection relies upon a high level of critical knowing based upon knowledge of self. This enables strategy selection and application in complex problems (HOA.4).

3.21   Higher-order thinking is a combination of critical and creative thinking and is considered to be complex thinking. It involves epistemic assumptions and epistemological judgments, and knowledge of their effect on problem solving (HOA.5)..

Chapter 4 affirms the relationship between reflection and metacognition through a discussion of self-knowledge.

4 Reflection and metacognition: Affirming the connection

This chapter confirms that the interaction between metacognition and reflection is dependent upon self-knowledge, an essential element of metacognition. Ascertaining self-knowledge as a core connection between reflection and metacognition stimulates discussion of other significant conceptual contributions, enabling a mapping of these theories.

Self-knowledge: Uniting reflection and metacognition

Earlier in Part I, historical discussions provided a foundation for strongly suggesting that self-knowledge is an essential, uniting core between reflection and metacognition. Contributions by Aristotle, Descartes and Augustine fundamentally imply that self-knowledge and self-understanding are essential in knowing oneself; this can only be achieved through deliberate reflection and introspection. If self-knowledge relies upon reflection and introspection, what are the differences between the two processes, and how do these processes relate to metacognition and contribute to self-knowledge?

The terms reflection and introspection have been used, to some extent, interchangeably in the literature (e.g. Rosenthal, 1986, 2000). Even though reflection is sometimes considered a process or part of introspection, the terms have different meanings. Reflection involves contemplative, focused thinking, whereas introspection is self-observatory and constitutes self-analysis through the awareness of feelings, thoughts and reactions. The term introspection has been derived from the Latin *spicere* (to look) and *intra* (within) (Lyons, 1986; Rosenthal, 2000).

The interaction between reflection and introspection brings about self-reflection or self-knowledge. Introspection relies upon self-knowledge and interaction involves a self-interpretative, conscious process influenced by past experiences and impacted by current situations (Rosenthal, 2000; Ryle, 1949). To reflect at a deep level or to reflect critically, it is necessary for consciousness of these reflective processes to be present. Reflection can be just reflecting, without a conscious application and awareness of reflectivity. When reflection is conscious, focused and applied, it involves consciousness and promotes the development of self-knowledge. This level of reflexivity begins to develop in adolescence (Blasi and Hoeffel, 1974). Therefore, consciousness and introspection are intertwined, and reliant upon self-knowledge and reflective processes.

Both Locke's concept of 'inner perception "reflexion"' (see Ryle, 1949, p. 159) and James' (1890a, p. 400) 'consciousness of Self' identified the connection between reflection, introspection and consciousness, based upon self-knowledge. James specifically describes consciousness of oneself as involving a stream of thought; identifying that knowledge of self is the core of consciousness. Considered a significant contributor to 'introspectionist psychology' (Urmson, 1960, p. 195), James' work focused on describing intellectual processes, and control and consciousness of thinking. This is now identified as an early conceptual discussion of cognition and meta-cognition (Brown, 1977; Flavell *et al.*, 2000; Fox and Riconscente, 2008; Langrehr and Palmer, 1998; Reeve and Brown, 1984).

Self is considered to be the essence of consciousness (Blasi and Hoeffel, 1974; Rosenthal, 2000; Ryle, 1949). Without a knowledge of self, it has been argued that consciousness may not be present. Consciousness enables knowledge differentiation, the 'content of knowledge' and the 'act of know-ing'; the latter is congruent with self-knowledge rather than only content knowledge of the object of consciousness. Consciousness reliant upon transparency of self provides a clear connection between knowing, under-standing, reflecting and, importantly, an understanding of the content of that knowledge (Blasi and Hoeffel, 1974). Self-knowledge can only be developed through a purposeful reflection of self, without which we could not develop an understanding of the world around us, and our place in it. This would also involve a self-awareness or autonoetic consciousness which is essential to self-knowledge and regulatory processes (Wheeler *et al.*, 1997).

Self-knowledge and consciousness are also affected by a wider, critical consciousness created by interactions with others, instigating change and critical problematisation. Critical consciousness develops through social interaction, which supports the identification of problem situations and the evolution of a specific conscious, critical problematisation of the problem, instigating the need for a solution (Freire, 1973; Habermas, 1987). Prob-lematisation seems congruent with the idea that knowledge development can occur in individual and collaborative problem-solving situations. These situations, fundamentally complex problems, rely upon self-knowledge of strategies, applications and processes necessary for problem solving; and involving metacognitive processes.

The literature does provide a number of instances where self-knowledge is related to reflection, introspection and metacognition (e.g. Bogdan, 2000; Borkowski, 1985; Rosenthal, 1999). Self-knowledge is in essence the founda-tion upon which introspection and reflection impact upon metacognition processes (e.g. Borkowski, 1985; Jonassen and Tessmer, 1996/1997; Pintrich, 2002; Rosenthal, 1999; Schraw and Dennison, 1994). The literature does refer to self-knowledge as an essential component of metacognition (e.g. Borkowski, 1985; Jonassen and Tessmer, 1996/1997; Pintrich, 2002; Rosenthal, 1999; Schraw and Dennison, 1994). However, Flavell (1979, 1987) did not use the term reflection in describing metacognitive knowledge, specifically within the 'person' variable, nor did he specifically use the term self-knowledge. Nevertheless, Flavell's component of metacognitive knowledge strongly suggests that self-knowledge is essential to metacognitive processes in problem-solving situations for it is an element of metacognitive knowledge which is affected by the beliefs of the learner and also their beliefs of themselves in the world (Flavell, 1979; Pintrich, 2002).

Knowledge of problem-solving strategies is affected by self-knowledge (Flavell, 1979; Pintrich, 2002; Schraw and Dennison, 1994). In considering this, Jonassen and Tessmer (1996/1997) also identify future research possibilities which focus on ascertaining the effects of the use of 'self-knowledge strategies upon (1) error type and rate during problem-solving learning, and (2) problem-solving performance in near and far transfer tasks' (p. 40). Near transfer refers to the ability to transfer knowledge and skills to problems that are similar in structure, or well-structured problems. Far transfer refers to the ability to transfer knowledge and skills to problems which are not similar in structure, or complex problems (Osman and Hannafin, 1992).

The literature has shown that the terms reflection, introspection and consciousness are at times used interchangeably, and it has been argued that reflection and introspection are not essentially the same process. However, they do interact and rely upon consciousness and each other, facilitating the development of self-knowledge. Gaining a deeper or higher level of reflection, or reflection reliant upon introspection, not being 'thinking about thinking', are reflective processes which depend upon the analysis of self-knowledge. Reflection may not be associated with introspection if reflection is not purposeful and dependent upon looking within, drawing from beliefs, prior knowledge and understandings, suppositions and assumptions. Also, understanding and awareness of the impact of feelings and thoughts about learning processes, abilities, contexts and challenges are essential to self-knowledge. The effect of challenges on problem-solving processes including reflexivity and introspection should not be underestimated. Complex problems can have a significant impact on problem-solving processes, being affected by beliefs about oneself as a learner and possibly instigating false beliefs and false self-knowledge. Self-knowledge is the foundation for metacognitive processes.

The following assertions identify that self-knowledge is essential to reflection and metacognition:

4.1   Self-reflection or self-knowledge is a combination of purposeful reflection and introspection reliant upon consciousness and is integral to metacognition.

4.2   Self-knowledge is the core of metacognition, specifically metacognitive knowledge, and involves knowledge of strategies and processes and develops in and is affected by complex problem-solving situations.

Figure 4.1 is an amplification of the relationships between self-knowledge, reflection, metacognition and consciousness.

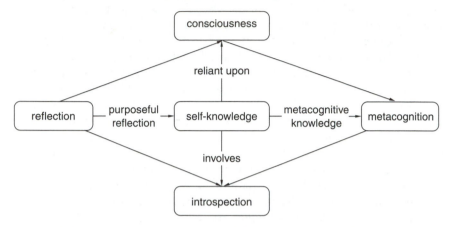

Figure 4.1 Amplification of the relationship between self-knowledge, consciousness and introspection in the conceptual framework of metacognition

The following discussion further considers the specific conceptual contributions which reaffirm the connection between metacognition and reflection.

Current discussions of metacognitive processes consider that 'reflective thinking is the essence of metacognition' (Hartman, 2001c, p. xi). Reflection, awareness and introspection of thoughts, processes, strategies and knowledge are synonymous with metacognition, and are especially important in problem-solving situations. The literature reasserts this many times over (e.g. Birenbaum and Amdur, 1999; Borkowski and Cavanaugh, 1981; Brown, 1987, 1997; Iran-Nejad and Gregg, 2001; Kemmis, 1985; McAlpine *et al.*, 1999; Mezirow, 1991; Nisbett and Wilson, 1977; Paris and Winograd, 1990; Schraw, 1998, 2001; Schraw and Dennison, 1994; Sitko, 1998; Weinert, 1987; Yussen, 1985). However, there are few conceptual explorations of the relationship between metacognition and reflection.

One contribution, by Yussen (1985), identifies reflective processes for three components of metacognition: metamemory – contemplating strategies to facilitate memory; metacomprehension – assessing comprehension; and metaattention – identifying variables impacting on concentration or observation. Paris and Winograd (1990) connect metacognitive knowledge with 'self-appraisal' processes. They refer to self-appraisal as 'personal reflections about one's knowledge states and abilities' (ibid., p. 17). Another contribution, by Bogdan (2000), describes the term 'metamentation or mental reflexivity' as essential to 'reflexive consciousness', judgment, self-evaluation, and forward thinking (p. xi). The term seems synonymous with meta-cognition, although he does not use the term.

Earlier, an empirical study by Hanley (1995) was reviewed which argued that expert learners applied, implemented and displayed attributes of critical thinking when relying upon their metacognitive knowledge and strategies during problem solving. Ertmer and Newby (1996) provide a theoretical supposition which supports these findings. They believe that reflection is central to metacognitive processes and essential to the development of expert learners. In support of this Ertmer and Newby depict a model illustrating reflection as the central and connecting process between metacognitive knowledge and self-regulation or 'metacognitive control' (ibid., p. 15). They consider that reflection directly impacts on metacognitive knowledge. However, they overlooked Flavell's (1979, 1981a; Flavell and Wellman, 1977) significant work which identified categories and sub-categories of metacognition, including metacognitive knowledge. Adopting similar subcategories to those of Flavell – task, strategy – and using the term 'self' instead of person without referring to his work is a substantial oversight. This is a theoretical flaw in their discussion, although their case for the interrelationship between metacognitive knowledge and metacognitive control based upon reflection is convincing.

A significant theoretical contribution connecting metacognition, knowledge and reflection is provided by Cornoldi (1998). He cogently establishes that 'metacognitive reflection' involves beliefs, perceptions and understandings of a problem or cognitive task or activity and is influenced by problem elements and variables affecting the problem-solving process (ibid., p. 139). Metacognitive reflection is directly associated with the problem and problem-solving process. It comprises various elements or components including 'metacognitive knowledge' and 'metacognitive judgments or metacognitive conceptualization' (ibid., p. 140).

Cornoldi (1998) refers to Cornoldi and Vianello (1992) in describing metacognitive knowledge as a form of 'preexisting reflection' (p. 140). This prior reflective knowledge encompasses beliefs and understandings about problems and problem solving, and exists before a new problem or cognitive task is first encountered. Reflective knowledge then develops during the problem-solving process and may include reflecting on whether the problem is harder or easier than anticipated and the identification of specific strategies to facilitate a solution(s). This is posited as metacognitive conceptualisation or metacognitive judgments. Metacognitive conceptualisation is affected by the problem itself, including context, multiplicity of variables, complexity, ambiguity and changes. Therefore, metacognitive conceptualisation, an element of metacognitive reflection, results as a combination of preexisting reflective, metacognitive knowledge and specific strategy metacognitive knowledge. Cornoldi also refers to metacognitive attitude and specific metacognitive knowledge as subcategories of metacognitive knowledge, both of which impact upon metacognitive reflection.

There is an interactive relationship between metacognitive attitude, specific metacognitive strategy knowledge (both subcategories of metacognitive knowledge) and metacognitive reflection. Metacognitive attitude may directly influence the development of metacognitive reflection and metacognitive knowledge. The inclination to attempt a complex problem, time spent on task, general attitudes or beliefs about the problem and one's ability affect metacognitive reflection. Metacognitive knowledge is also influenced by the interaction between metacognitive attitude and metacognitive reflection in the determination of appropriate task strategies (Cornoldi, 1998). A detailed discussion of metacognitive knowledge is covered in Part 3 – Metacognition: The Taxonomy. Table 4.1 provides an outline of Cornoldi's components of metacognitive reflection.

Table 4.1 Cornoldi's components of metacognitive reflection

Components of metacognitive reflection	
Metacognitive reflection	People's beliefs and interpretation of cognitive activity. It can be distinguished in two aspects: (a) metacognitive knowledge, and (b) metacognitive conceptualisation of a task
Metacognitive knowledge	People's beliefs concerning all possible aspects of cognitive activity (nature, functioning, self-evaluation, etc.), preexisting before actual cognitive tasks are carried out. It may be general or specific, more or less conscious, verbalisable, and so forth
Metacognitive conceptualisation of a task	Metacognitive reflection present at the moment of starting a task and during its execution
Metacognitive attitude	Overall level of metacognitive knowledge, with cognitive, emotional-motivational, and behavioral implications
Specific metacognitive knowledge	Knowledge concerning specific aspects of cognitive functioning

Source: Adapted from Cornoldi (1998).

Figure 4.2 depicts the major conceptual contributions to metacognition and reflection. It illustrates each of the core terms used by the theorists to describe their conception of metacognition and reflection. Depicting these contributions highlights the interchangeable use of metacognitive terms to describe similar processes. For example, metacognitive knowledge is used by Ertmer and Newby (1996), who incorporate interactions between metacognition, reflection and metacognitive control. Nisbet and Shucksmith (1984) refer to metacognition as the 'seventh sense . . . the awareness of one's mental processes, the capacity to reflect on how one learns, how to strengthen memory, how to tackle problems systematically – reflection, awareness, understanding, and perhaps ultimately control' (p. 1). Similarly, Schraw (2001) refers to metacognitive awareness which also incorporates

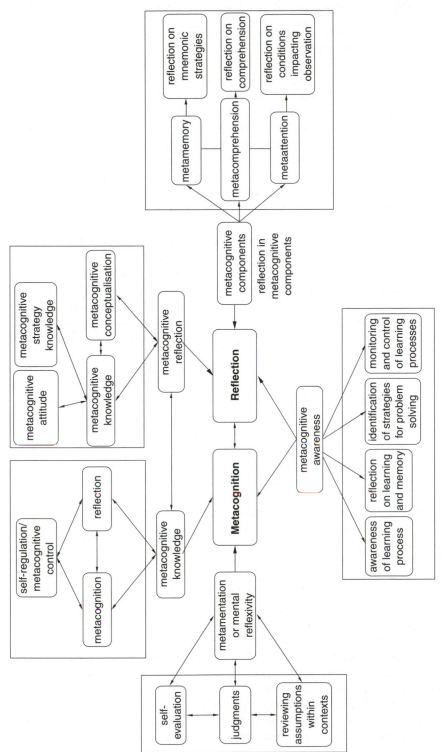

Figure 4.2 Amplification of major contributions to metacognition in the conceptual framework of metacognition

knowledge of strategies and monitoring and control, which are reliant upon reflection and metacognition.

Studies by McAlpine *et al.* (1999) and McAlpine and Weston (2000) investigated, through the use of interview and video data, the reflective teaching processes used by six university professors in the planning, teaching and evaluation of student work. The studies clearly identified a commonality between metacognitive processes and reflectivity. A model of metacognitive processes, including reflection, demonstrates the interactions between six elements: goals, knowledge, decision making, action, monitoring cues and corridor of tolerance. Goals are central to all of these elements. The teaching processes of the professors indicated that cues helped them to monitor their work to achieve particular goals, facilitate decision making, and build upon existing knowledge and experience. Reflection was identified as fundamental to facilitate these metacognitive processes. The studies identified that there is a definite relationship between metacognition and reflection. McAlpine *et al.* (1999) clearly identify a link between knowledge and access to that knowledge, via monitoring and reflection. These are all metacognitive processes. Although the professors in the study did not use reflective journals to record their metacognitive processes, many other studies have relied upon the use of reflective or cognitive tools to verify the connection between reflection and metacognition.

The use of cognitive tools or mind tools, scaffolding or reflection tools facilitates the solving of complex problems and supports metacognitive processes facilitating critical reflection (e.g. Brown *et al.*, 1994; Ferry and Brown, 1998; Hedberg *et al.*, 1998; Jonassen, 1996, 2000, 2003; Jonassen and Reeves, 1996; Jonassen and Wang, 2003; Lajoie, 1993; Lin *et al.*, 1999). Some types of cognitive tools are journals, which can be written, visual or multimedia. Other forms are concept mapping or mind mapping, and report writing. Concept maps or semantic networks are visual representations of knowledge and understandings which can effectively be used in collaborative learning environments and to facilitate metacognitive processes (Cicognani, 2000; Hedberg *et al.*, 1998; Hine *et al.*, 2001; Marra and Jonassen, 2002; Novak, 1990).

Hedberg *et al.* (1998) used concept mapping and report writing as cognitive tools to scaffold students' reflective processes during the solving of a complex problem. The results established that scaffolding, in the form of concept mapping, was successful in supporting students in the solving of complex problems. However, students needed to rely upon 'their abilities to re-focus and extend their information' more in the complex problem than the well-structured problem (Hedberg *et al.*, 1998, p. 325). Hedberg *et al.* alluded to the use of scaffolding to support reflection and higher levels of metacognitive processes. Hine *et al.* (2001) also identified that concept mapping supports metacognitive processes, specifically reflection on concepts and their interrelationships. The study found that the use of scaffolding by way of concept mapping supported students' self-reflection, metacognitive awareness and metacognitive skills. Similarly, Daley (2002) used concept mapping to support adult students' awareness and under-standing of their learning processes.

Studies such as those by McCrindle and Christensen (1995) found that journal writing can support metacognitive processes. Their quantitative study of 40 first-year university biology students involved the completion of a reflective journal or a report on their learning processes during the course. The study reports that the students who completed the journal were aware of and used more sophisticated metacognitive strategies and demonstrated a higher level of conceptual understanding of course content. The students demonstrated an increased awareness of metacognitive strategies and control of these strategies. As a result they performed significantly better in the final exam than the students who completed a report of their processes and did not keep a reflective journal. The study is based upon a strong theoretical framework where the authors carefully discuss the links between Flavell's (1979) metacognitive theories of person, task and strategy vari-ables. Similarly, a recent study by Rimor and Kozminsky (2003) developed a tool called the 'metacognitive tool for students' reflections'. It is based upon Flavell's (1979) person, task and strategy variables and was used to study students' metacognitive knowledge of these variables and their application in an online environment, specifically an online forum or discussion board conducted asynchronously.

A study by Birenbaum and Amdur (1999) also specifically identified an increased level of metacognitive awareness through the use of reflective journals. Their qualitative study of 25 graduate students' knowledge and understanding of constructivist, alternative assessments integrated the use of reflective journals to identify how these journals enhanced the learning process. Their results reflected findings by McCrindle and Christensen that students gained and developed their own personal knowledge, represented as metacognitive knowledge and awareness. This claim corresponds to Hatton and Smith's (1995) findings that describe critical reflection as a process which can be represented, to some extent, in journal writing.

Similarly, a study by Hine (2000) investigated the use of journal writing to support reflection and metacognitive processes with second- and third-year preservice teachers in the context of mentoring. The study found that journals can be successfully used to promote self-reflection and in turn enhance monitoring and promote reflective, meaningful learning. Accord-ing to Newton (1991), the use of journal writing as an effective metacog-nitive awareness and development tool facilitates the development of understanding and 'meaning making' of texts and supports students' devel-opment as 'critics of their own learning processes' (p. 478). This paper does not define metacognition in any sense although the writer is adamant that journal writing has helped to improve her first-year university students' responses to questions regarding their efforts to understand a demanding literary text and as a consequence has helped the development and assessment of their learning strategies. Hine *et al.* (2001) identified the use of journal writing as an effective strategy which enhances students' reflection and metacognitive awareness. Alternatively, Pugalee (2001) provides a strong argument for involvement of metacognitive processes as part of reflective writing during problem solving in mathematics. He explains that 20 Year 9 Algebra students were engaged in a range of metacognitive processes which were reflected in the journalising of their problem-solving processes. He discusses the importance of inner speech and the relationship between reflection, metacognition and writing during mathematical problem solving. Although a range of problems was used in the study, Pugalee did not indicate if they were well-structured or a combination of well-structured and complex problems.

According to Ferry and Brown (1998), the use of a multimedia (visual) journal helped preservice teachers develop reflective skills. They argue that their study demonstrates that the preservice teachers developed meta-cognitive knowledge through the use of the multimedia journal. However, they did not define what they considered to be metacognitive knowledge or provide any theoretical connection with their study and metacognition theory.

Many of the empirical studies used reflective journals to collect data establishing their relationship. However, it should be noted that there are potentially many other types of cognitive tools, such as knowledge representation, visualisation and modelling tools, which could also be effectively used to establish this link (Jonassen, 2003).

The following statements assert that the studies reaffirm the connections between metacognition and reflection:

4.3   Reflection is essential for metacognitive processes facilitating complex problem solving.
4.4   Reflection is the connection between metacognitive knowledge and self-regulation or metacognitive control.
4.5   Reflection and self-knowledge are essential for the identification, monitoring and control of problem-solving strategies.
4.6   Metacognitive tools support reflection and are important scaffolds for well-structured problem solving but more so for complex problem solving.

Conclusion

This chapter has described the relationship between metacognition and reflection as dependent upon self-knowledge. Self-knowledge is identified as the core foundation of metacognition. It is argued that self-knowledge is developed through the interaction between reflection, introspection and consciousness and is essential for metacognitive processes to occur.

The literature has shown that the terms reflection, introspection and consciousness are at times used interchangeably. It has been argued that reflection and introspection are not essentially the same process. However, they interact and rely upon consciousness and each other, facilitating the development of self-knowledge. A deeper or higher level of reflection, reliant upon introspection, depends upon and interacts with the analysis of one's self-knowledge. Reflection may not be associated with introspection if it is not purposeful and dependent upon looking within, drawing from beliefs, prior knowledge and understandings, suppositions, and assumptions. Also, an understanding and an awareness of the effect of feelings and thoughts about learning processes, abilities, contexts and challenges are essential to self-knowledge. The effect of challenges on problem-solving processes including reflexivity and introspection should not be underestimated. These challenges that also involve dealing with the realisation of false beliefs, false self-knowledge, and uncertainties such as self-doubt of oneself as a learner are instigated in complex problems and can have significant effects on problem-solving processes.

Self-knowledge or self-interpretation is dependent upon self-reflection or the interaction between reflection and introspection. It is fundamental for metacognitive processes to occur and specifically involves metacognitive knowledge, including knowledge of strategies and processes. Metacognitive knowledge and self-knowledge develop in, and are affected by, complex problem-solving situations.

Although the literature supports the theory that self-knowledge is essential for metacognitive processes to occur, there is scarcely any research or theoretical discussion which specifically describes the interrelationship between self-knowledge, reflection, introspection, consciousness and metacognition. Nor are there substantial studies on the effect of self-knowledge, as an element of metacognitive knowledge, on the solving of complex problems.

Both the conceptual and the empirical contributions support the argument, the foundation of this thesis, that reflection is the quintessence of metacognition. Researchers are still identifying the types and forms of metacognitive tools that can be successfully used to support problem solving and facilitate reflection and metacognitive processes in complex problem-solving contexts. It has been established that reflection, supported by metacognitive tools, is essential to metacognitive knowledge and the monitoring and control of problem-solving strategies. Scaffolding, however, is necessary to support these processes, especially during problem solving in complex problem contexts.

Moreover, research into the relationship between reflection and metacognition is sparse. Essential elements and components of metacognition which have been identified by theorists such as Kuhn, Cornoldi and Yussen do not appear to have been fully investigated. The potential for extensive research into the effect of reflective processes on metacognition in complex problem-solving situations is rich and diverse.

The following higher-order assertions are generated from the above discussion:

4.7   Self-knowledge is developed through the interaction between reflection, introspection and consciousness, and is essential for metacognition (HOA.6).

4.8   Self-knowledge is a form of metacognitive knowledge, including knowledge of strategies and processes. Metacognitive knowledge and self-knowledge develop in, and are affected by, complex problem-solving situations (HOA.7).

4.9   Self-knowledge is influenced by feelings, beliefs, false beliefs, self-doubt, prior knowledge and understandings, suppositions, assumptions, ability, contexts and challenges which can be instigated in complex problems and can affect problem-solving processes (HOA.8).

Conclusion to Part I

First, Part I has established that reflection is the core of metacognition by firmly rejecting the notion that it is simply 'thinking about thinking'. The assertions generated highlight the intricate connections between metacognition and reflection, and support the rejection of this colloquialism. To date little has been written about the multifarious connections between metacognition and reflection, raising the importance of reflection as the quintessence of metacognition. Clearly, if research is investigating metacognition in complex, challenging problems, researchers need to look beyond colloquialisms of metacognition, and the global use of the term reflection, to identify specifically the type of reflective processes – such as critical reflection, critical thinking and reflective thinking – which are instigated in these types of environments. Researchers also need to consider that immersed in these reflective processes is higher-order reasoning.

Second, metacognitive reflection and metareflection are intricate processes incorporating many higher levels of mental activity. These are identified as knowledge of self, knowledge of strategies, higher-order reasoning, self-regulatory processes such as monitoring and control, critical reflection, critical thinking, and reflective judgments. They also, to some extent, interact with each other, especially in problem-solving situations. Such complex, reflective processes are necessary to instigate, promote, and support metacognitive processes facilitating problem solving, especially in complex problems. This is still in need of validation through future empirical studies.

Third, metacognition can not exist without some form or level of reflection, fleeting or purposeful. Purposeful reflection is necessary to facilitate problem solving in complex situations and is essential to critical thinking, critical reflection and reflective thinking. It is also necessary for the development of self-knowledge so that metacognition can occur. Its development relies upon the interaction between reflection, introspection and consciousness. Relying upon self-knowledge, reflective processes facilitate the control, correction and monitoring of problem-solving strategies. The more complex the situation, the higher the level of reflective processes required, and learners need additional supports such as scaffolding and verbalisation for problem solving. Knowledge has been identified as essential to metacognition, although the extent to which reflection instigates and supports the development of metacognitive knowledge has received little attention. Also, self-knowledge is central to the development of metacognitive knowledge, and this too has received little attention by researchers, including the impact of beliefs on self-knowledge and metacognitive processes, especially during problem solving in complex contexts. It is important to understand how self-knowledge impacts on strategy knowledge, and the monitoring and control of these strategies.

Part II

Metamemory: The foundational construct

Part II establishes that metamemory is the foundation of the construct of metacognition. A number of theorists including Flavell, Corsini, Brown, Wellman, Metcalfe, Koriat and Nelson provide a basis for discussing the development of the constructs of metamemory and metacognition. Memory monitoring, feeling and knowing phenomena, and the categorisation of metamemory as a construct are discussed in light of their importance in regard to the development of the construct of metacognition. The development of the *conceptual framework of metacognition* and the *taxonomy of metacognition* continue in this part and, where relevant, assertions are made between metacognition and complex problem solving. It includes three chapters: Chapter 5 Memory monitoring and metamemory; Chapter 6 The foundation of metamemory; and Chapter 7 Metamemory and its components: The basis of metacognition.

5   Memory monitoring and metamemory

This chapter focuses on the early contributions to the development of the construct of metamemory in which memory monitoring and awareness of memory processes make important contributors to its conceptual development.

Metamemory: Early contributions and memory monitoring

Philosophers such as Plato and Aristotle, and 'early pedagogues' such as James (1890a), as well as others, contributed to current understandings of memory development and processes (Perlmutter, 1988). Plato refers to memory as a 'conversation of perception' (Beare, 1906, p. 264) which is akin to Aristotle's views of memory as the connection between perception and conception.

Aristotle considered the soul was vital to memory and recollection and he believed that memory recollection was not reliant upon remembering specific facts and experiences, but on associations of ideas and knowledge. Aristotle's views on memory involved perception and recollection via associationist processes such as reminiscence, contrariety, contiguity, contrast and similarity (Beare, 1906; Dunlosky and Bjork, 2008a; Perlmutter, 1988). Aristotle's associationist views of memory processes were also held by James (1890a). He emphasised the importance of mnemonic monitoring and the processes of association and attachment of memories with other memories. Thinking about memories was stressed by James as essential to weaving 'systematic' relationships through associative processes. Therefore, Aristotle and James contribute to an early conceptual dialectic linking memory processes and metamemory. Thinking about memory or making sense of and use of memory is a conscious cognitive approach to memory and memory monitoring, the fundamental foundations of metamemory. Historical contributions to memory development and processes provide a foundation for three complex forms of cognitive processes consisting of operative, metacognitive and epistemic knowledge (Perlmutter, 1988).

Flavell's early contribution to the development of metamemory

Flavell's contribution to the development of metamemory and metacognition is based upon, and developed from, his early interest in Piagetian theories and emerged from his research and discussion of memory and recall (see Cavanaugh and Perlmutter, 1982; Flavell, 1963, 1977; Flavell *et al.*, 1993, 2002; Gage and Berliner, 1984; Hacker, 1998; Osman and Hannafin, 1992). Even though his interest in memory and memory strategies developed from his work on Piagetian theory, Piaget himself 'did not argue explicitly that knowledge about memory is crucial for memory development' (Cavanaugh and Perlmutter, 1982, p. 13). Flavell had a keen interest in the relationship between memory and memory development, which is demonstrated in a number of his works (e.g. Flavell, 1970, 1971a; Flavell *et al.*, 1970; Flavell and Wellman, 1977; Kreutzer *et al.*, 1975).

An influential metamemory research paper by Flavell *et al.* (1970) investigated the relationship between memory and the strategy processes of children of different age groups whilst they were engaged in various types of memorisation activities. The study investigated their application of fundamental elements of metamemory: memorisation strategies, knowledge, awareness and monitoring of their own memory. The outcome indicated that older children used complex, specific memorisation strategies, naming items, and anticipating and rehearsing to monitor, prompt and increase recall readiness. Overall, the study showed that the nature and development of knowledge and awareness of one's own memory system are interrelated and in need of further research.

In another study, Flavell (1970) investigated the development of mnemonic-mediational processes and skills in children, such as verbal rehearsal. Mnemonic-mediation is a 'planful, instrumental, cognitive act, akin to problem-solving behavior' (p. 208), which is a metamemory process. Terms such as metamemory and metacognition evolved later, but these initial research papers provided an introduction and a foundation to these concepts.

Tulving and Madigan (1970) called for conceptual and empirical research on metamemory processes a year before Flavell (1971a) coined the term 'metamemory'. His paper is considered by some to be the foundational paper on metamemory (e.g. Kluwe, 1982, 1987). Tulving and Madigan identified knowledge of the knowledge stored in memory as unique to human memory. This was an early identification of knowledge of memory as an essential aspect of metamemorial processes. Flavell's (1971a) introduction to the term highlighted the categories of metamemory, including knowledge of memory processes and the monitoring and regulation of these processes. He called for the continued development of the construct of metamemory which further encouraged a number of conceptual and empirical papers on memory development (e.g. Appel *et al.*, 1972; Brown, 1978; Brown and DeLoache, 1978; Flavell, 1970, 1971a, 1977, 1978; Flavell *et al.*, 1970; Flavell and Wellman, 1977; Kreutzer *et al.*, 1975; Wellman, 1978; Yussen and Bird, 1979).

Flavell (1971a, 1977) stressed that constructive memory relies upon knowledge and cognition and is a form of 'applied cognition' that involves the application of 'intellectual weaponry' to facilitate the solving of mnemonic problems. This involves the ability to reason and make inferences and interpretations during the processing, storing and retrieval of information.

Corsini and Brown's contribution to memory development

Flavell *et al.*'s (1970) research stimulated a number of discussion papers on memory awareness and memorisation strategies (e.g. Corsini, 1971; Flavell, 1971a). Corsini (1971) reviewed a number of studies which investigated memory development, including the propensity and ability for representation, mnemonic strategies, and the development of a cognitive operative system. In light of these studies, he reviewed and discussed Bruner's (1964) work on the development of representational abilities. Corsini recognised the relationship between representational abilities and previous experience and the interaction between the learner and the situation.

This interaction between the task and prior experience relies upon memory development, including the development of mnemonic strategies applied to problem-solving situations. Corsini contends that the development of mnemonic routines or strategies should be discussed in terms of their association with task problem solving, ability and the situation, and not a particular stage or level of development.

He identified the emerging relationship between memory and awareness of one's mnemonic processes, metamemory, describing a 'cognitive operative system', which could be considered a metamemorial system, involving memory monitoring and control of memory processes which are stimulated and instigated in problem-solving contexts.

Figure 5.1 depicts Corsini's cognitive operative system showing the interaction between task and prior experience affecting memory development and the development of mnemonic strategies.

Similarly, Brown (1974) also considered that memory development and successful performance on memory tasks relies upon the effective use of 'plans, schemes, or mnemonic strategies' (p. 55). The use of planning and mnemonic strategies supports the organisation and modification of what can be the initial unsystematic input of information into controllable 'information-rich units'. Figure 5.2 represents the interaction between the memory task, mnemonic strategies and monitoring and control.

Corsini's (1971) cognitive operative system can be related to Brown's (1974) discussion of plans, schemes, or mnemonic strategies as processes or strategies applied during problem solving. She referred to the use of these strategies, as Corsini also does, to describe the processes and supports

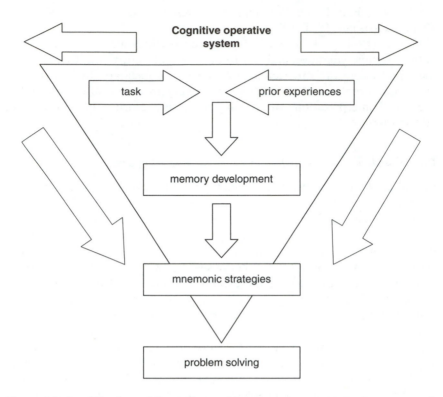

Figure 5.1 Amplification of Corsini's cognitive operative system in the conceptual framework of metacognition

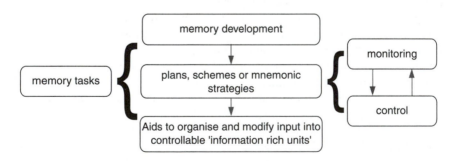

Figure 5.2 Amplification of the relationship between successful performance on memory tasks and memory development in the conceptual framework of metacognition

Source: Adapted from Brown (1974).

which contribute to memory development. These processes refer to monitoring and control processes facilitated by the use of mnemonic strategies. These initial discussions relate to Flavell's early description of metamemory and are its foundations. Early research determined that adults improved memory performance by using sophisticated acquisition and retrieval strategies. Children enhanced memory performance via the use of verbalisation. The use of strategies and, specifically, knowledge of memory strategies are directly linked to metamemory theory and therefore memory monitoring and include feeling and knowing phenomena. Studies such as those carried out by Hart (1965, 1966, 1967a, 1967b) and Brown and McNeil (1966) represent early research on feeling and knowing phenomena and memory monitoring to facilitate strategy control in problem-solving situations. These phenomena are discussed later in the chapter.

Referring to Corsini and Brown's theories, the following assertions identify key conceptual contributions to the foundation of metamemory:

5.1 The development of memory and mnemonic strategies relies upon the interaction between the task and prior experiences, especially in problem-solving situations.

5.2 The development and application of plans and mnemonic strategies facilitate the organisation and control of knowledge and are influenced by the problem and the problem-solving process.

5.3 Metamemory involves awareness and knowledge of memory storage and retrieval, memory representational abilities and strategies which affect successful problem solving.

5.4 Metamemory involves monitoring and control of mnemonic processes, especially in problem-solving situations.

Memory monitoring as a foundation of metamemory

In short, we make search in our memory for a forgotten idea, just as we rummage our house for a lost object. In both cases we visit what seems to us the probable neighbourhood of that which we miss. We turn over the things under which, or within which, or alongside which it may possibly be; and if it lies near them, it soon comes to view (James, 1890a, p. 654).

James (1890a) referred to memory monitoring or the use of memory strategies to monitor and facilitate recollection. He described memory as reliant upon monitoring, knowledge and awareness of a memory or associated memories. His statement also relates to current understandings of feeling and knowing phenomena. Feeling and knowing phenomena are essentially part of memory monitoring, including the use and application of acquisition and retrieval strategies. Memory monitoring involves an intricate process of judging the accuracy of one's memory which in essence is metamemory, knowledge of one's own memory. Knowledge of one's memory involves feeling and knowing phenomena as indicators of this knowledge (Butterfield *et al.*, 1988; Wellman, 1978). The interest in memory monitoring is evident by the vast number of studies on feeling and knowing phenomena, too many to review in this book. But, importantly, the following section aims to depict the fundamental relationship between feeling and knowing phenomena, memory monitoring, and metamemory.

Effective memory monitoring

At the same time as Corsini's (1971) discussion of memory development and research by Brown and McNeil (1966), Hagen and Kingsley (1968) and Hart (1965), Flavell (1971a) continued his own dialogue regarding the development and nature of memory. He referred to Corsini's cognitive operative system and its development, influenced by the interaction between the person and environment. The memory task, prior memory, task similarity and cognitive experience dictate the mnemonic strategies applied. Effective memory monitoring relies upon the development of deliberate memory or 'deliberate memorisation'. Deliberate memorisation involves 'planful, intentional, goal-directed, future-oriented behavior' (Flavell, 1971a, p. 276). Brown (1975) also described 'deliberate remembering' as a process of conscious memory involving the development of memory strategies through awareness and the active storing and retrieving of information. Therefore, effective memory monitoring is based upon a number of variables including deliberate, planful memorisation, and the development and use of mnemonic strategies.

It seems clear that these discussions posit a strong connection between memory and metamemory. However, debate continues regarding the extent of the relationship, especially considering that many studies have endeavoured to affirm the relationship between memory and metamemory with and without success.

The following assertions describe the main connections between memory, memory monitoring and metamemory.

5.5   Memory monitoring involves the acquisition, retrieval and application of mnemonic strategies and intelligent, deliberate and planful memorisation.

5.6   Deliberate remembering instigates the conscious development and use of mnemonic strategies, and the active storage and retrieval of information.

5.7   Memory monitoring involves judgments of memory accuracy and feeling and knowing phenomena as indicators of this knowledge.

5.8   Knowledge of memory processes, including the memory task, task similarity and cognitive experiences, influence the application of mnemonic strategies.

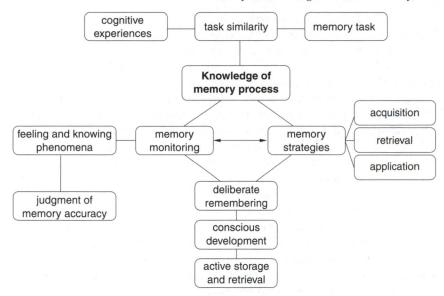

Figure 5.3 Amplification of knowledge of memory processes in the conceptual framework of metacognition

Figure 5.3 depicts the relationships between metamemory, mnemonic strategies, monitoring and control.

The following section draws from both theoretical and empirical studies to argue the connection between memory and metamemory.

Is there a memory–metamemory connection?

There has been, and there continues to be, a great deal of discussion about the form, strength of and issues surrounding the relationship between memory and metamemory (e.g. Borkowski *et al.*, 1988; Cavanaugh and Borkowski, 1979; Cavanaugh and Perlmutter, 1982; Cornoldi *et al.*, 1991; Cowan, 1997; Dunlosky and Bjork, 2008a; Joyner and Kurtz-Costes, 1997; Metcalfe, 2000; Pressley *et al.*, 1985; Schneider, 1985; Schneider and Bjorklund, 2003; Schneider and Lockl, 2002; Wellman, 1983). For a detailed conceptual description of the memory–metamemory connection, certain references are notable (see Borkowski *et al.*, 1988; Dixon and Hertzog, 1988; Dunlosky and Bjork, 2008b; Joyner and Kurtz-Costes, 1997; Pressley, Borowski and O'Sullivan, 1984; Schneider, 1985; Schneider and Bjorklund, 2003). The intention here is to identify the overall relationship between the two constructs.

Particular studies (e.g. Cavanaugh and Borkowski, 1980; Kelly *et al.*, 1976; Salatas and Flavell, 1976) are mentioned in the literature (see Flavell *et al.*, 1970; Joyner and Kurtz-Costes, 1997; Markman, 1977; Pressley, Borkowski and O'Sullivan, 1984; Wellman, 1983) as those which investigated the connection between memory and metamemory. These studies produced low correlations (Cavanaugh and Borkowski, 1979), mixed results (Joyner and Kurtz-Costes, 1997) and instigated 'gloom' about the strength of the relationship between metamemory and memory (Wellman, 1983). Despite this initial gloom, Wellman considered it necessary to review other research and not rely only on the findings of these studies.

A meta-analysis of memory–metamemory studies draws the conclusion that a 'significant and substantial relationship between memory and memory performance' exists (Schneider, 1985, p. 101). However, this relationship is influenced by issues of age and task difficulty, subsequently affecting memory performance. Difficult memory tasks where judgments, processes and actions are involved reinforce the metamemory–memory connection (Borkowski, 1985; Brown, 1978; Schneider and Lockl, 2002). The difficulty of the memory task affects the level of metamemorial processes applied (Brown, 1978). This is substantiated by studies investigating metamemory processes in children which have encountered a number of issues including the reliability of children's responses, inaccurate predictions of their memory on recall tasks, and task complexity involved in determining children's memory and metamemorial processes (e.g. Brown and Lawton, 1977; Flavell *et al.*, 1970; Markman, 1977). Studies generally found that young children have difficulty and lack experience in monitoring their memory, applying mnemonic strategies and demonstrating knowledge of their memory (e.g. Flavell *et al.*, 1970; Kreutzer *et al.*, 1975; Markman, 1977). For example, Markman (1977) investigated awareness of comprehension failure. She found that the ability to identify comprehension failure is related to the ability to monitor and evaluate cognitive processes as young children were passive comprehension monitors and memory monitors. However, conversely there have been a few studies which found that children do have some awareness and knowledge of their own memory (Joyner and Kurtz-Costes, 1997; Schneider, 1985). Adults are far better at monitoring their memories than children (Brown, 1977; Leal, 1987). They can review, assess and be aware of which memories are not retrievable and which are retrievable (Lindsay and Norman, 1972).

Perlmutter (1988) acknowledges the issues regarding age, task complexity and the advantages of developed metamemorial knowledge. She explains that:

> children's increasing *knowledge about the world* (i.e. epistemic memory), and in particular, their increasing *knowledge about the workings of the human memory system* (i.e. metamemory), allow them to use their memory systems more effectively. Therefore, young children show the greatest disadvantage on memory tasks that depend on epistemic or metacognitive knowledge. Epistemic knowledge in general, and

metacognitive knowledge in particular, also have an important role in memory development during adulthood.

(pp. 365–366)

Metamemory described as knowledge of one's memory and the use of mnemonic strategies to facilitate acquisition and retrieval warrants the question as to whether metamemory influences or is necessary for successful memory performance (Cavanaugh and Borkowski, 1979; Joyner and Kurtz-Costes, 1997; Schneider and Lockl, 2002). Analyses of other metamemory–memory studies have revealed that there are considerable differences between them, but overall they indicate that there is some relationship between metamemory and memory strategies and performance (Pressley, Borkowski and O'Sullivan, 1984; Schneider, 1985; Weinert, 1987).

A study by Cavanaugh and Borkowski (1979) explored if metamemory influenced memory performance in 50 grade-three students and investigated the relationship between metamemory and memory using a 'pre-post design in which strategy training and transfer intervened between metamemory assessment sessions' (p. 162). Referring to Flavell and Wellman's (1977) taxonomy of metamemory, they found that strategy knowledge, application and transfer improved strategy maintenance, and that metamemory was important for this to occur.

Confirming this connection, Wellman (1983) explained that the memory–metamemory relationship is based upon knowledge of memory, the use of specific purposeful memory strategies to facilitate memory retrieval, and knowledge of what is and is not known. Similarly, Pressley, Borowski and O'Sullivan (1984) also identified that the memory–metamemory connection is 'very likely in demanding strategy deployment situations such as on novel, difficult memory tasks' (p. 95).

Research by Short, Schatschneider and Friebert (1993) investigated the relationship between memory performance and metamemory. The study involved 62 average and 66 low achieving children and examined whether their age, development and skill differences were represented through memory performance and metamemory. Referring to Borkowski and Pressley's work on metamemory strategy knowledge, the study identified that specific task-related strategy knowledge was a better predictor of memory performance than general strategy knowledge. Strategy knowledge, but not task knowledge, especially of task parameters, was found to be a predictor of memory performance. Overall, age, skill, context and type of task affect memory and metamemory performance.

Generally, metamemory judgments, e.g. feeling-of-knowing judgments, facilitate the identification of specific memory strategies aiding memory retrieval and allocation to the particular required context (Wellman, 1983). The application of these strategies is affected by beliefs about memory performance, self-knowledge, strategy knowledge, and the motivation to facilitate memory retrieval (Dixon and Hertzog, 1988). This relates to

Wellman's (1983) view that the connection between memory and meta-memory is based upon a theory of mind involving the interaction between 'knowledge and action'. This interaction reflects memory performance relying upon knowledge of memory and then action upon this knowledge by using mnemonic strategies. The limitations of this study inhibit a detailed discussion of Wellman's theory of mind (see Wellman, 1983, 1985a, 1985b, 1988a, 1988b, 1990) including other contributions from Astington *et al.* (1988), Flavell (2004) and Schneider and Pressley (1997). There is a need for a detailed discussion of Wellman's theory of mind in the context of metamemory or metacognition.

Memory–metamemory approaches

Two main approaches to researching the memory–metamemory relation-ship are the 'direct-link approach', and the investigation of 'developmental differences' in memory knowledge (Borkowski *et al.*, 1988). The direct-link approach is also described in the context of investigating knowing and feeling phenomena as the 'trace-access' or 'direct-access' model or approach to metamemory judgment research (Koriat, 1995; Koriat and Levy-Sadot, 2000). It relied upon two main types of studies: correlational studies and training or intervention studies (Borkowski *et al.*, 1988). Two correlational studies (Kelly *et al.*, 1976; Salatas and Flavell, 1976) found no significant correlation between memory performance and metamemory (Borkowski *et al.*, 1988; Joyner and Kurtz-Costes, 1997), whereas Yussen and Berman's (1981) study found a significant correlation (Joyner and Kurtz-Costes, 1997). The training studies believed that mnemonic training would lead to a better understanding of memory and memory processes. Generally, training of mnemonics did improve immediate memory performance although it was not necessarily sustained and there was limited transferability (Borkowski *et al.*, 1988). Brown and Campione's (1977) study found that such training can be successful if it builds upon children's current strategy knowledge. They also noted that the older children in the study had a higher level of cognitive maturity and were able to adopt strategies and maintain them more successfully.

Poor correlations between memory–metamemory and the 'gloom' described by Wellman have affected the types of studies conducted. Borkowski *et al.* (1988) argued that studies should 'move beyond the direct-link approach, and instead describe metamemory as an integrated and interactive system of knowledge' (p. 79). Two types of studies identify the positive relationship between memory and metamemory: manipulation studies involving training and multiple assessments of metamemory per-formance (Borkowski *et al.*, 1988). Strategy training and new memory tasks provide a context in which to understand differences in metamemory performance (Borkowski *et al.*, 1988).

Listed below are assertions which describe the main connections between memory and metamemory.

5.9 Knowledge about the world (empirical knowledge) and knowledge about memory are important for memory development and performance.
5.10 Metamemory is important for strategy application, transfer and maintenance.
5.11 Age, task difficulty and demanding strategy application situations affect memory performance.
5.12 Difficult memory tasks involve judgments, processes and actions affecting the level of metamemorial processes applied.
5.13 Metamemory judgments facilitate the identification of mnemonic strategies supporting the retrieval and allocation of a memory to a context.
5.14 Beliefs about memory performance, self-knowledge, strategy knowledge and motivation affect memory retrieval and strategy application.
5.15 Strategy training and new memory tasks provide a context for understanding differences in memory performance and how metamemory influences memory performance.

Figure 5.4 (see p. 70) demonstrates the specific relationships between knowledge of memory processes and strategy usage which affect memory performance.

The following section identifies types of knowing and feeling phenomena and discusses the connection to memory monitoring, of both theoretical and empirical studies. The methodological issues which prevail in this field are noted.

Memory monitoring and knowing and feeling phenomena

The tip-of-the-tongue phenomenon is a reflection, assessment or subjective experience that an item, memory or word which cannot be currently recalled is imminently recallable (Brown and McNeil, 1966; Schwartz, 2002). The feeling-of-knowing phenomenon is a reflective judgment that an unrecalled memory or item is familiar (Hart, 1965; Wellman, 1977).

James (1890a, 1892) was a principal contributor to initial discussions of metamemory and metacognition. He was one of the first theorists to discuss tip-of-the-tongue (e.g. Hart, 1965) and feeling-of-knowing experiences (see Brown, 1977; Brown and Lawton, 1977; Brown and McNeil, 1966; Metcalfe, 2000; Schwartz, 2002). Bowne (1886, 1897) is also another significant contributor to awareness of memory knowledge (Cavanaugh and Perlmutter, 1982).

In the following statement, James referred to feeling and knowing phenomena in the sense that he believed that accessing memory involved different feelings of memory knowledge. He described these feelings as

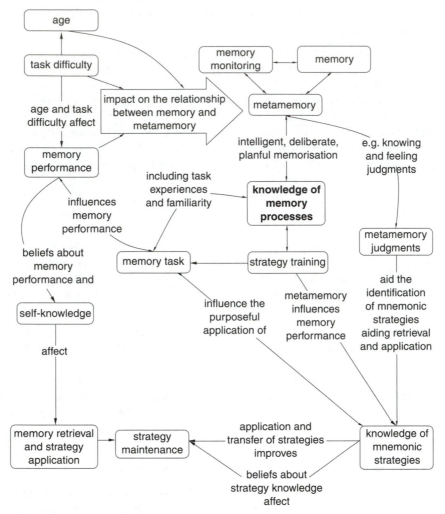

Figure 5.4 Amplification of the memory–metamemory connection in the conceptual framework of metacognition

reliant upon experience and feelings of 'warmth and intimacy' (James, 1890a). James acknowledged that feeling and knowing phenomena are indicators of the relationship between memory and knowledge, and are therefore indicators of knowledge of memory. James (1892) wrote:

> Suppose we try to recall a forgotten name. The state of our con-
> sciousness is peculiar. There is a gap therein; but no mere gap. It is a
> gap that is intensely active. A sort of wraith of the name is in it,
> beckoning us in a given direction, making us at moments tingle with
> the sense of our closeness, and then letting us sink back without the

longed-for term. If wrong names are proposed to us, this singularly definite gap acts immediately so as to negate them. They do not fit into its mould. And the gap of one word does not feel like the gap of another, all empty of content as both might seem necessarily to be when described as gaps . . . There are innumerable consciousnesses of want, no one of which taken in itself has a name, but all different from each other. Such feeling of want is *tota cælo* other than a want of feeling: it is an intense feeling.

(para. 26)

Knowledge is considered the basis of the tip-of-the-tongue phenomenon (Brown and McNeil, 1966). It is important for recall, for example, recall of specific information, methods and processes, patterns or structure (Bloom, 1956). Therefore, knowledge is an important element for understanding memory and for the process of recall, and serves as a guide during the reconstruction of information during retrieval (Brown, 1977; Cavanaugh and Perlmutter, 1982). Although the discussion has centred on knowledge as a basis upon which recall may be stimulated, Schwartz (2002, 2006) describes metacognitive experiences as the basis upon which tip-of-the-tongue phenomena occur. However, these experiences would rely upon knowledge to facilitate recall processes during tip-of-the-tongue states. Knowledge and experiences could be considered to be entwined to support memory retrieval.

Feeling-of-knowing judgments happen after or during acquisition and are judgments of whether at present the non-recallable knowledge is known or subsequently recallable (Izaute *et al.*, 2002; Leonesio and Nelson, 1990; Nelson, 1999; Nelson and Narens, 1990, 1994; Schneider, 1998). This knowledge of memory and the continued feeling of that knowledge prompts continued searching to support retrieval and then subsequent application of that knowledge (Narens *et al.*, 1994).

Literature on feeling-of-knowing (e.g. Dunlosky and Metcalfe, 2009; Funnell *et al.*, 1996; Izaute *et al.*, 2002; Janowsky *et al.*, 1989; Koriat, 1994, 1995, 1998; Metcalfe, 1986a, 2000; Miner and Reder, 1994; Nelson, 1999; Nelson and Narens, 1990, 1994; Nhouyvanisvong and Reder, 1998; Schneider, 1998; Shimamura and Squire, 1986; Sinkavich, 1995) and tip-of-the-tongue phenomena (e.g. Koriat, 1998; Schwartz, 2002; Smith, 1994) provides comprehensive discussions of these, and demonstrates the renewed interest in awareness and monitoring of one's memory and the effect of feeling-of-knowing judgments on mnemonic strategy selection and application.

Types of feeling and knowing research

Generally, feeling-of-knowing research has followed Hart's (1965, 1966, 1967a, 1967b) methodology, identified as the trace-access or direct-access approach (Janowsky *et al.*, 1989; Koriat, 1994, 1995; Koriat and Levy-Sadot, 2000; Miner and Reder, 1994; Son and Schwartz, 2002). Feeling-of-knowing judgments are tested by monitoring and then recall of no item or an incorrect item. The former is referred to as an omission error and the latter as a commission error. Commission errors and accurate recall are based upon confidence judgments (Izaute *et al.*, 2002; Narens *et al.*, 1994).

Although there is a history of applying the direct or trace-access view, there are other methods of investigating the relationship between memory performance and feeling-of-knowing phenomena (see Miner and Reder, 1994; Son and Schwartz, 2002). One alternative is the inferential view; judgments are based upon cueing and are influenced by the familiarity of the cues. Therefore tip-of-the-tongue and feeling-of-knowing states are inferred from information which is indirectly related to the memory (Funnell *et al.*, 1996; Koriat, 1995; Riefer, 2002; Son and Schwartz, 2002).

Current studies of tip-of-the-tongue states are combining the direct access and inferential views by using a number of stimuli including semantic, auditory and visual cues. Riefer's (2002) study found that tip-of-the-tongue experiences are instigated more by the 'nature of the response set than by the type of stimuli cues' (p. 565). The results did not support inferential theories of the tip-of-tongue states, e.g. cue familiarity, but supported direct-access theories.

Koriat's accessibility view or model is another alternative method of investigating feeling-of-knowing phenomena. The accessibility view considers that monitoring and retrieval processes are intertwined and are not independent processes, such as in the direct-access approach. The process of searching for specific memory draws from cues and facilitates the judgment of whether the item is retrievable from memory, stimulating continued searching. Therefore, both monitoring and retrieval are interdependent. However, they do not guarantee accuracy of the retrieval (Koriat, 1994, 1995; Son and Schwartz, 2002). A study by Kelemen (2000) found that judgments of learning were more accurate and accessible if they were delayed and prompted by 'knowledge-based cues'. He found that phrasing of cues can also affect the accuracy of memory monitoring.

Other metamemory phenomena

Other metamemory phenomena include judgments of learning (Dunlosky and Metcalfe, 2009; Hacker, 1998; Hertzog *et al.*, 2003; Kelemen, 2000; Koriat and Ackerman, 2010; Nelson and Dunlosky, 1991; Nelson and Narens, 1990, 1994; Schneider, 1998; Tobias and Everson, 2000) also known as judgments of knowing (Leonesio and Nelson, 1990; Zechmeister and Nyberg, 1982), ease-of-learning judgments (Hacker, 1998; Leonesio and Nelson, 1990; Nelson, 1999; Nelson and Narens, 1990, 1994; Schneider, 1998; Zechmeister and Nyberg, 1982), judgment of uncertainty (Nelson, 1992), judgment of agency or performance (Metcalfe and Greene, 2007), and judgment of prose (Zechmeister and Nyberg, 1982). Judgment of prose refers to the ability or the extent to which learners can remember from connected discourse or prose material (Zechmeister and Nyberg, 1982).

Judgments of learning or judgments of knowing refer to a person's knowledge of whether an item has been learned and if it can be remembered when needed. They involve monitoring and control of learning including the amount of application needed for the task. They are not the same as feeling-of-knowing judgments and confidence judgments, as judgments of learning rely upon a recall test (Narens *et al.*, 1994). Nelson and Narens (1994) contend that judgments of learning occur '*during or soon after acquisition* and are predictions about future test performance' (p. 16). Judgments of learning are used to monitor and regulate learning through the selection of strategies to facilitate memory acquisition and retention, enhancing memory performance (Nelson and Narens, 1990). They can be applied to different learning situations but are specifically discussed and researched in the context of study and exam preparation (Kelemen, 2000; Koriat and Ackerman, 2010; Nelson and Narens, 1990; Pressley, Borkowski and O'Sullivan, 1984). The accurate assessment of knowledge states leads to effective monitoring and control through the selection of appropriate and effective strategies. Inaccurate monitoring can lead to ineffective strategy selection and application, and inefficient use of study time (Kelemen, 2000; Metcalfe *et al.*, 2007). Beliefs regarding study time allocation to differing tasks influence judgment of learning and self-monitoring of study time can facilitate awareness of the study time allocated by others (Koriat and Ackerman, 2010; Metcalfe *et al.*, 2007).

Ease-of-learning judgments are judgments about how difficult or how hard it will be to learn something new within a particular domain of knowledge or context. This includes the ability to discriminate between hard and easier content (Hacker, 1998; Leonesio and Nelson, 1990; Metcalfe *et al.*, 2007; Nelson, 1999; Nelson and Narens, 1990, 1994; Schneider, 1998; Zechmeister and Nyberg, 1982). Strategy selection can be influenced by ease-of-learning judgments, judging whether a particular strategy would be easier to apply and be successful in attaining new knowledge or meeting task demands (Nelson and Narens, 1990). Nelson and Narens (1990, p. 130) contend that these 'judgments occur in advance of acquisition, are largely inferential, and pertain to items that have not yet been learned.' Underwood's (1966) study of the ease of recall of hard and easier items by adults is an example of early research on this phenomenon. Judgments of learning, ease-of-learning and feeling-of-knowing are not considered to be interrelated monitoring processes; that is they do not depend upon each other to occur and they monitor different memory processes. Additionally, judgment of uncertainty (Nelson, 1992) is another form of feeling and knowing phenomena. This refers to thinking one knows something about a topic but being uncertain about the depth of one's knowledge.

Narens, Jameson and Lee (1994) explain that confidence judgments relate to decisions to provide answers to problems during retrieval. Research by Roebers (2002) found that both children and adults tended to overestimate confidence in their answers regardless of whether they were unbiased, misleading or forced-choice recognition questions. Adults demonstrated higher levels of metamemory monitoring skills.

A study by Koriat *et al.* (2002) found that over and under confidence of judgments of learning can also affect the subjective monitoring of knowledge. Similarly, Sinkavich's (1995) research investigated the metamemorial judgments of the accuracy of information recalled by 67 Educational Psychology university students who were asked to judge their confidence judgments, the effect on performance in multiple-choice examinations and their actual performance. Whilst students completed their exam, they also documented their level of confidence. They were also given ten replacement items, including a range of easy and difficult items that could be used to replace test questions if they were not satisfied with their answers. The results identified that 'good' students had better judgment of confidence accuracy than 'poor' students. Overall, the findings showed that all students can improve their scores by using metamemorial judgments in tests by having access to replacement items which could improve their test scores (Sinkavich, 1995).

A study by Pallier *et al.* (2002) found that accuracy of confidence judgments is influenced by personality, cognitive ability and 'confidence trait'. Although the researchers did not specifically investigate this in the context of memory acquisition and retrieval, these findings can have possible implications for further research into confidence judgments and metamemory. Further research could consider the implications of individual differences on the accuracy of confidence judgments in different situations, including confidence judgments in eyewitness testimonies.

There are many factors that can influence accurate memory retrieval in eyewitness testimonies (Perfect, 2004). Confidence judgments about general knowledge are higher than confidence judgments about recognising faces. This occurs because people obtain ready feedback of their ability to recall general knowledge items. This feedback is not so readily available for eyewitness memory as these situations cannot easily be revisited or compared with the recollections of others, and therefore eyewitness testimonies are reliant on retrospective confidence judgments (Dunlosky and Metcalfe, 2009; Perfect, 2004).

Efklides (2002, 2003) discussed in detail a number of other feeling and knowing phenomena, such as feeling of familiarity, feeling of difficulty, judgment of solution correctness and feeling of satisfaction. These are also monitoring processes used throughout the whole task experience. She labelled all feeling and knowing phenomena as metacognitive experiences and then specifically metacognitive feeling and metacognitive judgments. Metacognitive experiences is a term coined by Flavell (1979, 1981a) and is discussed in Part 3.

A little-known metacognitive state has been identified by Metcalfe (1986a, 1986b) and Metcalfe and Wiebe (1987) as feeling-of-warmth judgments. During the problem-solving process, frequent judgments are made based upon feelings of solution closeness. Metcalfe (1986b) describes the essential difference between feeling-of-knowing and feeling-of-warmth judgments as being that the former are related to memory and 'do not predict problem-solving performance with insight problems' or complex problems (p. 623). She has investigated feeling-of-knowing and feeling-of-warmth judgments in the context of insight problems (e.g. Metcalfe, 1986a, 1986b, 1996, 1998). Insight problem solving involves a sudden awareness of the correct solution (Metcalfe, 1996). She does not use the term complex or ill-structured problem in her description of insight problems, but as they do not have a clear goal state, they could be considered a type of complex problem. She does, however, make the distinction between routine and insight problems and metamemorial/metacognitive judgments. During routine problems or well-structured problems, feeling-of-knowing judgments help to predict whether one will be able to remember or solve the problems later. However, feeling-of-knowing judgments are not prognostic for insight problems. Feelings-of-warmth judgments in routine problems or well-structured problems increase in a linear fashion towards the correct solution. Feeling-of-warmth judgments were also used by Jaušovec (1994b) to investigate metacognitive processes during problem solving.

These phenomena are used to explore the belief that we have knowledge of our own knowledge and the ability to accurately monitor knowledge and thought processes (Hacker, 1998; Nelson and Narens, 1990, 1994). Metamemory monitoring processes, such as feeling-of-knowing, judgments of learning or knowing and ease-of learning, are described by Nelson and Narens (1990, 1994) and Nelson (1999) as 'prospective monitoring', i.e. judgments about future or subsequent responses. Schraw (2009) describes prospective judgments as those made before testing.

Nelson and Narens (1990) provide a detailed amplification of their theoretical memory framework which identifies the specific interactions between monitoring and control based upon the interrelationship between ease-of-learning judgments, judgments of learning, feeling-of-knowing judgments and confidence judgments in the context of examination study. They explain that the judgments monitor, in this example, the process of studying and instigate strategy searching, retrieval and application. Control processes react to the monitoring processes instigated by feeling and knowing experiences by producing, continuing and terminating an action. A description of their theoretical framework of metamemory, which forms the basis for the interaction between monitoring and control, is discussed later in this chapter.

The following assertions arise from the discussion of feeling and knowing phenomena and memory monitoring:

5.16   Knowledge is essential to facilitate recall of information, methods, processes and structures and it facilitates the reconstruction of information during retrieval.

5.17   Tip-of-the-tongue and feeling-of-knowing states rely upon reflection, specifically reflective assessment and reflective judgments of the current memory state.

5.18   Feeling and knowing phenomena are feelings of memory knowledge reliant upon experience and awareness. They facilitate memory monitoring and instigate strategy selection and application.

5.19   Judgments monitor and instigate control processes such as strategy searching, retrieval and application to facilitate memory acquisition and retention to support memory performance.

5.20   Accurate assessment of knowledge states leads to effective monitoring, control and selection of appropriate strategies. Inaccurate monitoring can lead to ineffective strategy selection, application and time use.

5.21   Judgments are inferential, occur in advance of acquisition and concern items that have not yet been learned.

5.22   Judgments may be influenced by personality, self-concept, and overall confidence in knowing, retrieving and applying appropriate strategies.

Figure 5.5 builds on Figure 5.4 and demonstrates the relationships between metamemory judgments and metamemory. It depicts the connection between metamemory judgments and monitoring and control of mnemonic strategies. Self-concept, self-knowledge and confidence influence metamemory judgments. Metamemory judgments facilitate knowledge of memory strategies and processes. Memory monitoring and control processes are influenced by feeling and knowing phenomena.

There has been a great deal of research into feeling and knowing phenomena and the literature provides many in-depth reviews of empirical studies (e.g. Dunlosky and Metcalfe, 2009; Hall and Bahrick, 1998; Koriat, 1994; Miner and Reder, 1994; Narens *et al.*, 1994; Schneider, 1998; Son and Schwartz, 2002). The scope of this book does not allow for an extensive review of these. The following section, however, provides an overview of a selected number of foundational empirical studies which support some of the theoretical discussion thus far with a focus on studies of feeling-of-knowing and tip-of-the-tongue. Many of the studies are primarily interested in child and adult development and the application of feeling-of-knowing metamemorial knowledge and strategies. Therefore, this is the context in which these are discussed because of their significance, but overall they contribute to the argument supporting the view that complex, cognitive tasks are generally better performed by adults. There are few studies on knowing and feeling phenomena which relate to problem solving (e.g. feeling-of-warmth judgments) and these will be covered more appropriately in Chapter 9.

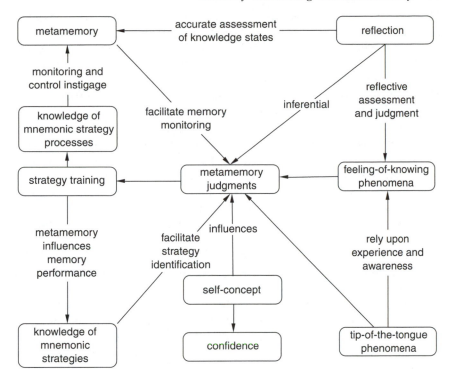

Figure 5.5 Amplification of the metamemory and metamemory judgments connection in the conceptual framework of metacognition

About the same time as Flavell and Corsini's discussions on memory processes, there were a number of researchers (e.g. Baker and Brown, 1984b; Belmont and Butterfield, 1969; Brown, 1974, 1975, 1978; Brown *et al.*, 1983; Brown and Campione, 1977; Brown and Lawton, 1977; Brown and Palincsar, 1982; Brown and Smiley, 1977; Hagen and Kingsley, 1968; Hart, 1965; Markman, 1977) who also contributed to early research in memory processes, metamemory, metacomprehension and metacognition. From these early studies, questions arose regarding memory, storage, retrieval, control and monitoring, leading to the foundations of what is known today as metacognitive research (Hacker, 1998). The following discussion provides an overview of a selection of these research papers.

An early study by Hart (1965) investigated feeling-of-knowing experiences and tip-of-the-tongue phenomena. Hart (1965) cited James (1890a, 1890b) as having contributed to initial discussions on feeling-of-knowing experiences. His study investigated the accuracy of feeling-of-knowing experiences as an indicator of memory storage. Hart (1965) referred to the 'memory monitoring process' as the intervening process between feeling-of-knowing, recall and recognition which contributes to the 'efficiency of the human information-processing system' (p. 215). The dominant research paradigm for feeling-of-knowing judgments is known as the 'recall-judgment-recognition paradigm' or RJR (Dunlosky and Metcalfe, 2009; Hacker, 1998; Metcalfe, 2000; Miner and Reder, 1994; Schwartz and Perfect, 2002). Hart contributed other works (such as Hart, 1966, 1967a, 1967b) which also discussed and investigated feeling-of-knowing experiences. Butterfield *et al.* (1988) consider that Hart's contribution to the understanding of feeling-of-knowing experiences and the measurement of them pioneered this field of inquiry and that his procedures have effectively assessed metamemory or metacognition processes. They have successfully been applied to a number of other studies involving the feeling-of-knowing phenomena, such as those by Brown and Lawton (1977) and Wellman (1977). Although Hart's methodologies are respectfully discussed, Koriat (1994) focuses on the limitations of Hart's approach to feeling-of-knowing research.

At the same time as Hart's study, studies by Brown and McNeil (1966), and later Wellman (1977), investigated and discussed tip-of-the-tongue and feeling-of-knowing experiences. These studies of tip-of-the-tongue phenomena highlighted that memory monitoring occurred because participants were able to judge successfully what they felt they knew, but could not retrieve (Cavanaugh and Perlmutter, 1982). This was also reflected in Belmont and Butterfield's (1969) research, which investigated short-term memory functioning including acquisition and retrieval in adults. They found that adults used a variety of sophisticated, effective acquisition and retrieval strategies. Focused application of specific acquisition and retrieval strategies are also discussed by Brown and Lawton (1977).

Brown and Lawton's (1977) study investigated the feeling-of-knowing phenomena in 69 educable children with learning disabilities and found that the older children demonstrated a higher level of sensitivity and awareness of feeling-of-knowing. The older children were able to predict in advance or judge confidently their recall accuracy prior to the task. This requires the ability to imagine future cognitive actions; this can be difficult for young children. Brown and Lawton stressed the importance of the reliability of data from children regarding their metamemorial knowledge explaining that it was important not just to accept single verbal responses as a measure of 'metacognitive insight' as this may not be an accurate representation of memory knowledge.

Similarly, Hagen and Kingsley's (1968) study investigated memory acquisition and recall in children. They found that verbalisation facilitated memory more effectively for younger rather than older children. They determined that spontaneous verbal rehearsal was also particularly significant in supporting memory performance. Although verbalisation can facilitate metamemorial processes, a study by Cunningham and Weaver (1989) found that kindergarten children who were not so articulate used a number of 'nonverbal predictions' in specific memory task situations. As well as Hagen and Kingsley's (1968) study, a number of other studies followed that investigated acquisition and retrieval strategies especially in children (e.g. Hagen and Stanovich, 1977; Kobasigawa, 1977; Moely, 1977; Paris and Lindauer, 1977; Wellman, 1977).

Age does affect feeling-of-knowing judgments especially in complex cognitive tasks. Adults' feeling-of-knowing judgments are more accurate than children's in complex, cognitive tasks. However, children can have accurate feeling-of-knowing judgments on a set task with specific guided instructions. These judgments aid in instigating metacognitive strategy selection and application in problem-solving contexts, therefore children are 'production deficient' in independently making feeling-of-knowing judgments or acting on those judgments (Butterfield *et al.*, 1988). In research studies, the effect of the complexity of the cognitive task on feeling-of-knowing judgments can lead to participants making judgments about what they think they should know, rather than what they actually do know (Cavanaugh and Perlmutter, 1982).

These significant studies have contributed to the foundations, discussion and development of metamemory and metacognitive research by providing an understanding of the complexities of memory monitoring in adults, and the understanding that children have limited experience and availability of tested and successful mnemonic strategies to facilitate memory performance. Both direct access and inferential views have been applied and tested in empirical studies and can be considered effective in identifying the memory–metamemory connection.

Overall, the studies reaffirm the memory–metamemory connection by identifying that:

5.23 Age and task difficulty affect feeling-of-knowing judgments.
5.24 Generally adults use more sophisticated acquisition and retrieval strategies to retrieve information accurately.
5.25 Children rely upon verbalisation and guidance in stimulating strategies to facilitate memory performance especially in complex memory tasks.
5.26 Feeling-of-knowing judgments instigate metamemory strategy selection and application in problem-solving contexts.
5.27 Mnemonic strategies facilitate acquisition, retrieval and memory performance reinforcing the connection between memory and metamemory.

Conclusion

Metamemory is supported by memory monitoring and control. This is reflected in feeling and knowing phenomena facilitating strategy selection and application in problem-solving contexts. Knowledge, monitoring and control of memory form the foundation of metamemory. Memory monitoring involves complex processes of reflection and judgment of the accuracy of one's memory, reliant upon one's own knowledge and awareness of memory. Knowledge of memory, i.e. metamemory, also includes the awareness of comprehension failure. As outlined earlier, adults are able, through experience and development of mnemonic strategies, to be more aware of comprehension failure. Memory development is supported by prior experiences that instigate the application of previously successful mnemonic strategies. Adults have the experience and knowledge of memory to apply deliberate, conscious memory processes, such as planning, to organise pieces of information to facilitate memory acquisition and retrieval (Brown, 1974, 1975; Flavell, 1971a).

The relationship between memory and metamemory is influenced by age, knowledge and task complexity (Borkowski, 1985; Brown, 1975, 1978; Brown and Smiley, 1977; Flavell, 1971a; Perlmutter, 1988; Weinert, 1987). Task complexity impacts on whether there is a consistent relationship between memory and metamemory (Weinert, 1987). Nevertheless, this relationship is influenced by strategy knowledge, retrieval, monitoring, control and transfer and affected by deliberate, planful memory strategies (Brown, 1975; Flavell, 1971a). Strategy maintenance and transferability are dependent upon the interrelationship between memory monitoring and memory knowledge, and are also influenced by task novelty and complexity. Beliefs about memory performance, motivation, self-knowledge of memory strategy retrieval and subsequent application are also affected by novelty and task complexity (Borkowski, 1985; Cavanaugh and Borkowski, 1979; Dixon and Hertzog, 1988; Pressley, Borkowski and O'Sullivan, 1984).

As outlined earlier, feeling and knowing phenomena are part of the memory monitoring process which involves mnemonic mediation and the application of mnemonic strategies. This relates to Corsini's (1971) cognitive operative system which involves the use of mnemonic strategies and links task and experience facilitating memory development. As identified by Flavell (1970) and Flavell and Wellman (1977), metamemory basically refers to knowledge of memory processes including knowledge of memory strategies, ability and environment. Feeling and knowing phenomena occur during memory tasks affecting memory development.

There is a lack of discussion connecting feeling and knowing phenomena and reflective processes. The studies reviewed have neither specifically connected nor discussed the interrelationship between reflection and memory monitoring. Chapter 3 argued for the existence of this interrelationship and that there are levels or types of reflective processes which are necessary for different metacognitive requirements. Metamemory relies upon knowledge of memory and the monitoring and control of memory processes. As identified by Nelson and Narens (1990), the interaction between monitoring and control processes is influenced by feeling and knowing phenomena that are forms of reflective processes. Both monitoring and control of memory would also be influenced and instigated by reflection.

Mnemonic acquisition and retrieval strategies interact with memory monitoring and affect memory development, influenced by feeling and knowing phenomena which occur during the process of reflection – essentially during memory acquisition and retrieval. There is a relationship between feeling and knowing phenomena and memory monitoring. As identified in the literature (Hart, 1965; Wellman, 1977), reflective judgment is part of the process of the experience of feeling-of-knowing and tip-of-the-tongue phenomena. Reflection is a critical part of memory monitoring, memory development and memory performance. As reflection is fundamental to memory, so too is knowledge. Knowledge of memory strategies, especially to facilitate the acquisition and retrieval of memory, informs the ability to experience tip-of-the-tongue and feeling-of-knowing phenomena but also enables the application and use of mnemonic strategies for successful memory performance. Reflection can only be supported by the knowledge of memory to facilitate retrieval. Reflective judgments would involve feeling and knowing states and facilitate memory monitoring especially in solving complex problems. Reflecting this, a discussion of feeling-of-warmth judgments and problem solving (e.g. Jaušovec, 1994a, 1994b; Metcalfe, 1986a, 1986b; Metcalfe and Wiebe, 1987) will be covered in Chapter 9.

The following higher-order assertions (HOA) are drawn from the above discussion.

5.28 Memory knowledge includes mnemonic strategy knowledge and instigates the monitoring and control of this knowledge (HOA.9).

5.29 Metamemory experiences instigate memory searching to facilitate retrieval and application of knowledge (HOA.10).

6   The foundation of metamemory

This chapter describes the conceptual contributions to metamemory and provides a foundation for Part 3, which discusses the categorisations of the construct.

The foundation of metamemory: Brown, and Flavell and Wellman

Brown (1975) and Flavell and Wellman (1977) made conceptual contributions that identified complex relationships between memory and metamemory. Brown's taxonomy of memory described metamemorial processes such as 'knowing about knowing' and 'knowing how to know'. Flavell and Wellman identified categories of metamemory in their taxonomy of metamemory. The relationships between the two contributions are discussed and the overall categories and elements of metamemory are identified.

Brown's metamemory

Brown (1975) described the relationship between memory and metamemory through her categorisation of three types of memory and memory processes, presented as a taxonomy of memory. These include knowing, knowing about knowing, and knowing how to know. All three categories are influenced by semantic memory which involves meaningful holistic memory experiences influenced by context. Briefly, knowing is the 'dynamic knowledge system' essential for cognitive activity. Knowing about knowing is 'introspective knowledge' of the processes involved in the knowledge system, and knowing how to know refers to the variety of mnemonic or metamemorial strategies and skills needed for deliberate memorisation. All three types of memorial knowledge are affected by human development and task experiences. It is argued in the following discussion that Brown's taxonomy of memory, specifically knowing about knowing and knowing how to know, set the foundation for current understandings of metamemory.

Knowing about knowing

Brown's conception of knowing about knowing referred to elements of Flavell's theories of knowledge about memory and the factors that influence memory performance (Brown, 1975; Flavell, 1971a). Both theories are based upon the conception of introspective knowledge of memory and strategic processes (Cavanaugh and Borkowski, 1979). Knowing about knowing is metamemorial knowledge or knowing about memory, memory strategies and plans. It involves strategic, deliberate planning to facilitate subsequent strategy application. Beliefs about memory processes influence the selection of strategies and application of plans. This introspective knowledge enables the selection, evaluation and modification of strategies during problem solving. The failure to apply metamemorial strategies effectively to different contexts is due to a lack of metamemorial awareness and control. Therefore, undeveloped knowledge of memory can affect the trans-situational application of these strategies (Brown, 1975).

Knowing about knowing involves not only knowledge of what is known, but also of what is not known. This knowledge is obtained through the interaction between knowledge and the monitoring of that knowledge. Self-awareness instigates knowledge of what is known and not known in problem-solving situations (Brown, 1978). Therefore, Brown's conception of knowing about knowing is akin to current understandings of knowledge of metamemory or declarative metamemory.

Knowing how to know

Knowing how to know involves memorial or mnemonic strategies, plans and actions which facilitate intelligent interactions with meaningful tasks and situations. Through experience and task complexity, many of these processes become implicit and are immersed in the process of active memorisation or problem solving. The application of mnemonic strategies to complex, meaningful problems is a result of 'involuntary remembering' and not 'deliberate remembering' or the 'reproduction' of memorisation strategies (Brown, 1975). Deliberate remembering or memorisation strategies are called upon in artificial or well-structured situations which 'demand exact reproduction of information as a goal in itself' (Brown, 1975, p. 106). Even so, deliberate attempts at memorisation involve the application of mnemonic strategies which first surface in the context of meaningful tasks.

Involuntary remembering is instigated in complex tasks where the identification of relationships between elements or information facilitates the 'reconstruction' of meaning and comprehensions. Knowledge of past experiences, including developed mnemonic strategies and ideas from meaningful situations, enables possible reconstruction of meanings and understandings. Memory reconstruction may not solely rely upon retrieving the actual situation from which the memory was first generated but may use strategies to render the memory task or situation meaningful and manageable. Retrieval of a memory, specifically of meaningful situations, can be made even if the information was involuntarily or automatically stored (Brown, 1975).

Planful, conscious mnemonic strategies can still be involved in the comprehension and retention of meaningful activities. Depth of comprehension is not necessarily the result of deliberate memory strategies, but the intent can enhance performance, especially if it is related to information which is engaging, of value and meaningful. These situations result in deeper levels of analysis, comprehension and understanding. The acquisition of mnemonic strategies and the ability to monitor and control them are essential skills. The ability to master these skills and apply them enables one to deal with the complexity of meaningful environments (Brown, 1975).

Knowing how to know can be regarded as procedural metamemory (Brown, 1977). Identifying the categories and elements of metamemory is important in developing an understanding of the dichotomy between declarative and procedural metamemory. Although the dichotomy may seem theoretically clear, the processes are not always totally separable. These connections are discussed later in this chapter.

Figure 6.1 depicts the elements of knowing about knowing and knowing how to know from Brown's work. Brown's theories reflect Flavell's contributions.

The following assertions list the main contributions by Brown which outline the metamemory category of knowing about knowing and knowing how to know:

6.1   Knowing about knowing (declarative metamemory) involves introspective knowledge of memory and awareness of what is known and not known, and is influenced by development and task experiences.

6.2   Knowing about knowing involves beliefs and deliberate planning which influence and facilitate strategy selection and application.

6.3   Knowledge about knowing aids the trans-situational application of memory strategies and, therefore, lack of metamemorial awareness and control is reflected in ineffective application of metamemorial strategies in different contexts.

6.4   Knowing how to know (procedural metamemory) involves the implicit or explicit application of mnemonic strategies, systems and plans needed for purposeful memorisation or learning.

6.5   Knowing how to know relies upon self-knowledge and awareness to facilitate monitoring in memory and problem-solving tasks.

6.6   Complex, meaningful memory or problem-solving tasks influence the development, selection and application of mnemonic strategies, and affect the comprehension and reconstruction of meaning.

6.7   Deep levels of comprehension, analysis, strategy monitoring and control are needed to render memory tasks or situations meaningful and manageable.

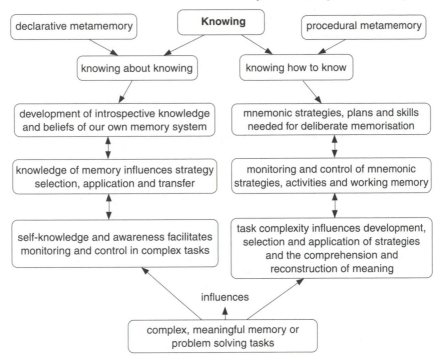

Figure 6.1 Amplification of Brown's theories of knowing in the conceptual framework of metacognition

Source: Adapted from Brown (1975).

There is a strong connection between Brown's theories of knowing about knowing and knowing how to know and Flavell and Wellman's (1977) taxonomy of metamemory, which identifies the elements of metamemory, such as knowledge of memory abilities and knowledge of memory strategies. This nexus is discussed further after an in-depth discussion of Flavell and Wellman's taxonomy of metamemory.

Flavell and Wellman's metamemory taxonomy

Although not intended to be a definitive model of metamemory, Flavell and Wellman's (1977) taxonomy of memory phenomena and metamemory is referred to as the foundation of metamemory and metacognition theory (e.g. Borkowski *et al.*, 1988; Brown, 1977; Brown and Campione, 1977; Cavanaugh and Borkowski, 1979; Kluwe, 1982; Pressley *et al.*, 1985; Schneider, 1985; Schneider and Lockl, 2002). Influenced by Brown's (1975) taxonomy of memory, Flavell and Wellman (1977) formed the basis of their taxonomy of metamemory on four broad theories or categories of memory phenomena. The second, third and fourth categories are 'reminiscent' of

Brown's (1975) 'distinction between "knowing", "knowing how to know", and "knowing about knowing", respectively' (Flavell and Wellman, 1977, p. 4). Table 6.1 presents the relationships between Flavell and Wellman's categories of memory and Brown's taxonomy of memory.

Table 6.1 Flavell and Wellman's four broad categories of memory phenomena matched with Brown's taxonomy of memory

Brown's taxonomy of memory	Flavell and Wellman's categories	Description
	First category	Basic, unconscious memory operations include processes applied in recognising an object, recall of absent objects or situations and cueing.
Knowing	Second category	Direct, involuntary and unconscious effects of the level of cognitive development on memory including the development of strategies to acquire, store, and retrieve information and find similar meaning and conceptual links. Adults find it much easier than children to do this.
Knowing how to know	Third category	Variety of conscious, voluntary, mnemonic strategies and control processes used to meet task requirements.
Knowing about knowing	Fourth category	Awareness and knowledge of memory and apprehension, storage and retrieval processes or specifically metamemory or knowledge about memory.

Sources: Adapted from Flavell and Wellman (1977) and Brown (1975).

The four categories of memory phenomena were developed to help understand knowledge of memory and the processes involved in the application of that knowledge. The development of mnemonic knowledge and the skills to acquire mnemonic knowledge are derived from cognitive growth and learning experiences. Knowledge of memory and associated skills are reflected in the categories and subcategories of the taxonomy which are based upon the four broad categories or theories of memory phenomena (Flavell and Wellman, 1977).

Metamemory incorporates a number of elements and to identify and organise these elements, Flavell (1977) proposed a classification scheme describing these facets of metamemory and the development of metamemory or 'knowledge about memory' (see Table 6.2). These are classified as categories and subcategories; the categories are sensitivity and the variables include subcategories of person, task and strategy (Flavell and Wellman, 1977). The taxonomy of metamemory identified that some tasks require planful mnemonic strategies and that performance in a memory situation or task is affected by conscious factors. These are classified as

Table 6.2 Flavell and Wellman's facets or varieties of metamemory as a foundation for the taxonomy of metacognition

Categories	Descriptions
Sensitivity	Perception or awareness of situations instigate memory strategies for storage and retrieval of information.
	Attunement to when storage strategies and retrieval strategies are needed is developed over time and through experience.
	Memory sensitivity development involves actively knowing when to use deliberate, goal-orientated strategies to memorise information intentionally, and when to allow spontaneous, passive use of memory strategies (Flavell, 1977, 1978, 1981a; Flavell and Wellman, 1977).
	Sensitivity to the requirements of the memory situation through attunement, adaptability and awareness.
	Awareness of which situations 'do and do not call for intentional memory-related behavior' (Flavell, 1978, p. 214), such as 'deliberate, strategic efforts to store or retrieve items' (Wellman, 1978, p. 24).

Variables
Knowledge of the factors, including knowledge of memory or person, task and strategy variables, which interact and affect memory storage and retrieval (Flavell, 1977, 1978, 1979, 1981a; Flavell and Wellman, 1977). The following are the three variables or subcategories of Flavell and Wellman's taxonomy.

Person	Knowledge of 'memory-relevant attributes' (Flavell, 1977) or 'enduring mnemonic characteristics and capacities' (Flavell, 1978, p. 216). This includes two elements of person memory development – knowledge and monitoring.
	Development of accurate understandings or knowledge of memory abilities, including beliefs of oneself and others as mnemonic beings.
	Proficiency at monitoring and interpreting mnemonic experiences and states such as feeling-of-knowing and tip-of-the-tongue (Brown and McNeil, 1966; Flavell, 1977, 1978; Flavell *et al.*, 1970; Flavell and Wellman, 1977; Hart, 1965; Wellman, 1977, 1978). 'Here-and-now monitoring' involves 'knowing how to detect and interpret transient mnemonic process and states' (Flavell, 1978, p. 217).
Task	Knowledge and awareness of the potential benefits and applications of various mnemonic strategies to aid task performance (Flavell, 1977; Wellman, 1978).
	Knowledge and awareness of task 'memory-relevant characteristics' (Flavell, 1977).
	Knowledge of the variety of tasks and task difficulty enables the differentiation between simple tasks and complicated mnemonic tasks which require greater retrieval demands (Flavell, 1977; Wellman, 1978).

continues

Table 6.2 (continued)

Categories	Descriptions
Strategies	Effective memory depends upon mnemonic ability, task complexity and the successful application of mnemonic strategies.
	Strategies involve executive function or control processes and are reliant upon knowledge of these strategies to be effectively adaptive to a particular task (Flavell and Wellman, 1977).
	Knowledge of potential strategies and solution procedures (Flavell, 1978; Wellman, 1978).

Source: Adapted from Flavell and Wellman (1977).

memory-relevant characteristics of the person, task and strategies and are based upon four categories of memory phenomena.

Sensitivity to task situations involves an awareness of and attunement to when to use particular mnemonic strategies and specifically relates to the task variable where awareness of task situations and the suitability of different mnemonic strategies interact with knowledge of various tasks, task difficulty and complexity. It is not specifically declarative knowledge but can be classified as procedural and conditional knowledge. Conditional knowledge will be discussed in Chapter 9.

The person variable involves personal knowledge of memory attributes and awareness through monitoring of feeling and knowing phenomena. Person attributes are classified as declarative metamemory, and monitoring and interpretation of feeling and knowing states are classified as regulation of metamemory. Memory performance is affected by the interaction between person and task and is facilitated by strategy knowledge. Strategic processes also involve executive functioning and control which prompt the use and termination of particular strategies.

Metamemory is considered to consist of and be influenced by these elements and processes. Flavell's (1978; 1981a) subsequent papers continued to discuss these categories of the taxonomy in a metamemory context and later Flavell's (1979; 1981a; 1987) discussion focuses on metacognition with a revised version of Flavell and Wellman's taxonomy which provided a framework for a model of metacognition and cognitive monitoring. Flavell (1981a) referred to the taxonomy of metamemory as the beginning or foundation of the cognitive monitoring model. This model is discussed in Chapter 8.

Listed are assertions derived from the discussion of Flavell and Wellman's (1977) taxonomy of metamemory.

6.8   Cognitive development, learning experiences, awareness and skills influence the development and acquisition of mnemonic knowledge or knowledge of memory and strategy knowledge (akin to 'knowing about knowing').

6.9   Conscious, voluntary mnemonic strategies and control processes are used to address task demands (akin to 'knowing how to know').

6.10 Sensitivity involves actively knowing when to use deliberate, goal-orientated strategies to intentionally memorise information and when to allow spontaneous, passive use of memory strategies in different task situations.

6.11 Knowledge of memory attributes and abilities (person variable), including beliefs of oneself and others as mnemonic beings, support monitoring and interpreting mnemonic experiences such as feeling and knowing states.

6.12 Knowledge and awareness of task characteristics (task variable), including types of tasks, difficulty and the benefits and applications of various mnemonic strategies, aid task performance.

6.13 Knowledge of strategies (strategy variable) mnemonic ability, task complexity and the successful application of mnemonic strategies involve executive function processes and are affected by adaptability to a particular task.

Figure 6.2 (see p. 90) depicts the factors of metamemory and the inter-relationship between the subcategories of each factor. This diagram is based upon Flavell and Wellman (1977) and Flavell's (1978, 1979, 1981a) description of these metamemory elements.

Conclusion

Knowledge of memory processes, and mnemonic strategies and abilities have an important effect upon memory development. Memory development is not isolated from cognitive development, including the development of perception, comprehension, inference, language, problem-solving skills and trans-situational skills. The monitoring of memory via the use of mnemonic-mediation processes, memorisation strategies and knowledge of memory affects the further development of memory ability and strategies (Brown, 1975, 1978; Flavell, 1977, 1978; Flavell and Wellman, 1977; Kreutzer *et al.*, 1975). A number of other dedicated works investigated and discussed memory, comprehension and cognitive development (e.g. Brown and DeLoache, 1978; Kail and Hagen, 1977; Paris and Lindauer, 1977).

Knowledge of memory is the foundation of Brown's, and Flavell and Wellman's taxonomies. Flavell and Wellman acknowledge the influence of Brown's work on the development of their taxonomy. She proposed three types of memory knowledge in the context of knowing, knowing about knowing and knowing how to know which are specifically related to Flavell and Wellman's four broad categories of memory. The following discussion draws together both contributions under the titles of knowing, knowing how to know and knowing about knowing, and distinctly identifies the

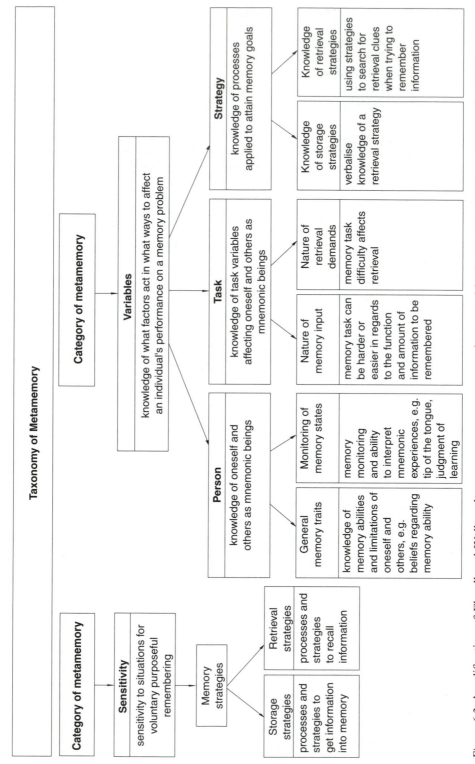

Figure 6.2 Amplification of Flavell and Wellman's metamemory taxonomy as interpreted in the conceptual framework of metacognition

Source: Adapted from Flavell and Wellman (1977).

processes which comprise knowledge of memory. It is obvious that there are distinctions between the specific metamemorial processes of knowing how to know and knowing about knowing and interactions between the two.

Knowing is affected by cognitive development and involves unconscious, involuntary mnemonic processes and strategies of recognition, recall and cueing. A form of metamemory knowledge, knowing about knowing, is the introspective awareness and knowledge that facilitates the development of memory knowledge. Knowing about knowing can be considered a form of declarative metamemory. Cognitive development, experiences and skills affect the development and acquisition of memory knowledge. Strategy knowledge, an aspect of metamemory knowledge, is facilitated by awareness, promoting planning and strategy selection. Self-knowledge and awareness help to facilitate monitoring, control and strategy transfer in memory and problem-solving tasks. Strategy selection, application, monitoring and control can be influenced by beliefs. Lack of metamemory knowledge and awareness leads to ineffective strategy application and monitoring and control of these strategies in various situations.

Flavell and Wellman's variables category incorporated factors such as person, task and strategies, considered as forms of declarative knowledge and reflective of Brown's knowing about knowing. These factors directly and indirectly influence memory performance and can impact positively or negatively on meeting complex, task demands, and influence success in solving various types of problems. Therefore task complexity, including the situated context of the cognitive activity, can have important implications for metamemory processes. Cavanaugh and Perlmutter (1982) considered that an additional variable could be the task or problem context. It is that 'knowledge of the context in which memory processing occurs' that can have important effects on task or problem success (ibid., p. 15). Brown also consistently referred to influences of task complexity and demands on the application of metamnemonic processes and strategies. More so than Flavell and Wellman, Brown stressed the effect of knowledge and application of executive processes on meeting task demands. The combination and interaction of these variables in complex problems would provide an interesting focus of an empirical study.

Knowing how to know or procedural metamemory includes purposeful strategy and plan application to facilitate memory and learning. This involves conscious, voluntary application of memory strategies to meet task requirements. Although in her early work Brown (1975) identified monitoring and control processes as knowing how to know or procedural metamemory, she later clearly re-classifies monitoring and control as part of regulation processes (see Brown, 1978, 1987; Brown *et al.*, 1983; Brown and DeLoache, 1978). Of course all of these processes interact and rely upon each other for effective memory development and performance on memory tasks. Task complexity and meaningfulness affect the development, selection and application of mnemonic strategies. Complexity also influences the reconstruction of knowledge and the attainment of the problem solution. Therefore, effective strategy selection and application facilitate analysis and assist the attainment of deeper, meaningful levels of comprehension. This also influences efficient strategy monitoring and control, rendering complex memory tasks or problems manageable and meaningful. Knowledge and application of strategies and processes can be implicit or explicit. They are more likely to be explicit in complex task and problem situations. Flavell and Wellman's sensitivity category could be considered to be akin to Brown's knowing how to know. Sensitivity involves the awareness of the applicability of mnemonic strategies in different task situations and awareness is necessary for the instigation of planful, mnemonic strategies. It is actively knowing when to use deliberate, goal-orientated strategies intentionally to memorise information and when to allow spontaneous, passive use of memory strategies.

Knowledge, awareness and the application of mnemonic strategies are essential for problem solving. Knowledge of metamemory processes, including beliefs about one's own memory ability, may affect problem solving and can have a greater effect on solving of complex problems. Well-developed memory processes, strategies, intelligent monitoring and the use of plans facilitate the solving of complex, contextualised problems. It is this conscious, deliberate reliance on metamemory processes that supports complex problem solving. These suppositions need further investigation as the relationship between problem solving and metamemory has not been fully identified.

The following higher-order assertions (HOA) are drawn from the above discussion:

6.14 Knowledge of memory involves introspective awareness and self-knowledge which influences planning, strategy selection and application (HOA.11).

6.15 Knowledge of procedural memory processes involves conscious, purposeful strategy and plan application (HOA.12).

6.16 Effective strategy selection and application facilitates task analysis and assists the attainment of deeper, meaningful levels of comprehension. This influences efficient strategy monitoring and control, facilitating the problem solution (HOA.13).

6.17 Situational knowledge and task complexity influence the reconstruction of memory knowledge and strategy knowledge and their application in problem-solving situations (HOA.14).

7 Metamemory and its components: The basis of metacognition

This chapter identifies and discusses the specific categories and elements of metamemory, including declarative and procedural metamemory. This review of metamemory forms a foundation for discussing metacognition in Part III. Overall this discussion provides an important contribution to the *conceptual framework of metacognition* and *taxonomy of metacognition.*

Categories of metamemory: Knowledge of memory and regulation of memory

This section builds upon the taxonomic contributions of Brown, and Flavell and Wellman whose contributions to metamemory provide a significant foundational representation of the development and the current view of the construct. Their works provide the foundation for two distinct but interrelated dichotomies of metamemory: knowledge of memory and regulation of memory. A number of subcategories are identified within these two categories. Knowledge of memory includes Flavell and Wellman's person, task and strategy variables. These are connected to Brown's knowing about knowing, identified as declarative metamemory or knowledge, and knowing how to know, identified as procedural metamemory or knowledge. Regulation of memory includes mnemonic experiences, specifically memory monitoring and feeling-of-knowing phenomena. An outline of Nelson and Narens' metamemory monitoring and control framework adds to the discussion of the interaction between monitoring and control processes.

It has been argued that metamemory should only involve knowledge of memory as the inclusion of regulatory processes of memory complicates the construct (Cavanaugh and Perlmutter, 1982; Chi, 1987). Whether metamemory includes regulatory processes in addition to knowledge of memory has been a continued area of discussion and contention (Cavanaugh and Perlmutter, 1982; Flavell, 1977; Schneider, 1998; Schneider and Lockl, 2002; Weinert, 1988; Wellman, 1983). This uncertainty has contributed to the problems in defining the construct and therefore its fuzziness.

Nevertheless, the literature consistently identifies regulatory processes such as monitoring and control as essential to memory storage and retrieval. Therefore, metamemory involves knowledge of memory including memory ability and strategy knowledge (Brown, 1978; Cavanaugh and Perlmutter, 1982; Flavell and Wellman, 1977; Leonesio and Nelson, 1990). It also involves monitoring, predicting, coordinating, control and focused application and efforts to solve problems. Essentially this also involves self-monitoring and regulation of memorial processes (Brown, 1978; Flavell and Wellman, 1977; Leonesio and Nelson, 1990).

The inclusion of regulation of memory reflects the evolution of both metamemorial and metacognitive theories, considering too that the core metamemory theory is the foundation of metacognition. Flavell's (1978; Flavell and Wellman, 1977) initial works on metamemory focused on knowledge about memory but his later works on metacognition also emphasised regulatory processes such as planning, evaluating, testing, revising and remediating (see Flavell, 1979, 1981a). Brown discussed knowledge about memory but also identified regulatory processes as an integral category of metamemory including mnemonic strategies such as rehearsal, planning, monitoring and checking processes (Baker and Brown, 1984a; Brown, 1978).

Although it is important to distinguish between knowledge of memory and regulatory processes, the difficulty lies in clearly differentiating between them as they are interdependent and interact with each other in task situations. These delineations and their specific elements are discussed and assertions are drawn which contribute to the *conceptual framework of metacognition* and the *taxonomy of metacognition*. Relevant and selected studies are reviewed in the light of these particular dichotomies.

Knowledge of memory: Person, task and strategy

Memory proper, or secondary memory as it might be styled, is the knowledge of a former state of mind after it has already once dropped from consciousness; or rather *it is the knowledge of an event, or fact*, of which meantime we have not been thinking, *with the additional consciousness that we have thought or experienced it before*. (James, 1890a, p. 648)

James' statement is historically significant in terms of metamemory theory. He identified knowledge of memory as the 'meta' in metamemory. Knowledge of memory is inherent in, and fundamental to, current conceptual understandings of metamemory. The first central distinction is the difference between remembering and knowledge about memory – metamemory – which is essentially cognitive knowledge versus engaging in cognition. This distinction is based upon reflective processes applied during the cognitive activity which encourages engagement. Knowledge about memory includes examples such as tip-of-the-tongue knowledge (Brown and McNeil, 1966; Hart, 1965; Schwartz, 2002; Wellman, 1977) – where someone knows about his or her cognition in spite of an inability to execute the cognitive act right then – and knowing that rehearsal facilitates short-term memory, without currently engaging in rehearsal itself.

A number of theorists have also mirrored James' view of knowledge of memory by defining metamemory as knowledge about or of memory, memory tasks, memory strategies and personal memory ability (e.g. Brown, 1975, 1978; Cavanaugh and Perlmutter, 1982; Chi, 1978; Flavell, 1971a, 1977; Flavell and Wellman, 1977; Gathercole, 1998; Hertzog and Dixon, 1994; Leonesio and Nelson, 1990; Pressley, Borkowski and O'Sullivan, 1984; Schneider, 1985, 1998; Schneider and Bjorklund, 2003; Wellman, 1978, 1983).

Knowledge of memory is affected by beliefs and self-knowledge, including ability knowledge. It is also affected by memory awareness and self-system knowledge of memory processes including memory capacity, strategies and skills (Borkowski and Cavanaugh, 1981; Brown, 1978; Brown and Campione, 1977; Cavanaugh and Perlmutter, 1982). It is also reliant upon judgments and language and is important for problem solving (Gathercole, 1998; Hertzog and Dixon, 1994; Wellman, 1983). It includes variables such as person, task and strategy knowledge and involves a particular sensitivity towards this knowledge to enable effective memory storage and retrieval (Flavell, 1977; Flavell and Wellman, 1977; Weinert, 1987; Wellman, 1978, 1983). Overall, it is delineated into two subcategories, declarative meta-memory and procedural metamemory. Although Flavell and Wellman's (1977) taxonomy has been labelled as a 'taxonomy of declarative meta-memory' (Schneider, 1998, p. 1), their taxonomy represents knowledge of memory, including both declarative and procedural metamemory. It also identifies, in the person variable, the monitoring of memory states including feeling and knowing phenomena categorised in this book as regulation of metamemory. Schneider and colleagues (see Schneider, 1998; Schneider and Bjorklund, 2003, p. 380; Schneider and Lockl, 2002, p. 230) categorise memory monitoring as procedural metamemory. This book will only categorise procedural metamemory as specifically 'knowing how to know' and not inclusive of monitoring and control. This stance reflects the categorisation in the metacognition literature which consistently identifies a separate category, regulation of cognition, which includes monitoring and control processes (see Baker and Brown, 1984b; Borkowski, 1985; Brown, 1981; Brown *et al.*, 1983; Brown and Palincsar, 1982; Flavell, 1981a; Flavell *et al.*, 1993, 2002; Hartman, 2001a; Joyner and Kurtz-Costes, 1997; Paris and Winograd, 1990; Pintrich *et al.*, 2000; Schraw, 1998; Schraw and Moshman, 1995). The following subsections outline and clarify these two forms of knowledge of metamemory.

Assertions identifying the essential aspects of knowledge of memory follow:

7.1   Knowledge of memory includes variables such as person, task and strategy knowledge and involves sensitivity towards this knowledge facilitating memory storage and retrieval.

7.2   Knowledge of memory involves knowledge of memory tasks, strategies and personal memory attributes, and is affected by beliefs, ability and self-knowledge, and memory awareness of processes such as memory capacity, strategies and skills.

7.3   Knowledge of memory is reliant upon judgments and language and is important for problem solving.

Declarative metamemory: Knowing about knowing (person, task and strategy)

Declarative metamemory involves factual, explicit, truthful and conscious knowledge about person memory characteristics, memory task demands and their information requirements, and knowledge of mnemonic strategies to facilitate memory acquisition, storage and retrieval (Flavell, 1977, 1978, 1979, 1981a; Flavell and Wellman, 1977; Hertzog and Dixon, 1994; Joyner and Kurtz-Costes, 1997; O'Sullivan and Howe, 1998; Schneider, 1998; Schneider and Bjorklund, 2003; Schneider and Lockl, 2002; Wellman, 1983). It has also been referred to as 'stored metamemory' which involves knowledge, understandings, information and representations (Hertzog and Dixon, 1994). It is also identified as important for memory problems which occur in 'everyday-life situations' (Knopf *et al.*, 1988; Lockl and Schneider, 2002).

Declarative metamemory is reliant upon memory schemas, also described as schematic knowledge, schematic propositional networks or node-link networks (Bellezza, 1996; Chi, 1978, 1987). Instigation of this existing schematic knowledge is prompted by mnemonic images and cues which support inferences and the storage of new information (Bellezza, 1996; Chi, 1978, 1987; Schneider and Pressley, 1997). Chi considered that the declarative nature of knowledge supported by schematic or node-link networks facilitates metamemorial processes. This factual label is questioned by O'Sullivan and Howe (1995, 1998) who considered that declarative metamemory is limited by its label as factual knowledge about memory which neglects personalised beliefs about memory and that a new conceptualisation should include interpretive and personally constructed knowledge of verifiable and naive beliefs about memory and knowledge of their effects on memory processes. However, in the light of Flavell and Wellman's taxonomy, specifically the person variable, this is not necessarily a totally new conceptualisation of declarative metamemory. Supporting this, Flavell stated that 'the person category encompasses everything that you could come to believe about the nature of yourself and others as cognitive processors' (Flavell, 1979, p. 907). Although Flavell and Wellman did not discuss in detail the accuracy of naivety of beliefs, they did emphasise the effect of intra-individual beliefs on memory processes (see Flavell, 1978, 1979; Flavell and Wellman, 1977). Therefore, even though they did not specifically highlight the effect of the naivety and verifiability of beliefs, it is not a neglected part of the foundational conceptualisation of metamemory but an overlooked aspect of declarative metamemory.

Flavell and Wellman's works (see Flavell, 1977, 1978, 1979; Flavell and Wellman, 1977; Wellman, 1978) did not specifically differentiate between declarative and procedural metamemory.

The elements classified as declarative person metamemory in the person variable relate to specific knowledge of oneself including memory attributes, abilities, mnemonic self-concept, capabilities and limitations. This also incorporates knowledge of others as mnemonic beings. Declarative task metamemory involves specific knowledge of task characteristics as well as task difficulty and knowledge of the variety of mnemonic tasks. Declarative strategy metamemory is knowledge of the variety of mnemonic strategies and is also affected by person and task knowledge.

Table 7.1 refers to these contributions to identify those elements of each knowledge of memory variable which reflect the categorisation of declarative metamemory.

Knowledge about memory, such as task and mnemonic strategies, develops earlier than person knowledge, including mnemonic self-concept

Table 7.1 Declarative metamemory in person, task and strategy variables

Person metamemory	Knowledge of memory-relevant attributes or abilities essential to person memory development
	Mnemonic self-concept including accurate understandings or knowledge of memory ability including beliefs of oneself and others as mnemonic beings
	Knowledge of enduring mnemonic qualities, capabilities and limitations
Task metamemory	Knowledge and awareness of task 'memory-relevant characteristics' (Flavell, 1977)
	Attunement to memory ability in different memory tasks. This interacts with person variable
	Knowledge of the variety of tasks and task difficulty enables the differentiation between simple tasks and complicated mnemonic tasks which require greater retrieval demands
Strategy metamemory	Effective memory depends upon mnemonic ability, task complexity and the successful application of mnemonic strategies
	Knowledge of various mnemonic strategies and awareness of their potential effectiveness in specific memory task situations

(Chi, 1978). Chi described knowledge of stimuli present in memory task situations as another knowledge of memory variable or factor.

Knowledge of mnemonic strategies or strategy metamemory, including the potential effectiveness of these strategies in different memory task situations, is insufficient for strategy development and application in challenging memory tasks (Hertzog and Dixon, 1994). Importantly, the interaction with person metamemory, such as beliefs regarding the ability to apply specific mnemonic strategies, effectively affects strategy development and application. Strategy selection in complex mnemonic tasks is affected by the interaction of person, strategy and task variables supported by monitoring processes and influenced by 'memory self-efficacy' (Hertzog and Dixon, 1994). Memory self-efficacy is also influenced by awareness of mnemonic processes, estimation of task difficulty and the evaluation of mnemonic knowledge and imagery (Campione and Brown, 1977). Memory self-efficacy affects knowledge of memory, specifically the person variable and the regulation of memory. Mnemonic beliefs and self-efficacy can be categorised as knowledge of memory; however, it is important to note these influence regulatory processes, specifically monitoring processes, and this in turn affects knowledge of memory. The influence of memory self-efficacy and beliefs on metamemory will be explained further in the subsection entitled Influences on metamemory: Memory, beliefs and self-efficacy.

Interaction among person, task and strategy variables facilitates metamemory and therefore knowledge of the interaction of these memory variables (Wellman, 1978). For example, memory task demands and characteristics interact in determining task difficulty. The interaction between person and strategy knowledge influences memory ability and performance (Flavell and Wellman, 1977; Wellman, 1978). Therefore, memory task complexity places increased demands upon the interaction between the types of metamemory. Memory tasks, especially complex tasks, instigate mnemonic mediation and are similar to problem solving situations (Brown, 1974). The interaction of all declarative metamemory variables forms the knowledge basis for procedural metamemory to occur.

Assertions which describe the essential aspects of declarative metamemory are:

7.4   Declarative metamemory involves factual, explicit, truthful and conscious knowledge about memory. Person memory characteristics, memory task demands and knowledge of mnemonic strategies facilitate memory acquisition, storage and retrieval.

7.5   Person declarative metamemory or mnemonic self-concept involves knowledge of person memory-relevant attributes, abilities and limitations including beliefs of oneself and others as mnemonic beings.

7.6   Task declarative metamemory involves knowledge of task variety, characteristics and difficulty facilitating an understanding of task demands. This is also affected by person metamemory.

7.7   Strategy declarative metamemory involves knowledge of various mnemonic strategies and the awareness of their effectiveness in memory task situations. This is affected by person metamemory.

7.8   Interaction among person, task and strategy variables facilitates metamemory and therefore knowledge of the interaction of these memory variables.

7.9   Memory task complexity increases demands upon the interaction between the metamemory variables.

Figure 7.1 draws from the above assertions to depict the relationship between knowledge of memory and declarative metamemory. It also illustrates the interaction between person memory attributes, task variety and characteristics, and knowledge of mnemonic strategies.

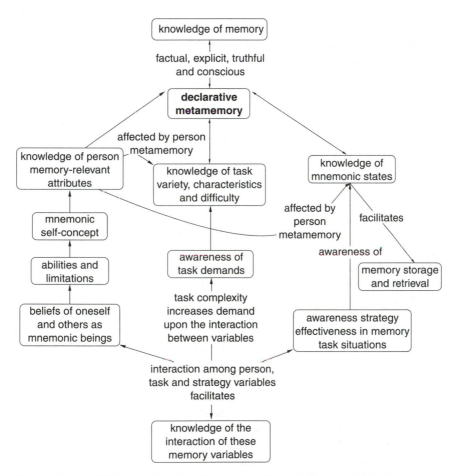

Figure 7.1 Amplification of declarative metamemory in the conceptual framework of metacognition

Procedural metamemory: Knowing how to know (strategy application)

Procedural metamemory is knowledge about how to do things or knowing how to know. This includes 'motoric, perceptual, and cognitive procedures involved in the performance of a skill' or strategy (Healy and Sinclair, 1996, p. 538). It also involves decisions regarding specific domain strategies and procedures applied to memory tasks which can be described also as production rules or processing rules (Chi, 1978, 1987; Pressley *et al.*, 1985). It also includes knowledge of the appropriateness of strategies for a particular task, strategic application knowledge, and the execution of strategies.

The difficulty lies in describing procedural metamemory without reference to declarative metamemory and also clearly distinguishing between the two types of knowledge of memory. Nevertheless, there are certain core differences and interrelationships which can be identified and described (Chi, 1987). Declarative metamemory informs and implicates procedural metamemory in terms of strategy selection and application and involves knowledge and understandings of memory strategies which facilitate knowledge of how to use different memory strategies including the selection of the most applicable strategy for particular memory tasks. The complexity of the learning task affects the need for a variety of advanced metamemory strategies. The conscious and deliberate use of these strategies facilitates storage and retrieval of multifaceted, meaningful information as well as uncomplicated knowledge (Brown, 1975; Flavell, 1977; Flavell and Wellman, 1977; Osman and Hannafin, 1992).

Procedural metamemory is also described as 'strategic action' reliant upon knowledge of the '*value* of a strategy, its *range* of applicability, and *mode* of execution' in memory task problems (Pressley *et al.*, 1985, p. 113). This also involves an awareness of encoding, strategic processes and memory systems (Best, 1986; Osman and Hannafin, 1992). As domain knowledge represented as schematic knowledge and task knowledge increases, the use of strategic knowledge also increases. Even with appropriate strategy selection, limited task knowledge can affect memory performance (Kail, 1990).

The application of strategies, the knowing of when, where (conditional) and how (procedural) to apply a specific strategy or strategy transfer, is considered to be a metamemorial (Campione and Brown, 1974) or meta-cognitive, process (Borkowski and Turner, 1989). Therefore, strategy transfer is an important part of procedural metamemory. Knowledge of memory facilitates strategy application and transfer from one contextual situation to another. A number of papers describe studies on strategy transfer including the development and application of strategies to enhance and promote performance (see Brown, 1981; Brown and Campione, 1977; Brown and Palincsar, 1982; Campione, 1987).

Table 7.2 identifies those particular elements of Flavell and Wellman's task and strategy variables which can be classified as procedural metamemory. This involves knowing which particular strategies are suitable for a particular task and knowledge of the processes of their application. Procedural strategy metamemory is affected by mnemonic ability and task complexity. It also incorporates the knowledge and awareness of strategy processes for specific tasks which are needed to obtain a task solution. Correlations between metamemory and performance are generally higher for applications of knowledge or procedural processes than declarative knowledge or knowledge about memory.

Table 7.2 Procedural metamemory in task and strategy variables

Task metamemory	Knowledge and awareness of the potential benefits and applications of various mnemonic strategies to enhance task performance (Flavell, 1977; Wellman, 1978)
Strategy metamemory	Effective memory depends upon mnemonic ability, task complexity and the successful application of mnemonic strategies
	Strategies involve executive function or control processes and are reliant upon knowledge of these strategies to be effectively adaptive to a particular task (Flavell and Wellman, 1977)
	Knowledge of different potential strategies and solution procedures (Flavell, 1978; Wellman, 1978)

Note: There are no procedural metamemory processes in the person variable. The monitoring aspect of the person variable is categorised as regulation of memory.

The aim here is not to describe in detail the application of strategic knowledge or the types of memory strategies. Detailed discussions on metamemory and strategy use are provided by a number of researchers including Paris and Lindauer (1982) and Pressley and Borkowski (see Pressley *et al.*, 1985; Pressley, Borkowski and O'Sullivan, 1984). As well as describing types of memory strategies or factual or declarative knowledge of memory strategies, Paris and Lindauer (1982) consider that procedural metamemory includes understanding how to select and apply mnemonic strategies for various memory task situations.

Pressley and Borkowski (Pressley *et al.*, 1985) also describe interrelationships between declarative knowledge or factual knowledge about strategies and procedural knowledge about strategies. Their metamemory about strategies (MAS) describes the interrelationship between declarative and procedural metamemory of strategies. There are six MAS components including procedural metamemory identified as metamemory acquisition procedures (MAPs). In later works on metacognition they label the MAS as the Good Information Processing Model (see Borkowski, 1985; Borkowski, Carr and Pressley, 1987; Borkowski *et al.*, 1990; Borkowski *et al.*, 2000; Borkowski *et al.*, 1988; Borkowski and Turner, 1989; Pressley *et al.*, 1985;

Pressley, Borkowski and O'Sullivan, 1984; Pressley *et al.*, 1987; Pressley, Levin and Ghatala, 1984). This will be described in more detail in Chapter 8.

The following assertions outline the overall aspects of procedural metamemory which is knowing how to know:

7.10 Knowledge and awareness of the potential benefits and applications of various mnemonic strategies and solution procedures facilitate task performance.

7.11 Procedural knowledge involves knowledge of strategy appropriateness, benefits and application of various mnemonic strategies for a particular task and the execution of strategies or actions.

7.12 Strategies involve executive function or control processes and are reliant upon declarative knowledge of these strategies to be effectively adaptive to a particular task.

7.13 Strategy selection is affected by task complexity and the interaction of person, strategy and task variables. This is supported by monitoring processes and influenced by memory self-efficacy.

Figure 7.2 draws from the above assertions to depict the relationship between knowledge of memory and procedural metamemory. It also illustrates the interaction between knowledge of strategy appropriateness, knowledge of the application of mnemonic strategies, and execution of strategies. Knowledge of strategy application is affected by the task and its complexity which influences task performance. These processes are supported by monitoring and control and memory self-efficacy.

Figure 7.3 (see p. 104) depicts the relationship between procedural metamemory and declarative metamemory and their variables.

Regulation of memory: Monitoring, control and executive function

Regulatory processes of memory are discussed in the context of the central executive, central processor, interpreter or executive processes. The central processor, through self-awareness, evaluates its processes and this facilitates efficient problem-solving processes (Brown, 1978; Gathercole, 1998). Memory monitoring interacts with the executive control of mnemonic activities and working memory facilitating memory performance in memory tasks (Brown, 1977, 1978; Butterfield *et al.*, 1973; Gathercole, 1998; Koriat and Goldsmith, 1998; Spearman, 1923).

Regulation of memory, also labelled as 'concurrent' metamemory, involves the monitoring, control and awareness of memory knowledge and processes (Hertzog and Dixon, 1994). Monitoring of memory or assessments of current memory or self-monitoring involves evaluations, intuitions and unconscious feelings such as feeling and knowing phenomena during memory tasks (Flavell, 1977; Kail, 1990; Kluwe, 1982; Leonesio and

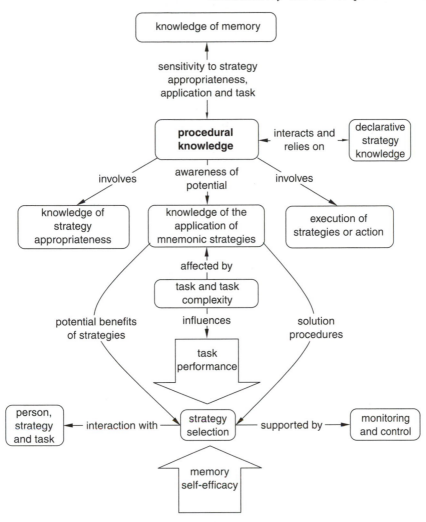

Figure 7.2 Amplification of procedural metamemory in the conceptual framework of metacognition

Nelson, 1990; Schneider and Bjorklund, 2003; Weinert, 1987; Wellman, 1977, 1983). Self-monitoring provides essential information via feeling and knowing phenomena such as ease of learning, judgment of knowing and feeling of knowing to facilitate control processes during memory tasks (Leonesio and Nelson, 1990).

Although monitoring and control processes are sometimes discussed jointly, they are distinct processes (Nelson and Narens, 1990; Reder and Schunn, 1996; Umilta and Stablum, 1998). Control processes involve the regulation and organisation of knowledge of memory which facilitates

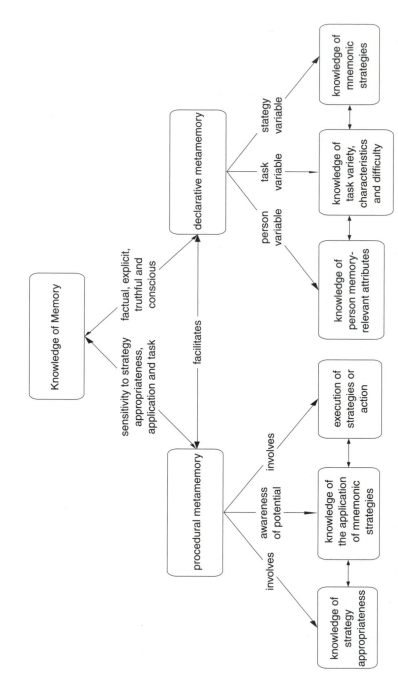

Figure 7.3 Amplification diagram of the connections between declarative and procedural metamemory from Figure 7.1 and Figure 7.2.

action such as task sequencing, time allocation and the allocation of other task-related resources. They are conscious, modifiable, adaptable and stimulated by past control experiences but also limited by short-term memory storage. Control processes are stimulated in complex, demanding memory task situations especially where there is task and strategy novelty, difficult and complex sequencing and execution of actions (Campione and Brown, 1977; Koriat and Goldsmith, 1998; Umilta and Stablum, 1998). The general view of control processes is that they are explicit and conscious (Campione and Brown, 1977; Shimamura, 1996). Another view, espoused by Reder and Schunn (1996), is that they are implicit processes developed through implicit learning and past implicit control experiences. In addition they are not always verbalisable because of their implicit, unconscious nature. Both views are correct. Control processes can be both implicit and explicit.

The assertions listed below identify the essential aspects of regulation of memory.

7.14 Regulation of memory involves the monitoring, control and awareness of memory knowledge and processes.
7.15 Memory monitoring interacts with the executive control or functioning of mnemonic activities and working memory, facilitating memory and performance in memory tasks.
7.16 Memory monitoring involves evaluations, intuitions and unconscious feelings, such as feeling and knowing phenomena, which facilitate control processes during memory tasks.
7.17 Control processes can be conscious and explicit or implicit processes. They involve regulation and organisation of mnemonic knowledge facilitating strategic processes.
7.18 Control processes are conscious, modifiable, adaptable and stimulated by past control experiences but also limited by short-term memory storage.
7.19 Control processes are stimulated in complex, demanding memory task situations especially where there is task and strategy novelty that evoke difficult and complex strategy sequencing and execution.

Nelson and Narens' metamemory monitoring and control framework

Nelson and Narens' (1990, 1994) well-known and cited model of metamemory or metacognition (they use the terms interchangeably) outlines the interactive process of monitoring and control (see Figures 7.4 and 7.5). In contrast to their framework, which describes the regulatory processes of metamemory, Flavell and Wellman's (1977) taxonomy generally focused on knowledge of memory. They specifically describe the monitoring and control processes in terms of feeling and knowing phenomena (discussed in Chapter 5). It seems relevant, therefore, to discuss Nelson and Narens'

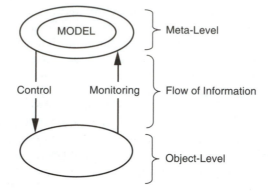

Figure 7.4 Nelson and Narens' model depicting the flow of information between the meta-level and the object-level

Source: Adapted with permission from Nelson and Narens (1990).

metamemory monitoring and control framework in this chapter and to refer to their contributions in Part 3.

The framework or model identifies three critical abstract principles of metamemory (see Figure 7.4). Cognitive processes are divided into two interrelated levels – meta-level and object-level. Information flows between the meta-level and the object-level. This flow of information is a dynamic interrelationship between the meta-level and object-level, incorporating the processes of control and monitoring.

The direction of flow of information is the foundation upon which the model works. The control process starts at the meta-level and changes the object-level. This may create an action at the object-level such as starting, continuing and finishing an action. Although it is an important function of control processes to start and stop an action or strategy at the object-level, control processes can also modify the object-level by the use of new mnemonic strategies. However, to support the control process and to provide the information necessary to make these control decisions, monitoring must take place.

This starts at the object-level and informs the meta-level, changing its state. The meta-level holds a model of the object level. This information is used by the meta-level to support the monitoring process. Understanding of this metamemorial monitoring process can be gained by the use of introspective reports although veridical reliability is questioned (Nelson and Narens, 1990, 1994). The overall effectiveness of the regulatory system depends upon the interaction between the object-level and the meta-level and therefore on the interaction between the monitoring and control of memory. Generally, the view is that control processes modify the object-level and the meta-level is informed via monitoring of the object-level (Nelson, 1996; Nelson and Narens, 1994).

Koriat and Goldsmith (1998) provide a descriptive example of the interaction between the meta-level and the object-level in Nelson and Narens' model:

> The student apparently first thought that he or she knew the answer (monitoring) and wrote it down (control), but then changed his or her mind about the correctness of the answer (monitoring) and decided to cross it out (control). The monitoring aspect, then, involves the subjective assessment of how likely it is that an answer that comes to mind is correct, whereas the control aspect concerns the operational decision to write down the answer or withhold it, or to cross out an answer that one has just written or leave it for inclusion in the final scoring.
>
> (pp. 98–99)

This description highlights the interrelationships between the critical processes of the model represented in the dynamic interaction between the object-level and the meta-level, goal state, and the interpretation and application of knowledge and strategies to control or change the object-level to attain the meta-level goal (Schwartz and Bacon, 2008; van Overschelde, 2008).

Nelson and Narens (1990, 1994) provide an extended depiction of their model or framework that describes in detail the interaction between monitoring and control processes in terms of knowledge acquisition, retention and retrieval (see Figure 7.5 p. 108).

Monitoring processes are described in terms of retrospective and prospective monitoring judgments. Retrospective monitoring is confidence judgments about prior responses. Prospective monitoring includes feeling and knowing phenomena such as ease-of-learning judgments which occur before acquisition, judgments of learning which occur during or shortly after acquisition and feeling-of-knowing judgments which occur during or after acquisition. Importantly, each of these feeling and knowing phenomena monitors various facets of metamemory. Nelson and Narens (1990, 1994) provide a detailed description of the acquisition, retention and retrieval stages including their interaction with the monitoring and control processes. In addition, Plude *et al.* (1998) discuss the possibility of expanding Nelson and Narens' metamemory monitoring and control framework to include 'motivational and capacity components' (p. 32). The *Handbook of Memory and Metamemory* is dedicated to discussing, reviewing and analysing Nelson and Narens' model and its application in metamemory and metacognition theory and research (see Dunlosky and Bjork, 2008b).

The following assertions identify key aspects of Nelson and Narens' model and specifically the interaction between monitoring and control:

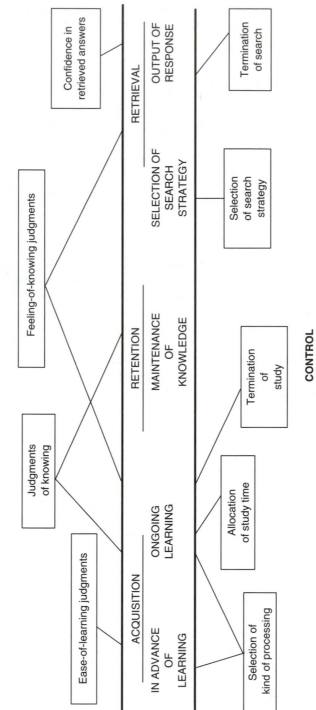

Figure 7.5 Nelson and Narens' theoretical metamemory framework

Source: Adapted with permission from Nelson and Narens (1990).

7.20 The interaction between the monitoring and control of memory reflects the view that control processes modify the object-level and the meta-level is informed via monitoring processes of the object-level.

7.21 Retrospective monitoring is confidence judgments about prior responses and prospective monitoring involves feeling and knowing phenomena which occur before, during or shortly after acquisition.

Figure 7.6 (see p. 110) draws from the above assertions to depict the relationship between regulation of memory, memory monitoring and control processes.

THE BRAIN: FRONTAL LOBE AND PREFRONTAL CORTEX

The human biological relationship between metamemory monitoring and control is its connection to the prefrontal cortex or the frontal lobe of the brain, the main function of which is to monitor functions and organise, coordinate, maintain and update information facilitating goal-direction and self-regulation (Fletcher and Henson, 2001; Romine and Reynolds, 2004; Wheeler *et al.*, 1997). Therefore the function of the frontal lobe, including damage, for example, through alcohol abuse labelled as Korsakoff's syndrome, has been and continues to be a focus for metamemory and metacognitive research (e.g. Hirst, 1982; Janowsky *et al.*, 1989; Shimamura and Squire, 1986; Squire and Zouzounis, 1988). As there are other works which discuss in detail the theoretical and empirical contributions in this complex field, this book highlights but does not delve deeply into the connections between the frontal lobe, regulatory processes such as monitoring and control, and metamemory (see Darling *et al.*, 1998; Parkin, 1997; Schwartz and Bacon, 2008; Shimamura, 1994, 1996, 2000, 2008). Shimamura (2008) considers that Nelson and Narens' metamemory framework is a useful model to help analyse frontal lobe functioning.

Wheeler *et al.* (1997) identified three levels of frontal lobe functioning. The first involves the organisation and integration of information including the ability to create meaningful mental representations of this information. The second or executive function involves monitoring, conscious control, goal setting and planning. Executive functioning is essential for solving complex, non-routine contexts that necessitate new solutions. The third involves autonoetic consciousness or self-awareness including reflection and introspection. Self-awareness is essential for executive functioning including the co-ordination of intricate processes such as goal setting, planning, monitoring, control and the anticipation and strategic application of these processes. Therefore, self-awareness is not only needed for knowledge of memory, but also for the effective regulation of memory processes. Other theorists also emphasise the relationship between frontal lobe damage and impairment of monitoring and control processes of metamemory (e.g. Metcalfe, 1996; Umilta and Stablum, 1998). Romine and Reynolds (2004)

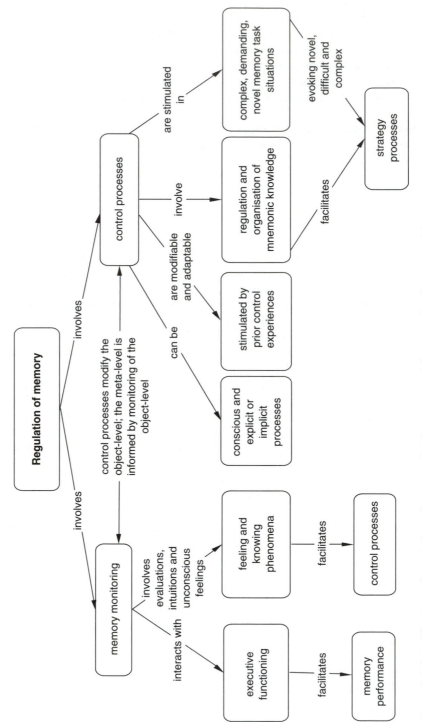

Figure 7.6 Amplification of regulation of memory in the conceptual framework of metacognition

also consider that frontal lobe functioning continues to develop in late adolescence and adulthood and that there is a strong connection between metacognition and frontal lobe functioning.

The effect of frontal lobe damage in the case of patients with Korsakoff's syndrome includes impairment of learning, memory and metamemorial functioning (Shimamura, 1994, 1996), specifically limited and impaired knowledge of mnemonic strategies, monitoring and control of mnemonic strategies, and feeling and knowing (Hirst, 1982; Janowsky *et al.*, 1989; Shimamura and Squire, 1986; Squire and Zouzounis, 1988).

The following assertions outline the basic relationships between frontal lobe functioning, executive functioning and self-awareness:

7.22 Frontal lobe functioning involves executive processes or functioning including monitoring, conscious control, goal setting, planning and the organisation and integration of information all necessary for complex problem solving.
7.23 Self-awareness including reflection and introspection supports frontal lobe or executive functioning including the coordination of intricate processes such as goal setting, planning, monitoring, control and the strategic application of these processes.
7.24 Self-awareness is necessary for knowledge of memory and regulation of memory processes.

Figure 7.7 draws from the above assertions to depict the relationship between frontal lobe functioning, executive functioning and self-awareness.

MONITORING STRATEGIES

Flavell and Wellman's person variable also identifies memory monitoring, a 'here-and-now monitoring', as essential in overseeing and guiding mnemonic strategies. This is essentially a regulatory process which involves the interpretation of mnemonic experiences or states (Brown and McNeil, 1966; Flavell, 1977, 1978; Flavell *et al.*, 1970; Flavell and Wellman, 1977; Hart, 1965; Wellman, 1977, 1978). This interpretation also relies upon knowledge of these experiences (Wellman, 1978). Monitoring strategies also involve processes or 'mechanisms that orchestrate cognition' (Cavanaugh and Perlmutter, 1982, p. 13). These mechanisms influence strategy selection, monitor strategy efficiency, influence the development of new strategies to meet task demands and monitor task completion (Brown, 1978; Cavanaugh and Perlmutter, 1982; Joyner and Kurtz-Costes, 1997; Wellman, 1977).

Memory monitoring is affected by learned mnemonic strategies and knowledge of these strategies. Over time, the utilisation of these becomes automated and 'quasi-reflective' (Flavell and Wellman, 1977). Although selection may be automated, the effectiveness or result of the particular strategy is known (Flavell and Wellman, 1977; Reder and Schunn, 1996). Complex, novel task situations instigate the development and application of

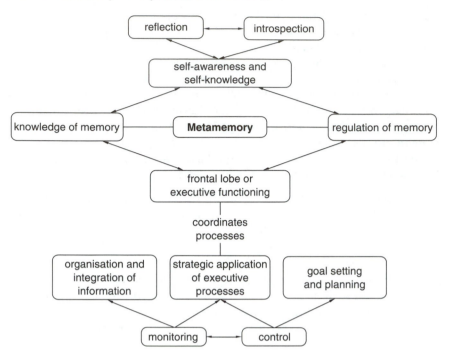

Figure 7.7 Amplification of the relationship between executive functioning and self-awareness in the conceptual framework of metacognition

novel strategies. These may not be automated but, rather, highly conscious, monitored and controlled processes. The conscious regulatory processes are important to help determine strategy effectiveness.

The following assertions identify the key relationships between memory monitoring and mnemonic strategies:

7.25 The person variable involves memory monitoring or 'here-and-now monitoring' necessary for overseeing and guiding mnemonic strategies.

7.26 Monitoring strategies involve mechanisms or processes that influence the development of new strategies, strategy selection and efficiency to meet task demands and task completion.

7.27 Memory monitoring is affected by the selection and application of learned mnemonic strategies which become automated and quasi-reflective processes, especially in predictable task outcome situations.

7.28 Complex, novel task situations instigate the development and application of novel strategies which are highly conscious, monitored and controlled processes facilitating the determination of strategy effectiveness.

Figure 7.8 draws from the above assertions to depict the relationship between monitoring and mnemonic strategies.

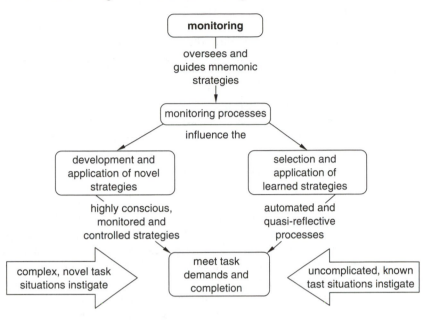

Figure 7.8 Amplification of the relationship between monitoring and mnemonic strategies in the conceptual framework of metacognition

Influences on metamemory: Memory, beliefs and self-efficacy

The literature provides a link between memory and beliefs often labelled as memory self-efficacy (Bandura, 1989; Cavanaugh, 1996; Dunlosky and Hertzog, 1998; Hertzog and Dixon, 1994; Light, 1996; Rebok and Balcerak, 1989). This is beliefs about one's memory ability and its effectiveness in different memory task situations (Cavanaugh, 1996; Dunlosky and Hertzog, 1998; Light, 1996; McDonald-Miszczak *et al.*, 1999). Memory demanding situations can elicit various emotions and beliefs about capabilities and successful performance (Bandura, 1989; Hertzog and Dixon, 1994; Joyner and Kurtz-Costes, 1997; Light, 1996).

In some instances, the literature is undecided as to whether memory self-efficacy should be included in the conceptualisation of metamemory. There are, however, strong proponents who consider that 'self-referent beliefs about memory' (Hertzog and Dixon, 1994, p. 234) affect monitoring processes and should be viewed as a component of metamemory (Bandura, 1989; Berry, 1989; Cavanaugh, 1996; Hertzog and Dixon, 1994; Hertzog *et al.*, 1989; Joyner and Kurtz-Costes, 1997; O'Sullivan and Howe, 1995, 1998). A study by McDonald-Miszczak *et al.* (1999) reaffirmed the memory self-efficacy and metamemory relationship. Their study found that memory self-efficacy significantly influenced memory performance, especially in prospective memory tasks.

The literature neglects to acknowledge adequately that Flavell and Wellman specifically identify, within the person category, beliefs about oneself as a mnemonic being. Hertzog and Dixon (1994) categorise aspects of mnemonic beliefs in the following statement:

> Representations of one's own tendency to react affectively to memory-demanding situations, as well as declarative knowledge about relationships between affective states and memory performance, are aspects of metamemory that can be subsumed under the categories of memory-related beliefs and knowledge, respectively.
>
> (p. 229)

Memory monitoring can activate positive or negative self-beliefs of oneself as a learner or of memory ability. These can either promote or inhibit memory performance and influence strategy selection and engagement in the monitoring process. Negative self-referent beliefs about memory may impede the willingness during memory monitoring to determine and select alternative mnemonic strategies or to use particular strategies to facilitate effective memory retrieval. This can be evident in complex, demanding memory task or problem-solving situations. Attributional beliefs – beliefs about success or failure – are relevant to this discussion but will not be covered in this chapter.

The following assertions identify the influences of beliefs on metamemory:

7.29 Memory self-efficacy comprises beliefs about one's memory ability and its effectiveness in different memory task situations.
7.30 Memory demanding situations and memory monitoring can elicit various emotions, positive and negative self-beliefs about capabilities and successful performance.
7.31 Beliefs can promote, inhibit or influence memory performance, strategy selection and engagement in the monitoring process especially in complex, demanding memory task or problem-solving situations.

Figure 7.9 (see p. 115) draws from the above assertions to depict the relationship between memory self-efficacy and self-beliefs.

Although Flavell and Wellman's taxonomy provides a rich theoretical framework for empirical metamemory research, there has been scant research in the past few decades investigating the interactions between the person, task and strategy variables. Nor has there been a great deal of research into the relationship between the variables and the sensitivity category. Studies which have investigated Flavell and Wellman's metamemory taxonomy researched it in the context of the potential of strategy

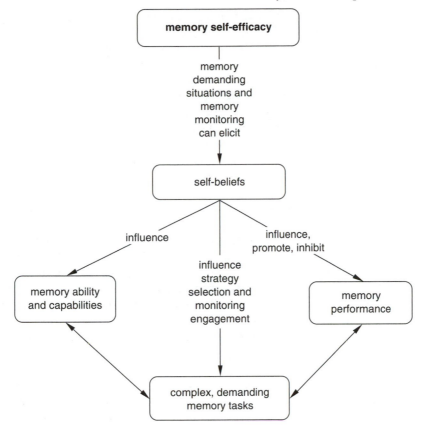

Figure 7.9 Amplification of the relationship between memory self-efficacy and beliefs in the conceptual framework of metacognition

training to improve metamemory and task performance and found positive results (e.g. Brown and Campione, 1977; Cavanaugh and Borkowski, 1979). Also, research on Flavell and Wellman's taxonomy, specifically the variables, investigated the difference in memory performance between young and older children, and the development of young children's metamemory ability (see Trepanier, 1982). Trepanier called for more research into the interactions between the variables.

Drawing from the conceptual contributions made in Flavell and Wellman's metamemory taxonomy, Wellman (1978) investigated the interaction between the metamemory variables of person, task and strategy, specifically the development of knowledge of the interaction between memory variables. This knowledge could be demonstrated through knowledge of item difficulty and the use of specific mnemonic strategies or the manipulation or breakdown of difficult aspects of the task. The participants, 20 five-year-olds and 20 ten-year-olds, were presented with judgment tasks where they judged either the memory relevance or memory irrelevance of a depicted knowledge of memory variable, and where they judged the interaction of two memory variables. The younger children 'judged memory performance on the basis of only one of the relevant variables' and had difficulty understanding that the interaction between variables could affect memory performance (ibid., p. 28). The study presented the children with only a restricted number of singular and inter-active memory judgment tasks but concluded that the children only later develop a knowledge of the interaction between variables. This knowledge is developed from an initial 'lack of understanding of memory-relevant phenomena to acquisition of an array of certain separate facts' (ibid.). Knowledge of individual or simple variables develops simultaneously with the development of knowledge of the interaction between these variables.

These findings reflect a statement by Brown and Campione (1977) in which they refer to a number of studies of children and their metamemory development and memory performance (e.g. Brown, 1974, 1975; Brown and Barclay, 1976). Brown and Campione (1977) explained that as children increase in age, maturity and metamemorial awareness, they progressively increase their strategy knowledge and application in simple and complex memory and problem-solving tasks. Their study was also based on Flavell and Wellman's taxonomy – specifically the interaction between task and strategy variables based on study apportionment and strategy training in 70 children with learning disabilities. They found that it was necessary to develop training strategies which recognise children's current knowledge of strategies and 'cognitive maturity' rather than trying to transfer sophis-ticated adult memory strategies. They also considered that Flavell and Wellman's metamemory variables are 'developmentally sensitive'. This developmental sensitivity is also related to the ability to monitor and control memory and learning strategies. This also relies upon sensitivity to the person, task and strategy variables (Schneider, 1998).

The interest in memory and metamemory strategy training, especially in children with learning disabilities, spurred a number of other research studies (e.g. Brown and Barclay, 1976; Brown and Palincsar, 1982; Campione and Brown, 1977; Digby and Lewis, 1986). These showed that children with learning disabilities could be taught to apply different task-related strategies, such as rehearsal, resulting in significant improvements in their performance (Borkowski, 1985; Campione, 1987). A study by Keeler and Swanson (2001) found that children with a mathematical disability were helped by strategy training to enhance their declarative metamemory strategy knowledge, working memory and mathematical performance.

Research such as that by Pressley, Borkowski and O'Sullivan (1984) has shown that knowledge of memory strategies and systems relates to successful metamemory monitoring and performance. Procedural and strategy knowledge is an indicator of metamemory success rather than just knowl-edge of metamemory processes. Knowledge of memory strategies or metamemory strategies interact in conjunction with 'person variables, such as a feeling of knowing and judgment of recall readiness, as well as task and strategy variables, such as the value or significance of the strategy' (Osman and Hannafin, 1992, p. 84). Borkowski and Cavanaugh (1981) contend that 'metamemory strategy connections are strengthened by feedback procedures following strategy training and are more likely discovered when an acquired strategy is applied to a new problem' (p. 256). A number of studies have found that strategy training facilitates the development of metamemory. They identified the connections between knowledge of metamemory variables, strategy use and memory performance (e.g. Ghatala *et al.*, 1985; Huet and Marine, 1997).

Andreassen and Waters (1989) used verbal reports as data to investigate the relationship between metamemory, organisational strategy application and memory performance during study. Sixty first-grade students with a median age of six years and nine months and 48 fourth-grade students with a median age of nine years and ten months were asked metamemory strategy questions before and after a memory task. The children reflected on their strategic processes to help recognise their specific organisational strategies and develop knowledge of organisation strategies and whether they facilitated memory performance. Results from the study suggest that reflection facilitates strategy awareness and instigates future planning and organisational strategies to support memory performance. They also found that children did not 'spontaneously' develop knowledge of organisational strategies and overall strategy application as adults seem to do. Thus children must be prompted to reflect on their strategic processes to enable the development of knowledge of these processes. Overall the findings demonstrate that metamemory strategies develop through age and experience. This study demonstrates that reflective verbal reports can be effective to help identify knowledge about strategy use. Research by Bray *et al.* (1999) also found that self-reports or verbal reports facilitated strategy use and the development of strategy knowledge in children with and without learning disabilities.

Adolescents (eleventh grade) were found to have higher levels of knowledge of memory variables and used more sophisticated strategies than children (seventh grade) (Suzuki Slakter, 1988). This is also supported by Kail (1990), who considered, after reviewing a number of studies, that 'developmental advances in knowledge can influence memory directly' (p. 78).

Overall, the studies reaffirm that Flavell and Wellman's taxonomy provides a foundation for research on metamemory. Variables and the interaction of these variables – person, task and strategy – provide scope for investigating knowledge of metamemory and the relationships between different forms of declarative and procedural knowledge. The studies have not investigated the potential relationships between sensitivity and the other variables. Sensitivity would involve self-knowledge, awareness and understanding of the applicability of strategy and task knowledge to meet task demands. It also relies upon the development and application of monitoring and control processes. The studies affirm that the variables develop simultaneously with the development of knowledge of the inter-actions between these variables. The studies have also confirmed that metamemory development increases with age, maturity and awareness. Most studies have investigated this increase in metamemorial knowledge specifically in terms of declarative and procedural strategy knowledge and used strategy training to determine improvements in memory performance and metamemory.

Mostly research has investigated the connection and interrelationship between memory and metamemory especially focusing on children's mem-ories and their ability to retrieve and then verbalise them using whatever mnemonic strategies they have developed. Memory monitoring, then, has been a major research focus in this field. It seems as though metamemory research has neglected to investigate specific metamemorial processes, including some of the feeling and knowing phenomena, although there has been a great deal of research on feeling-of-knowing and tip-of-the-tongue phenomena. Many artificial memory tasks have been given to participants rather than investigating their knowledge of their memory processes in real-life situations. Many research tasks test participants' ability to draw from their short-term memory in controlled task environments using picture cards and pictures collected from various sources relevant to the particular age group (e.g. Brown and Lawton, 1977; Wellman, 1978).

These significant studies affirm the following assertions regarding meta-memory:

7.32 The person, task and strategy variables and sensitivity are essential elements of metamemory and form components of declarative and procedural knowledge of memory.
7.33 Strategy knowledge – declarative and procedural – can develop through strategy training and improves memory performance.
7.34 Metamemory strategies develop through age and experience.
7.35 Verbal reports are useful in determining strategy knowledge and application in children, adolescents and adults.
7.36 Verbal reports facilitate strategy use and the development of strategy knowledge in children with and without learning disabilities.
7.37 Reflection facilitates strategy awareness and instigates planning and organisational strategies to support memory performance.

Conclusion

This chapter has established that knowledge of memory encompasses declarative and procedural metamemory. Declarative metamemory involves factual, explicit and conscious knowledge about memory and procedural metamemory involves strategic knowledge including appropriateness, benefits, application and execution of strategies for a specific memory task.

Knowledge of memory involves personal memory attributes which are affected by beliefs, memory self-efficacy, mnemonic self-concept, beliefs regarding memory ability and capability. Person declarative metamemory involves knowledge and beliefs of oneself and of others as mnemonic beings. Knowledge of memory facilitates memory acquisition, storage and retrieval and relies upon judgments and language to support memory performance and problem solving. Task declarative metamemory comprises knowledge of task variety, characteristics, difficulties and task demands. Strategy declarative metamemory involves knowledge of various mnemonic strategies, awareness of their effectiveness in memory task situations. Person declarative metamemory interacts with both task and strategy variables.

Procedural metamemory involves knowledge and awareness of the benefits, appropriateness and applications of various mnemonic strategies. It is dependent upon declarative knowledge of these strategies, affected by task complexity and the interaction of the variables. Strategy adaptivity, selection, execution and solution procedures facilitate task performance. Memory monitoring and control support and regulate strategy use.

Complex, demanding tasks instigate the development and application of novel strategies which are conscious, monitored and controlled to determine their effectiveness and application, facilitating task performance and completion. These types of tasks evoke difficult, multifaceted strategy sequencing and execution and instigate regulatory processes. Regulation of memory involves the monitoring, control and awareness of memory knowledge and processes. Memory monitoring involves evaluations, intuitions and unconscious feelings such as feeling and knowing phenomena. These processes promote the development of new strategies and strategy efficiency to meet demands and facilitate memory performance in novel tasks. Learned strategies are automated, quasi-reflective processes, especially in well-structured memory tasks.

Demanding memory tasks and monitoring processes can instigate beliefs, memory self-efficacy and emotions about one's ability, capability and memory performance. Beliefs can promote, inhibit and influence memory performance, strategy selection and engagement in monitoring processes, especially in complex, demanding memory tasks or problem-solving situations. There is also a connection with Flavell and Wellman's person variable as it involves and affects memory monitoring. Therefore, both declarative person metamemory and procedural strategy metamemory are influenced by memory self-efficacy. Underlying all these processes is the influence and importance of self-knowledge and reflective processes which are essential to knowledge of memory and regulation of memory.

Control processes are explicit or implicit, modifiable, adaptable and stimulated by past control experiences. They involve regulation and organisation of mnemonic knowledge and facilitate goal setting, planning and other strategic processes. Frontal lobe functioning or executive functioning involves self-awareness, reflection and introspection and is essential for both monitoring and control processes.

Flavell and Wellman (1977) do not specifically categorise aspects of their knowledge of memory, person, task and strategy variables as declarative or procedural. This categorisation is discussed in this book. This is important because it reflects the later categorisation by many other theorists of metacognition – knowledge of cognition – into declarative and procedural. Flavell and Wellman's category of sensitivity has been categorised by Schneider and Lockl (2002) as knowledge of memory, specifically pro-cedural metamemory, and they also subcategorised monitoring and control as part of procedural metamemory. This conceptualisation fails to identify monitoring and control as part of regulation of memory. However, Schneider and Lockl (2002) do correctly categorise sensitivity as procedural knowledge in terms of sensitivity to task, sensitivity to strategy application and initiation; but they also fail to recognise the interaction between sensitivity and the other variables of task and strategy. Interaction among person, task and strategy variables facilitates metamemory and therefore knowledge of the interaction of these memory variables. Memory task complexity increases demands upon the interaction between the meta-memory variables. As discussed in the review of empirical studies, the interaction between the variables has received little attention. There is the potential here for further research into the categorisation role of sensitivity as procedural metamemory and its interaction with the other variables.

The following higher-order assertions (HOA) are drawn from the above discussion:

7.38 Knowledge of memory involves personal memory attributes which are affected by memory self-efficacy, mnemonic self-concept and beliefs regarding memory ability and capability (HOA.15).

7.39 Knowledge of memory facilitates memory acquisition, storage and retrieval, and relies upon judgments and language to support memory performance and problem solving (HOA.16).

7.40 Task complexity increases demands upon the interaction between the metamemory variables and facilitates the development of knowledge of the interaction of these variables (HOA.17).

7.41 Strategy adaptivity, selection, execution and solution procedures facilitate task performance (HOA.18).

7.42 Regulation of memory involves the monitoring, control and aware-ness of memory knowledge and processes (HOA.19).

7.43 Memory monitoring involves evaluations, intuitions and unconscious feelings such as feeling and knowing phenomena (HOA.20).

7.44 Control processes involve regulation and organisation of mnemonic knowledge including facilitating goal setting, planning and other strategic processes (HOA.21).

7.45 Memory monitoring and control support and regulate strategies and promote strategy efficiency and the development of new strategies, especially supporting performance in novel, complex memory tasks (HOA.22).

7.46 Frontal lobe functioning or executive functioning is essential for monitoring and control and involves self-awareness, reflection and introspection (HOA.23).

Conclusion to Part II

It has been argued that the development of the construct of metamemory is based upon early discussions and empirical studies of memory and memory monitoring. This has re-established memory monitoring as a regulatory core function of metamemory and that it is not solely knowledge of memory, including declarative and procedural knowledge, but also regulation of memory. Even recent conceptualisations of metamemory identify monitoring and control as procedural metamemory within knowledge of memory and not as a separate categorisation of regulation of memory (Schneider and Bjorklund, 2003; Schneider and Lockl, 2002). Although there has been continued debate regarding the inclusion of regulatory processes in the definition of metamemory, the significance of these processes in terms of overall metamemorial functioning is hard to ignore. Schneider and Lockl's (2002) categorisation of monitoring and control as knowledge of memory, specifically procedural metamemory, is not convincing. As discussed earlier, there are clear differentiations between what is procedural metamemory and what are regulatory processes. Procedural metamemory involves knowledge of the application of specific strategies in different contexts. Although knowledge of memory, including both declarative and procedural metamemory, interacts with monitoring and control processes, monitoring and control should not be categorised as a type of knowledge of memory, but categorised as regulation of memory. The intricate interaction of regulatory processes with all types of knowledge of memory lends the categorisation of monitoring and control to regulation of memory.

Part II has established that the study of metamemory is historically the foundation of the study of metacognition. Metamemory theory has provided a framework for the development of the construct of metacognition. An advance in knowledge in this field is the drawing together of the conceptual contributions of major theorists such as Flavell and Wellman, and Brown to identify the core categories and subcategories. The conceptual mapping of these contributions and reflection on the connections with metacognition literature has enabled an integrated categorisation of metamemory. An extension of Flavell and Wellman's taxonomy is the categorisation of the specific aspects of person, task and strategy variables and the sensitivity category into knowledge of memory including declarative and procedural metamemory. Brown, Nelson and Narens and others' contributions to memory monitoring, control and executive functioning have been categorised as regulation of memory.

Part III

Metacognition: The taxonomy

Part III establishes the main conceptual contributions to metacognition theory and builds upon the conceptual contributions identified in Part II. Flavell's model of cognitive monitoring, an extension of Flavell and Wellman's taxonomy of metamemory into metacognition theory, is reviewed. Brown's conceptualisation of metacognition is analysed and Borkowski and Pressley's Good Information Processing or Good Strategy User Model of Metacognition is reviewed as well as Kuhn's Model of Metastrategic Knowledge. These contributions to metacognition theory and the taxonomies developed from the assertions in Parts I and II form a foundation to identify the elements, key elements, subcategories, super-categories and categories of metacognition which are represented in the *taxonomy of metacognition*. The *conceptual framework of metacognition* provides a depiction of the taxonomy.

8 Models of metacognition

The aim of this chapter is to review the significant models which contribute to the structure of the construct of metacognition and describe their components and their relationship to each other.

Conceptual contributions to metacognition theory

Models of metacognition

A number of key models from different theorists provide important conceptual contributions to metacognition. An analysis of these not only provides a framework to identify the essential elements, key elements, subcategories, supercategories and categories of metacognition but also builds upon contributions to metamemory by theorists such as Flavell and Wellman, and Brown, as mentioned in Chapter 4. Flavell and Wellman's (1977) taxonomy is extended in Flavell's (1979, 1981a) model of cognitive monitoring which develops the metamemory categorisations to metacognition theory. For example, knowledge of memory is extended to knowledge of cognition which includes the variables of person, task and strategy categorised as metacognitive knowledge. He also described metacognitive experiences, cognitive goals and cognitive actions or strategies as fundamental to metacognition. Metacognitive experiences are categorised in this book as a regulation of cognition.

Brown's (1978, 1981) contributions to metacognition are drawn together to identify her main categorisations. As well as Flavell, Brown provides a solid foundation of the construct. She does not specifically describe her work as a model of metacognition although the analysis of a number of her works provides a detailed categorisation of the construct.

Borkowski and Pressley's Good Information Processing or Good Strategy User model describes metamemory and metacognition strategy knowledge (see Borkowski, 1985; Borkowski, Carr and Pressley, 1987). Their model initially described metamemory strategy knowledge and acquisition strategies. As metacognition theory developed, it also evolved to refer to metacognitive strategy knowledge.

Kuhn's (1999a, 2000a, 2000b) model of meta-knowing takes a broader view by encompassing it within the term meta-knowing. Meta-knowing includes metastrategic, metacognitive and epistemological meta-knowing. The following subsections describe in detail each of these models and contribute to the *conceptual framework of metacognition* and the *taxonomy of metacognition.*

Flavell's model of cognitive monitoring

> Knowledge is an activity which would be better described as a process of knowing.
>
> (Polanyi, 1969, p. 132)

Flavell (1979, 1981a) developed the model of metacognition and cognitive monitoring based upon Flavell and Wellman's (1977) metamemory taxonomy. The model conceptualises four categories of metacognition: *metacognitive knowledge, metacognitive experiences, cognitive goals or tasks,* and *cognitive actions or strategies*. These categories are interactive and are central to the monitoring and regulation of tasks or problems.

Other literature which discusses cognitive monitoring provides a foundation to describe in detail Flavell's (1979, 1981a) model specifically within the context of the four components.

Cognitive monitoring is the reflective awareness and monitoring of mental states and processes including the ability to control, judge, evaluate and regulate the status of knowledge within one's cognitive system. It enables a person to know when information is known and understood, or not known or understood, and to have awareness of cognitive states such as imagining and visualising (Wellman, 1985a, 1985b). It is the ability to control this knowledge and apply decision-making processes to realise task goals through the matching of knowledge and action (Baker and Brown, 1984a; McAlpine *et al.*, 1999; Wellman, 1985a, 1985b). Wellman referred to this as 'knowing how', specifically knowing how to apply knowledge to facilitate task success and completion (Wellman, 1985a).

Flavell and Wellman's (1977) metamemory taxonomy served as a solid foundation for discussing the main components of metacognitive knowledge including variables of person, task and strategy and sensitivity. It provides a link between metacognitive knowledge and knowledge of metamemory, and sensitivity to metamemory processes and variables (Flavell, 1978, 1979, 1981a, 1987).

To understand the operation of the model, it is necessary to examine briefly the function of each component – cognitive goals, cognitive actions, metacognitive knowledge and metacognitive experiences.

Cognitive goals and subgoals (or tasks and subtasks) can be either implicit or explicit objectives which aim to facilitate the initiation, progression and completion of the problem or 'cognitive enterprise'. They can be both self-determined and governed by the problem or the interaction with others and be task specific, comprising a number of subgoals. Knowledge and awareness of the levels or types of cognitive goals and the role they play in problem solving develops over time with exposure to and experience in solving different problems. This knowledge includes the ability to clarify unclear goals, pursue several goals, set explicit goals intentionally, and adopt and deliberately pursue goals which are not self-selected (Flavell, 1979, 1981a, 1981b).

Cognitive actions or strategies are procedures facilitating the attainment of the cognitive goals of the problem or cognitive enterprise. Both goals and actions interact with metacognitive knowledge and involve and instigate metacognitive experiences (Flavell, 1979, 1981a, 1981b). They are categorised later in this book as procedural strategy knowledge. Cognitive goals, including subgoals, influence cognitive actions or strategies in complex problems. Identifying the actions to meet goals and subgoals in complex problems is gained through understanding how to determine and change actions or strategies relative to changes in goals (Flavell, 1981a).

Metacognitive knowledge is the accrued long-term knowledge, understandings and beliefs about situations, environments, variables such as person, task, and strategies and sensitivities that interact to affect the representation and outcome of tasks or problems. It can be either declarative or procedural. Metacognitive knowledge can have various levels of lucidity, intricacy, complexity, accuracy, or consistency. It can also influence the selection, evaluation and termination of cognitive actions or strategies and cognitive goals in the light of person and task influences and variables (Flavell, 1979, 1981a, 1981b, 1987).

Metacognitive knowledge is not necessarily always the conscious or explicit application of knowledge. It can be stimulated implicitly and be automatically applied to the problem or task. If unsuccessfully retrieved and applied, metacognitive knowledge may not always be effective in facilitating the problem solution. Ability, task interest and context affect metacognitive knowledge which in turn influences problem solving by guiding strategic processes facilitating the problem solution and task completion (Flavell, 1979, 1981a, 1981b, 1987).

Reflection on metacognitive knowledge interacts with, facilitates, affects and assists the understanding and interpretation of metacognitive experiences and cognitive actions or strategies. Metacognitive experiences can also be derived from metacognitive knowledge and include cognitive or affective experiences associated with the task, self, strategies or problem (Flavell, 1981a, 1981b; Hacker, 1998).

Person metacognitive knowledge involves beliefs and intuitions regarding the cognitive ability and nature of oneself and others. It encompasses three subcategories: intra-individual differences, inter-individual differences and 'universals of cognition'. Intra-individual differences are beliefs about oneself as a learner and inter-individual differences are beliefs of others and their ability as learners compared with oneself. Universal cognitions relate to beliefs and intuitions, understandings, misunderstandings, perceptions, conceptions, impressions regarding general abilities, properties and processes of oneself and others (Flavell, 1979, 1981a, 1981b).

Task metacognitive knowledge includes two subcategories: task information and task demands. Task information refers to the information provided by the task which is available during problem solving. This can be detailed, informative, inconsistent, dense, sparse, known, unknown, engaging, disengaging, structured or ill-structured. Task demands refers to the complexity and difficulty of various types of tasks. It involves knowledge, awareness and understanding of the elements and variables affecting the task including how to manage task characteristics and awareness of progress, success or failure. This knowledge develops through experience (Flavell, 1979, 1981a). The task dictates how the task information will be processed and presented and influences how task demands are met, both of which reflect variations in complexity such as the differences in characteristics of problem types. Sensitivity, an element of task metacognitive knowledge, also plays an important role in helping to match information and task components with types of processes and applications to facilitate task completion (Flavell, 1981a, 1981b).

Strategy metacognitive knowledge is knowledge of which strategies are effective in meeting task demands and achieving the desired outcome. This knowledge is gained through the interaction between person and task knowledge and through metacognitive experiences. Metacognitive knowledge of effective and non-effective strategies is based upon the learnt experiences of applying strategies to different tasks and problems. Strategy knowledge facilitates the application of strategies to various tasks (Flavell, 1981a, 1981b).

Metacognitive experiences are conscious cognitive and affective states which involve awareness, unexpected awareness, thoughts, intuitions, perceptions, feelings and self-judgments of oneself as a cognisor during problem solving and task completion. They rely upon conscious recognition of identifiable cognitive and affective states and involve appreciative or responsive awareness and recognition of attitudes. They can be momentary or prolonged and in some situations can interact with metacognitive knowledge to facilitate the development and evaluation of theories and strategies. The problem situation can influence the simplicity or complexity of the metacognitive experience and in turn these experiences can influence current goals and instigate the development of new goals. Although metacognitive experiences are generally conscious that does not mean they are always intentional for they can occur unintentionally and monitor processes unintentionally (Flavell, 1981a, 1981b).

They can influence and inform the development of metacognitive knowledge by increasing or revising this knowledge. Metacognitive knowledge can also be informed by metacognitive experiences that facilitate the inter-actions and relationships between strategies or actions, goals and the variables. Some experiences are conscious metacognitive knowledge objects, but others play the role of interpreting or providing information to meta-cognitive knowledge (Flavell, 1981b).

Metacognitive knowledge is informed by metacognitive experiences, such as judgments, via the monitoring of processes during problem solving. Monitoring of metacognitive experiences and metacognitive experiences themselves can prompt the retrieval and application of strategies to facili-tate the attainment of task goals. Metacognitive strategies and the use of monitoring processes can also instigate metacognitive experiences about the progress of goal attainment (Flavell, 1981b). Cognitive goals can prompt the retrieval of metacognitive knowledge relevant to particular goals and metacognitive experiences can be stimulated by the development of and reflection on those goals (Flavell, 1981a).

Figure 8.1 depicts the four fundamental components of the model of cognitive monitoring: cognitive goals or tasks, cognitive actions or stra-tegies, metacognitive knowledge and metacognitive experiences (Flavell, 1979, 1981a). The model does not, however, demonstrate the significant interaction which Flavell (1979, 1981a, 1981b) describes between meta-cognitive knowledge and metacognitive experiences.

The model also does not provide a strict representation of the actual processes of cognitive monitoring but illustrates the interrelationship between the components and processes.

Flavell (1981a) believes that other elements could be added to the model, such as the cognitive problem and problem setting, which could possibly further explain the interrelationship between the components. He explains that there could be multiple interactions between the cognitive problem and

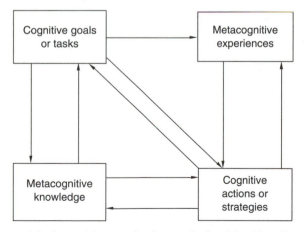

Figure 8.1 A model of cognitive monitoring as depicted by Flavell

Source: Adapted with permission from Flavell (1981a, p. 40).

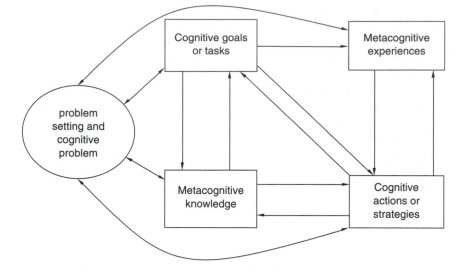

Figure 8.2 A model of cognitive monitoring incorporating the additional elements of the model as suggested but not depicted by Flavell.

Source: Adapted from Flavell (1981a).

problem setting and the four metacognitive components or processes. For example, knowledge of the problem context and situation would inform knowledge of the specific problem requirements and the attributes of the problem. This would then help to determine cognitive goals and actions which would be influenced by metacognitive experiences. A model incorporating these additional elements could provide a more comprehensive depiction of the process of cognitive monitoring. These additional elements, the problem setting and the cognitive problem, are not metacognitive processes but influence and are influenced by the four components of the model. Figure 8.2 provides an example of the possible interrelationships between the four components or processes and the problem context and cognitive problem.

The following assertions represent Flavell's contribution to the elements of metacognition:

8.1 Cognitive monitoring describes the interaction between metacognitive knowledge, metacognitive experiences, cognitive goals or tasks, and cognitive actions.

8.2 Cognitive monitoring involves reflective awareness of knowledge and monitoring, control and regulation of this knowledge during problem solving.

8.3 Cognitive monitoring facilitates knowing how to apply and control knowledge to enable the realisation of task goals.

8.4   Cognitive goals (tasks) and subgoals (subtasks) are either implicit or explicit objectives which are self-determined, identified through social interaction and by the specific task.

8.5   Knowledge and awareness of cognitive goals includes the ability to clarify, set and pursue several goals, facilitating the problem solving process.

8.6   Cognitive actions or strategies (procedural strategy knowledge) are procedures which facilitate the realisation of cognitive goals related to a problem.

8.7   Cognitive goals and cognitive actions interact with metacognitive knowledge and involve and instigate metacognitive experiences.

8.8   Cognitive goals influence cognitive actions in complex problems.

8.9   Knowledge and understanding of how to determine and change actions relative to changes in cognitive goals are necessary for the solving of complex problems.

8.10 Metacognitive knowledge is either declarative or procedural knowledge.

8.11 Metacognitive knowledge is accrued knowledge and beliefs about situations, variables (person, task, and strategies) and sensitivities that interact affecting the problem outcome.

8.12 Metacognitive knowledge influences the selection, evaluation and termination of cognitive actions and goals in the light of person and task variables.

8.13 Metacognitive knowledge can be explicitly or implicitly applied.

8.14 Metacognitive knowledge is informed by ability, interest and task context which then influences strategic processes by either facilitating or impeding the problem solution.

8.15 Reflection on metacognitive knowledge supports the understanding and interpretation of metacognitive experiences and cognitive actions.

8.16 Person metacognitive knowledge (includes three subcategories: intra-individual differences, inter-individual differences and universals of cognition) involves beliefs and intuitions regarding the cognitive ability and nature of oneself and others.

8.17 Task metacognitive knowledge includes two subcategories: task information and task demands. Sensitivity is also an element of task metacognitive knowledge.

8.18 Task information includes all available information provided by the task including task context.

8.19 Task demands involve knowledge of task complexity and characteristics. This knowledge develops through experience and includes the awareness of progress, success or failure. This is important for complex problem solving.

8.20 Sensitivity to task demands supports matching task information and components with strategies to facilitate completion.

8.21 Strategy knowledge is knowledge of strategy attributes, applicability and effectiveness in meeting task demands and successful outcomes.

8.22 Strategy knowledge develops through the interaction of person and task knowledge and metacognitive experiences applying strategies to different tasks.

8.23 Metacognitive experiences can be derived from and inform meta-cognitive knowledge through the cognitive or affective experiences associated with the person, task, or strategies.

8.24 Metacognitive experiences involve awareness, thoughts, intuitions, perceptions, feelings, judgments and monitoring during problem solving and task completion.

8.25 Metacognitive experiences can be implicit or explicit.

Figure 8.3 represents an amplification of Flavell's cognitive monitoring model. It links metacognitive knowledge with person, task and strategy knowledge and shows the relationship between sensitivity and task knowledge and strategy knowledge. Figure 8.3 draws from Figures 8.1 and 8.2 to represent the key contributions of Flavell's cognitive monitoring model in the *conceptual framework of metacognition* and the *taxonomy of metacognition*. It links metacognitive knowledge to knowledge of cognition and metacognitive experiences. It also demonstrates the interaction between metacognitive knowledge, metacognitive experiences, cognitive goals and actions.

Brown's conceptualisation of metacognition

A great deal of Brown's work on metacognition was specifically in the field of reading where she coined the term 'metacomprehension'. Although this section draws from those papers, her contributions are discussed in terms of metacognition. The scope of this book does not allow for a full discussion of metacomprehension although key contributions in this field are referred to. Brown (1978, 1981) identified what are considered to be the current categorisations or 'clusters' of metacognition, knowledge of cognition and regulation of cognition. The literature refers to both Flavell and Brown's contributions and uses the terms interchangeably without clear connections to the theoretical source. Their contributions are later drawn together to produce a cohesive categorisation of metacognition in the *taxonomy of metacognition*.

Brown (1978, 1981) labelled this category or cluster of metacognition as 'knowledge about cognition' but in subsequent works refers to it as 'knowledge of cognition' (Brown, 1987; Brown and Campione, 1981; Brown and Palincsar, 1982). She explains that it is a form of 'self-awareness' (Brown, 1977; Brown and Smiley, 1977) and 'knowledge about one's cognitions rather than the cognitions themselves' (Brown, 1978, p. 79), and is the central fundamental process of metacognition. Regulation of

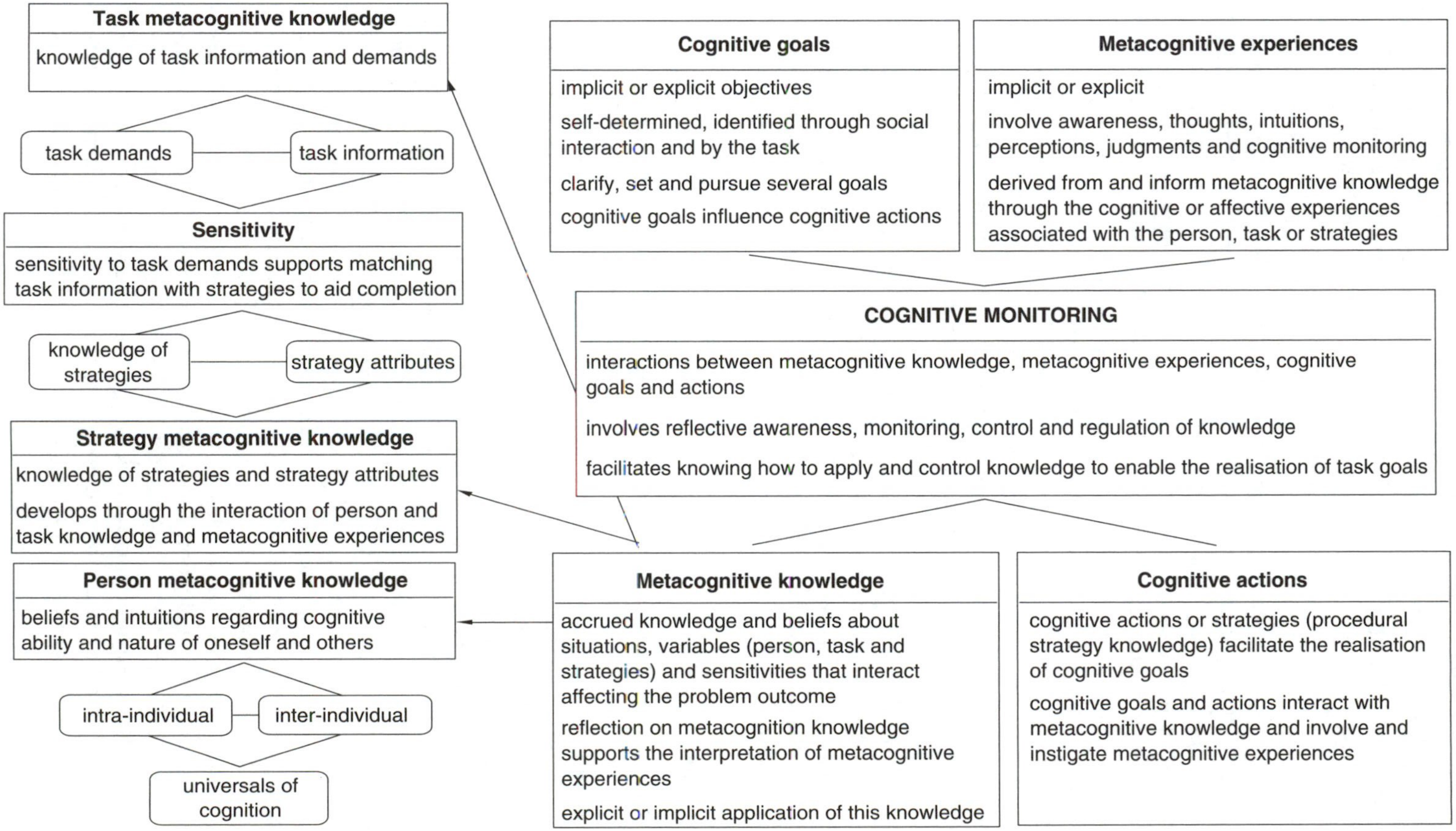

Metacognitive experiences

implicit or explicit

involve awareness, thoughts, intuitions, perceptions, judgments and cognitive monitoring

derived from and inform metacognitive knowledge through the cognitive or affective experiences associated with the person, task or strategies

Cognitive goals

implicit or explicit objectives

self-determined, identified through social interaction and by the task

clarify, set and pursue several goals

cognitive goals influence cognitive actions

COGNITIVE MONITORING

interactions between metacognitive knowledge, metacognitive experiences, cognitive goals and actions

involves reflective awareness, monitoring, control and regulation of knowledge

facilitates knowing how to apply and control knowledge to enable the realisation of task goals

Cognitive actions

cognitive actions or strategies (procedural strategy knowledge) facilitate the realisation of cognitive goals

cognitive goals and actions interact with metacognitive knowledge and involve and instigate metacognitive experiences

Metacognitive knowledge

accrued knowledge and beliefs about situations, variables (person, task and strategies) and sensitivities that interact affecting the problem outcome

reflection on metacognition knowledge supports the interpretation of metacognitive experiences

explicit or implicit application of this knowledge

Task metacognitive knowledge

knowledge of task information and demands

task information

task demands

task information

Sensitivity

sensitivity to task demands supports matching task information with strategies to aid completion

strategy attributes

knowledge of strategies

Strategy metacognitive knowledge

knowledge of strategies and strategy attributes

develops through the interaction of person and task knowledge and metacognitive experiences

Person metacognitive knowledge

beliefs and intuitions regarding cognitive ability and nature of oneself and others

intra-individual

inter-individual

universals of cognition

Figure 8.3 Amplification of cognitive monitoring in the conceptual framework of metacognition

Source: Adapted from Flavell (1981a).

cognition is considered by Brown (1978, p. 79) to be the secondary process of metacognition, applied in problem-solving contexts as the 'evaluation and control of one's own cognitive processes'. The following section describes each 'cluster' of metacognition.

The foundation of metacognition is knowledge. Knowledge informs the regulatory processes and so underpins both knowledge of cognition and regulation of cognition (Baker and Brown, 1984b; Brown, 1981). The literature has provided a source for confusion as metacognition has been used to refer to two distinctive but interrelated areas of inquiry, 'knowledge about cognition and regulation of cognition' (Brown, 1981, p. 21; 1987, p. 67). The confusion lies in the close relationship between the two clusters of metacognition. Oversimplification can occur when attempting to separate these two elements, but for clarity and research purposes, it is necessary (Brown, 1981; Brown et al., 1983; Brown and Palincsar, 1982).

The following assertions identify the primary and secondary clusters or categorisations of metacognition as discussed by Brown:

8.26 Knowledge of cognition is a form of self-awareness about one's cognitions. It is the primary 'cluster' or categorisation of metacognition.
8.27 Regulation of cognition is the monitoring and control of one's cognitive processes. It is the secondary 'cluster' or categorisation of metacognition.

Knowledge of cognition

Knowledge of cognition relies upon self-knowledge involving conscious reflection of knowledge and cognitive processes and awareness of their 'cognitive resources' and task demands (Baker and Brown, 1984b; Brown, 1981; Brown and Palincsar, 1982). This self-knowledge is described as 'stable, statable, fallible and late-developing' (Brown, 1981, p. 21; 1987, p. 67; Brown et al., 1983, p. 107; Brown and Palincsar, 1982, p. 1).

Knowing what or that (declarative knowledge) is considered stable knowledge (Brown, 1977, 1978, 1981, 1987; Brown and Palincsar, 1982). Stable means it is familiar, constant and established declarative knowledge about oneself and others in different knowledge domains and contexts. This also includes knowledge of tasks and their demands, self-knowledge and knowledge of others as cognitive beings, and strategy knowledge to meet task requirements. Brown et al. (1983) made a connection between knowledge of cognition, specifically declarative knowledge, and Flavell's person, task and strategy variables. This knowledge is then statable and involves reflection and communication about and of this knowledge, but it can also be fallible, meaning that facts known about cognition can be untrue or incorrect. Knowledge of cognition develops later in childhood and in adolescence as it relies upon reflection of cognitive processes. Reflection is essential to facilitate effective active planning to address task demands for it promotes awareness of task complexity, learner limitations and cognitive processes. This instigates a search for strategies to meet task demands and requirements. Knowing how to address these demands is procedural knowledge (Baker and Brown, 1984a, 1984b; Brown, 1977, 1978, 1981, 1987; Brown *et al.*, 1983; Brown and Palincsar, 1982; Reeve and Brown, 1985).

Knowledge of cognition involves the ability to judge knowledge accessibility and the awareness of information that is not known and information inferred from what is already known. This also involves inferential reasoning and also relies upon complex and rich structural or semantic knowledge (Brown, 1977).

Brown (1980) identified a number of types of knowledge including knowing when and what you know, knowing what you need to know, and knowing strategy effectiveness. Knowing when you know and when you do not know involves self-awareness, sensitivity to and evaluation of knowledge. Effective monitoring is influenced by task complexity and the extent of strategy knowledge. Knowing what you know and do not know relies upon awareness and the checking of understandings. This also involves feeling and knowing phenomena and reasoning processes to help to determine which knowledge is and is not known and what can be deduced from available information. Knowing what you need to know involves knowing what type of knowledge and information is needed to meet task demands. This involves identifying what is already known and being aware of and determining what is needed for successful task completion. This develops later in childhood and in adolescence and involves strategy knowledge as well as feeling and knowing phenomena such as ease-of-learning. Knowing strategy effectiveness involves the ability to identify appropriate strategies which match the task and will expedite successful task completion.

The following assertions identify the main conceptual contributions to knowledge of cognition and declarative knowledge by Brown:

8.28 Knowledge of cognition relies upon self-knowledge, awareness and reflection of whether information is or is not known and cognitive processes. It develops later in childhood and in adolescence.
8.29 Knowledge of cognition involves inferential reasoning and relies upon rich structural or semantic knowledge.
8.30 Knowledge informs regulatory processes and underpins knowledge and regulation of cognition.
8.31 Declarative knowledge is stable knowledge (familiar, constant and established).
8.32 Declarative knowledge includes self-knowledge and knowledge of others as cognitive beings, knowledge of tasks and task demands, and strategy knowledge.
8.33 Declarative knowledge can be statable, involving reflection and communication about and of this knowledge.

8.34 Declarative knowledge can also be fallible; facts known about cognition can be untrue or incorrect.

8.35 Declarative knowledge is knowing when and what you know, do not know and need to know, and knowing strategy effectiveness.

8.36 Declarative knowledge involves self-awareness, sensitivity to and evaluation of knowledge, awareness of understandings, and knowledge and identification of appropriate strategies.

8.37 Declarative knowledge is informed by feeling and knowing phenomena, and reasoning processes, and knowledge of information is needed to meet task demands.

8.38 Knowing strategy effectiveness involves identifying strategies which match the task and expedite completion.

8.39 Procedural knowledge is knowing how to address task demands.

Figure 8.4 presents an amplification of Brown's knowledge of cognition or metacognitive knowledge and identifies the elements of declarative and procedural knowledge.

Regulation of cognition

Regulation of cognition is often described in terms of executive control or executive functioning. With its conceptual beginnings derived from information processing theories, it includes regulatory abilities and processes such as planning, control, monitoring, testing, revising and evaluating (Baker and Brown, 1984a, 1984b; Brown, 1981; Brown et al., 1983; Brown and Palincsar, 1982). It involves processes which are, to some degree, 'unstable', rarely 'statable', to an extent age independent and dependent upon the problem, task or situation (Brown, 1981, 1987; Brown et al., 1983).

Brown and her colleagues label it metacognitive skills; specifically describing regulation as skills (Baker and Brown, 1984b; Brown, 1978; Brown et al., 1986; Brown and DeLoache, 1978; Brown and Palincsar, 1982). Brown (1978) first used the term metacognitive skills when describing their connection, role and interaction with knowledge of cognition. They involve processes such as awareness, planning, checking, monitoring and the conscious 'deployment of compensatory strategies' (Baker and Brown, 1984b, p. 355; Brown, 1978; Brown et al., 1986; Brown and Palincsar, 1982). Brown also referred to executive processes such as 'predicting, planning, checking, monitoring, reality testing, revising, evaluating, coordinating and controlling' as metacognitive skills which are essential for successful problem solving (Brown, 1978, 1980, 1981; Brown and DeLoache, 1978). Metacognitive skills are 'trans-situational', facilitated by knowledge of the applicability of strategies to various tasks, and are essential to solving all types of problems and tasks (Brown, 1978; Brown

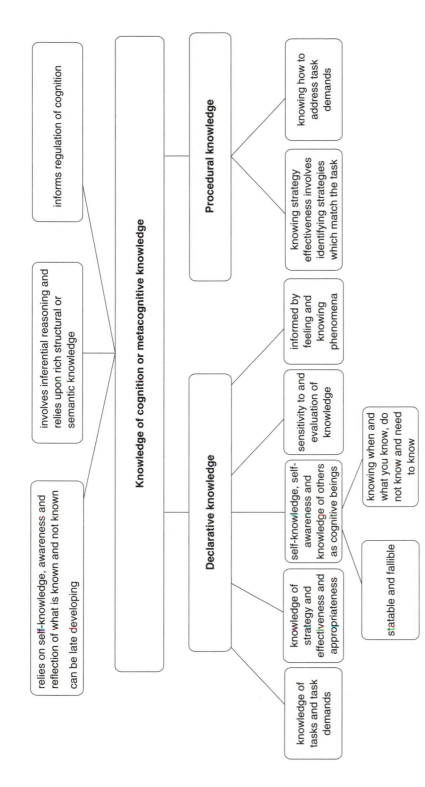

Figure 8.4 Amplification of Brown's knowledge of cognition in the conceptual framework of metacognition

et al., 1986). Trans-situational metacognitive skills involve judgments as to the applicability of the form of regulation in a particular problem-solving situation. This level of executive functioning develops later in adolescence (Brown, 1977). Although such skills are considered to be trans-situational, not all forms would be automatically transferred to another problem and in some instances they may be task dependent (Brown, 1978; Reeve and Brown, 1985). Reflection is an essential aid and a facilitator of metacognitive skills and therefore a regulation of cognition (Brown and Palincsar, 1982). Reflection involves conscious 'self-review', 'self-regulation' and 'self-interrogation' (Baker and Brown, 1984b; Brown, 1980, 1981, 1997; Brown *et al.*, 1986). Through conscious or voluntary control and regulation, reflection provides insights into learning and problem-solving processes, supporting the effective selection and application of strategies and the development of problem-solving skills (Baker and Brown, 1984b; Brown and DeLoache, 1978; Brown and Palincsar, 1982; Reeve and Brown, 1985).

Drawing from information-processing models, Brown and her colleagues identified executive functioning as an essential facilitator of metacognitive processes and an element of regulation of cognition (see Brown, 1978, 1987; Brown *et al.*, 1983; Brown and DeLoache, 1978; Reeve and Brown, 1985). Executive functioning oversees processes and operations such as interpreting, guiding, directing, orchestrating, supervising, overseeing, managing, predicting, planning, scheduling, selecting options, checking, tracking, evaluating, revising, monitoring, controlling and regulating processes and strategies during deliberate problem solving (Baker and Brown, 1984a; Brown, 1977, 1978, 1980, 1987, 1997; Brown and Palincsar, 1982; Reeve and Brown, 1985). It also involves instigating, starting and concluding processes by overseeing their progress, including the awareness of the likelihood of failure or success, especially in complex problem-solving situations (Brown, 1977; Reeve and Brown, 1985). Executive functioning relies upon self-awareness and self-knowledge to support its self-regulatory processes, labelled as metacognitive skills or cognitive monitoring. Executive functioning also interacts with awareness of task demands and applicability of strategies for particular problem-solving tasks and situations (Baker and Brown, 1984a; Brown, 1977, 1978; Reeve and Brown, 1985).

Across a range of Brown's papers (see Baker and Brown, 1984b; Brown, 1980, 1981, 1997; Brown *et al.*, 1983; Brown *et al.*, 1986; Brown and DeLoache, 1978; Brown and Palincsar, 1982; Reeve and Brown, 1985), but specifically in her 1977 and 1978 papers, an outline is provided of a number of requirements or abilities of executive functioning which are essential for effective and efficient problem solving. The list below draws together Brown's contributions to provide a comprehensive outline of regulatory and executive functioning processes and abilities. These abilities include:

(a) predicting the executive system's 'capacity limitations' and problem-solving limitations;

(b) an awareness of the range and repertoire of strategies and their appropriateness and applicability to different problem-solving tasks and situations;

(c) identification and characterisation of the problem or task;

(d) predicting, determining and understanding task demands by clarifying and identifying elements/aspects, focusing attention on the major content;

(e) planning, organising and scheduling of appropriate and applicable problem-solving strategies;

(f) supervising, tracking, reviewing and monitoring strategy effectiveness in light of the success or failure of their implementation; and

(g) consciously evaluating and checking strategy effectiveness in the light of the strategy success or failure, ensuring termination occurs when necessary.

These processes interact with knowledge of cognitive processes to support regulation and facilitate successful problem solving. They also involve external and internal verbalisation, self-questioning and self-interrogation of the process and progress of goal attainment and successful task completion. They are influenced and facilitated by context and social cognitive interactions and stimulate regulatory processes, all metacognitive processes (Baker and Brown, 1984b; Brown, 1980, 1987; Brown and Campione, 1986; Reeve and Brown, 1985).

The following assertions describe the main conceptual contributions made by Brown to the regulation of cognition, metacognitive skills and executive functioning:

8.40 Regulation of cognition is labelled as metacognitive skills and regulation of skills, and is described in terms of executive control, functioning or cognition.

8.41 Regulation of cognition involves processes which can be 'unstable', rarely 'statable' and can be late developing and task dependent.

8.42 Metacognitive skills involve processes such as awareness, predicting, planning, revising, checking, reality testing, evaluating, coordinating, monitoring and control, which are essential for successful problem solving.

8.43 Metacognitive skills can be trans-situational involving judgments regarding the applicability of strategies and type of regulation for problem-solving situations.

8.44 Executive functioning involves interpreting, guiding, directing, orchestrating, supervising, managing, predicting, planning, scheduling, selecting options, checking, tracking, evaluating, revising, monitoring, controlling and regulating processes and strategies during problem solving.

8.45 Executive functioning involves instigating, starting and concluding processes by overseeing their progress.
8.46 Executive functioning facilitates the awareness of failure or success in complex problem-solving situations.
8.47 Executive functioning relies upon self-awareness and self-knowledge to support its self-regulatory processes.
8.48 Executive functioning interacts with awareness of task demands to determine the applicability of strategies for particular problem-solving situations.
8.49 Regulation of cognition and executive functioning involves determining and understanding task demands by clarifying and identifying task elements.
8.50 Regulation of cognition and executive functioning includes planning, organising and scheduling of appropriate and applicable problem-solving strategies.
8.51 Regulation of cognition and executive functioning includes tracking, reviewing and monitoring strategy effectiveness in the light of implementation success or failure.
8.52 Reflection promotes awareness of task complexity, learner limitations and cognitive processes, and facilitates planning to address task demands.
8.53 Reflection instigates a search for strategies to meet task demands and requirements.
8.54 Reflection is an essential facilitator of metacognitive skills through conscious self-review, self-regulation and self-interrogation.

Figure 8.5 presents an amplification of Brown's regulation of cognition. It identifies the elements of metacognitive skills or regulation of skills and executive functioning.

Borkowski and Pressley's good information processing model

> Knowledge informs perceptions, provides a home for new memories amidst the storage of old ones, and informs cognitive routines and strategies in the face of complex problems.
>
> (Borkowski, 1985, p. 112)

This section builds upon discussions in Chapter 4 of metamemory about strategies (MAS) and metamemory acquisition procedures (MAPs) (Borkowski *et al.*, 1988; Pressley *et al.*, 1985; Pressley, Borkowski and O'Sullivan, 1984). The MAS and MAPs identify the elements and components of effective metamemory strategy use and are later redefined in terms of metacognitive strategy use in the Good Information Processing or the Good Strategy User Model by Borkowski and his colleagues (e.g. Borkowski, Carr and Pressley, 1987; Borkowski *et al.*, 1990; Borkowski

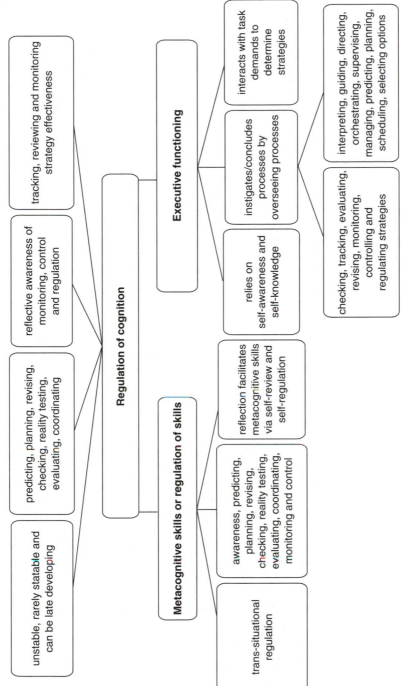

Figure 8.5 Amplification of Brown's regulation of cognition in the conceptual framework of metacognition

et al., 2000; Borkowski *et al.*, 1988; Borkowski and Turner, 1989; Pressley, Borkowski and O'Sullivan, 1984; Pressley *et al.*, 1987; Pressley, Levin and Ghatala, 1984). The major characteristics of the model include meta-cognitive knowledge about specific strategies or specific strategy knowledge, general strategy knowledge, beliefs about efficacy, and metacognitive acquisition procedures (Borkowski *et al.*, 2000; Pressley *et al.*, 1985; Pressley, Borkowski and O'Sullivan, 1984; Schneider and Pressley, 1997).

Metacognitive knowledge about specific strategies or specific strategy knowledge involves knowledge of strategy attributes and their effectiveness in different situations and contexts. It involves an understanding and awareness of the extent of possible applications for different tasks and problems, and the influence of task demands on strategy selection and application. Knowledge of strategy attributes facilitates the development of knowing and selecting when, where and how to use, apply and revise particular strategies, supported by monitoring and control processes. 'Informed strategy knowledge' includes knowledge of strategy goals, their effectiveness in different task and learning contexts, and knowledge of the outcomes of using particular strategies in certain types of tasks and problems (Borkowski, Carr and Pressley, 1987; Borkowski *et al.*, 2000; Borkowski and Turner, 1989; Pressley *et al.*, 1985; Pressley, Borkowski and O'Sullivan, 1984; Schneider and Pressley, 1997). Complex learning situations and domains provide further opportunities to enrich and develop specific strategy knowledge. This knowledge then enables appropriate strategy selection for specific tasks and supports problem solving through strategy monitoring (Borkowski *et al.*, 2000; Borkowski and Turner, 1989; Pressley *et al.*, 1985; Pressley, Borkowski and O'Sullivan, 1984; Short *et al.*, 1993).

General strategy knowledge involves an understanding of general strategy processes. Awareness of the value of being strategic develops and can be transferable to various tasks and across contexts. The attainment of general strategy knowledge leads to the development of higher-order skills which facilitates the selection and monitoring of appropriate strategies for specific tasks. General strategy knowledge also supports the identification of strategy components even if they have not been adequately or directly taught (Borkowski and Turner, 1989; Pressley *et al.*, 1985; Pressley, Borkowski and O'Sullivan, 1984; Short *et al.*, 1993).

Context and situational elements, as well as the self-system, influence the continued development of both specific strategy knowledge and general strategy knowledge. The self-system involves attributional beliefs, self-efficacy, motivation, self-regulation and self-esteem. It influences strategy selection and monitoring of strategy application and helps to develop an understanding of the importance of strategy knowledge. Monitoring is essential in providing the feedback needed regarding the success or failure of strategy application (Borkowski *et al.*, 1990; Borkowski *et al.*, 2000; Borkowski, Johnston and Reid, 1987; Borkowski and Muthukrishna, 1992; Schneider and Pressley, 1997).

The model indicates that declarative and procedural strategy knowledge and the applicability of particular strategies for different tasks, problems and situations are important for transferability. Strategy use is reliant upon knowledge of the most appropriate or most effective strategy to use in a particular context (Pressley *et al.*, 1987). Strategy selection and application are supported and facilitated by monitoring and control processes, including the ability to set meaningful goals and match metacognitive processes to achieve these. Strategy training or instruction in different contexts and situations promotes trans-situational and lifelong application of strategies, effective strategy use and continued metacognitive system development. Effective strategy use and transferability are also affected by beliefs about task difficulty, positive or negative self-concepts as a problem solver, self-efficacy and intrinsic motivation (Borkowski, Carr and Pressley, 1987; Borkowski *et al.*, 1990; Borkowski *et al.*, 2000; Borkowski *et al.*, 1989; Borkowski *et al.*, 1988; Borkowski and Muthukrishna, 1992; Borkowski and Turner, 1989; Brown, 1978; Osman and Hannafin, 1992; Pressley *et al.*, 1987). Supporting the relationship between metacognition and transferability, Campione (1987) contends that the inability to generate strategies and to transfer strategies from one problem to another is a metacognitive deficit. Relational strategy knowledge is essential for the demonstration, application and knowledge of the similarities and differences between multiple strategies in a task or problem (Borkowski and Turner, 1989; Pressley *et al.*, 1985; Pressley, Borkowski and O'Sullivan, 1984).

Metacognitive acquisition procedures incorporate two higher-order processes identified as executive processes and self-regulation. They are important for the evaluation of strategy processes and are the 'heart of metacognition giving it trans-situational applicability' (Borkowski and Turner, 1989, p. 161; Schneider and Pressley, 1997). Both higher-order processes are needed for the successful generalisation of a study skill or strategy and they affect general strategy knowledge including attributional beliefs (Borkowski and Turner, 1989; Pressley *et al.*, 1985; Pressley, Borkowski and O'Sullivan, 1984). Borkowski and Turner (1989) described executive functioning as a 'powerful determinant of strategy use' (p. 161). They identified a number of executive functions which facilitate and support strategy application, transfer and regulation. These include identifying the type of problem and its components, selecting strategies to match components and support problem solving, facilitating the mental representation of components and strategy application, supporting the allocation of mental resources and capabilities to promote problem completion, and monitoring solution processes. In later works metacognitive acquisition procedures are labelled as executive processes (e.g. Borkowski *et al.*, 2000).

As previously discussed, higher-order thinking, identified as executive control and self-regulation, is attained through the development of strategy knowledge and its application to different tasks (Borkowski and Muthukrishna, 1992; Borkowski and Turner, 1989) and is influenced by the self-system or one's beliefs (Borkowski *et al.*, 1990; Borkowski *et al.*, 2000). The augmentation of the original model depicts a greater emphasis on executive processes, and the personal, motivational and self-knowledge or self-system, as integral elements of metacognition.

Borkowski and colleagues have progressively developed their model of metacognition to incorporate extended self-system components such as self-knowledge and 'personal-motivational states' (see Borkowski *et al.*, 2000). Each model represents the relationship between general strategy knowledge, specific strategy knowledge, executive processes or metacognitive acquisition procedures, and attributional beliefs (see Borkowski *et al.*, 2000; Borkowski *et al.*, 1988; Borkowski and Muthukrishna, 1992; Borkowski and Turner, 1989; Pressley *et al.*, 1985). Borkowski *et al.* (2000) provide the most recent details of the model which is labelled as the 'cognitive, motivational, and self-system components of metacognition: The complete model' (p. 10).

In summary, the centrepiece of metacognitive theory is strategy selection and use. Not only are specific strategies essential for effective learning and problem solving, they also provide the context for training higher-level planning and executive skills explicitly as well as representing the basis for restructuring attributional beliefs and enhancing self-efficacy (Borkowski *et al.*, 2000, p. 9).

The following assertions represent the main conceptual contributions by Borkowski and colleagues to knowledge and regulation of strategies:

8.55 Metacognitive knowledge about specific strategies involves knowledge of strategy attributes and their effectiveness and application in different tasks and contexts.

8.56 Metacognitive knowledge about specific strategies involves awareness of the influence of task demands on strategy selection and application.

8.57 Knowledge of strategy attributes facilitates knowing and selecting when, where and how to use, apply and revise strategies. This is supported by monitoring and control.

8.58 Informed strategy knowledge is knowledge of strategy goals, their effectiveness in different task contexts, and knowledge of the outcomes of using particular strategies in certain types of tasks.

8.59 General strategy knowledge involves awareness of general strategy processes and the value of being strategic. It develops and is transferable to different tasks.

8.60 General strategy knowledge facilitates the development of higher-order skills which support the selection and monitoring of appropriate strategies for specific tasks.

8.61 Context and situational elements as well as the self-system influence the continued development of both specific strategy knowledge and general strategy knowledge.

8.62 The self-system involves attributional beliefs, self-efficacy, motivation, self-regulation and self-esteem.

8.63 The self-system influences strategy selection and monitoring of strategy application and helps to develop an understanding of the importance of strategy knowledge.

8.64 Strategy use is reliant upon knowledge of the most appropriate or effective strategy to use.

8.65 Declarative and procedural strategy knowledge including the applicability of strategies for different tasks and situations are important for transferability.

8.66 Strategy selection and application are supported and facilitated by monitoring and control processes which are essential for trans-situational application.

8.67 Effective strategy use and transferability are affected by beliefs about task difficulty, positive or negative self-concept as a problem solver, self-efficacy and intrinsic motivation.

8.68 Metacognitive acquisition procedures (labelled as executive processes) incorporates executive and self-regulatory processes necessary for strategy evaluation and generalisation.

8.69 Executive functions facilitate strategy selection, application, transfer and regulation.

8.70 Executive functions facilitate mental representations of task components, support the allocation of mental resources and capabilities and monitor solution processes.

8.71 Metacognition incorporates self-system components including self-knowledge, personal and motivational states, and attributional beliefs which influence executive functioning and self-regulation.

Figures 8.6 and 8.7 (see pp. 148 and 149) are amplifications of the elements of Borkowski and Pressley's Good Information Processing Model. They draw from assertions 8.55–8.71.

Kuhn's theory of meta-knowing

Kuhn's description of meta-knowing or meta-level processes or understanding is akin to metacognition. She describes her theory as 'knowing processes' which includes 'any cognition that has cognition (either one's own or others') as its object' (Kuhn, 1999b, p. 260; 2000b, p. 302). It comprises three forms: 'reflective awareness' of one's own and others' cognition, an understanding of the content of cognition, and the influencing of one's cognition through monitoring, control and self-regulation. As well as knowledge of one's own cognitive processes, it also refers to the broader conceptualisation of meta-knowing to include 'one's personal theories about the self's knowing capacities and dispositions' (Kuhn, 2000b, p. 316).

Kuhn uses the dichotomy of declarative knowing (knowing that) and procedural knowing (knowing how) to categorise her two major components of meta-knowing respectively into 'metacognitive knowing' and

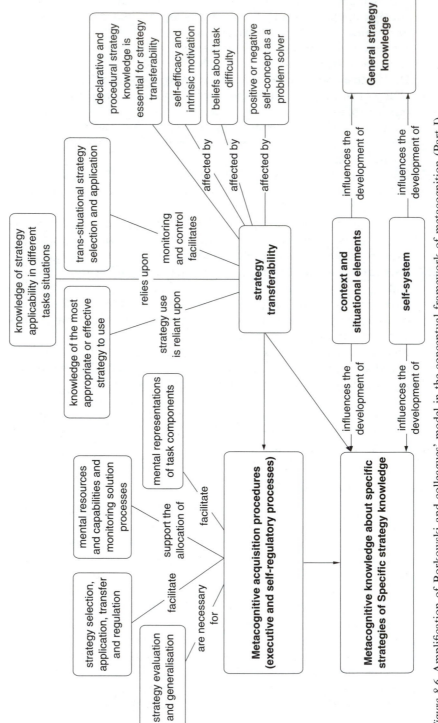

Figure 8.6 Amplification of Borkowski and colleagues' model in the conceptual framework of metacognition (Part I)

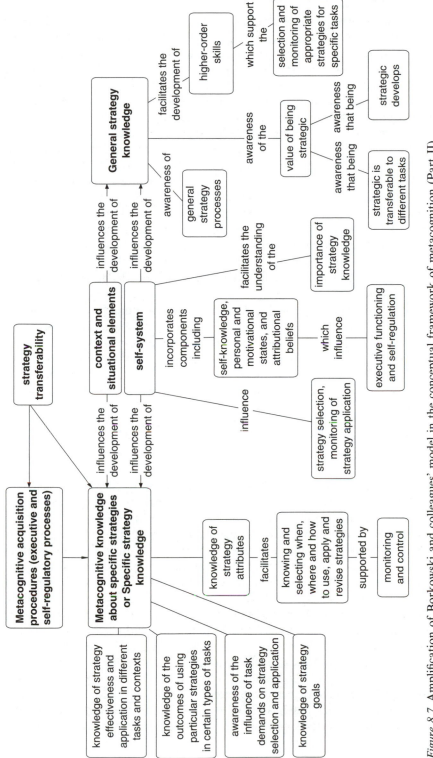

Figure 8.7 Amplification of Borkowski and colleagues' model in the conceptual framework of metacognition (Part II)

'metastrategic knowing' (Kuhn, 1999a, 1999b, 2000a, 2000b). In an earlier work, the terms 'metacognitive competence' and 'metastrategic competence' were used to describe the currently used terms of metacognitive knowing and metastrategic knowing (Kuhn et al., 1995, pp. 109–110). Kuhn and Udell (2001) also used the terms 'metastrategic operations' (procedural knowing) and 'metacognitive operations' (declarative knowing) (p. 262). Metacognitive knowing is knowing about the products or objects of knowledge, including beliefs about this knowledge, and involves reflecting on the content of this knowledge. Metastrategic knowing involves an awareness and knowledge of cognitive processes (Kuhn, 1999a, 1999b, 2000b; Kuhn and Dean, 2004; Kuhn et al., 1995; Kuhn and Pearsall, 1998).

Metacognitive knowing is further subdivided into 'specific and situational' knowledge, and 'general and abstract' knowledge. General and abstract knowledge involves what Kuhn describes as 'epistemological meta-knowing' (Kuhn, 2000b, p. 302). It refers to an 'individual's broader understanding of knowledge and knowing' and includes two types of knowing, labelled as personal and impersonal knowledge (Kuhn, 1999a, p. 18; 2000b).

The terms metastrategic knowledge, knowing, understanding, competence, or procedural meta-knowing are used interchangeably by Kuhn to describe 'awareness, understanding, monitoring, and management of one's strategic performance of many kinds of cognitive tasks' (Kuhn, 2001; Kuhn and Pearsall, 1998, p. 227). Metastrategic knowledge directly influences strategy selection and application. It is knowledge of how to apply the strategy, its effectiveness, ineffectiveness and limitations in different problem-solving situations. Essentially, it is 'knowing how, when and why the strategy should be used' (Kuhn et al., 1995, p. 109).

Metastrategic knowledge or understanding consists of two components – 'knowledge of task objectives' or 'metatask' and 'knowledge of strategies' or 'metastrategic' (Kuhn, 2000a, p. 179; 2001, p. 6; Kuhn and Pearsall, 1998, p. 227). It involves inferences and reasoning which influence strategy selection and application (Kuhn and Pearsall, 1998).

Knowledge of task objectives or metatask understanding involves knowledge, understanding and awareness of the task including its nature, structure, goals and objectives. This knowledge supports the selection and application of task-specific strategies, facilitating task completion and problem solution. Lack of task knowledge and limited understanding of the task objectives can affect selection and application of appropriate strategies. Both are essential to assist task completion and performance (Kuhn, 2000a; Kuhn et al., 2000; Kuhn et al., 1995; Kuhn and Pearsall, 1998).

Knowledge of strategies or metastrategic understanding is the awareness and understanding of the applicability of strategies for a particular task which addresses task objectives. Strategy selection is made from the range of strategies of which one has knowledge and needs to be matched with the task elements, objectives and goals to facilitate successful problem solving in different contexts (Kuhn, 1983, 2000a; Kuhn *et al.*, 2000; Kuhn *et al.*, 1995; Kuhn and Pearsall, 1998). Both knowledge of task objectives and knowledge of strategies interact and depend upon each other for successful task outcomes (Kuhn *et al.*, 2000; Kuhn and Pearsall, 1998).

In an earlier work, Kuhn (1983) refers to two types of executive strategy. Type one involves the strategy application and type two is knowledge of strategy to task appropriateness. These two early types of strategy knowledge relate to her more recent work on metastrategic knowing, the two subcomponents of which are knowledge of strategies and knowledge of task objectives. Kuhn describes the relationship between metacognitive knowing and metastrategic knowing as influenced by the specific task. The task influences strategy selection which Kuhn points out is not a strategic process but a metastrategic process (Kuhn, 2000b). Although Kuhn's conception of meta-knowing identifies regulatory processes as a form of meta-knowing, her conception does not describe this in detail and her model relates more directly to metacognitive knowledge rather than descriptions of metacognitive regulation. She includes aspects of metacognitive regulation in her description of metastrategic knowing.

Epistemological meta-knowing, epistemological understanding or epistemic understanding – Kuhn uses the terms interchangeably – is a component of metacognitive knowing or declarative knowing and is part of the process of metacognitive development (Kuhn, 2001, 2003; Kuhn and Dean, 2004; Kuhn and Udell, 2001). Kuhn's epistemological meta-knowing is categorised in this book as epistemic cognition.

The following assertions represent Kuhn's contribution to a discussion on meta-knowing, specifically metacognitive knowing and metastrategic knowing:

8.72 Meta-knowing is a broad term to describe knowledge of cognition including personal theories about knowing capabilities.

8.73 Meta-knowing includes reflective awareness and understanding of the content of cognition and the influence of monitoring, control and self-regulation on cognition.

8.74 Meta-knowing is categorised as metacognitive knowing or competence or operations (declarative knowing – knowing that) and metastrategic knowing (or competence, operations, understanding) or procedural meta-knowing (procedural knowing – knowing how).

8.75 Metacognitive knowing is knowing about and reflection on objects of knowledge, including beliefs about this knowledge.

8.76 Metacognitive knowing is subdivided into 'specific and situational' and 'general and abstract' knowledge.

8.77 General and abstract knowledge includes epistemological meta-knowing or epistemic cognition.

8.78 Epistemological meta-knowing is a person's wider understanding of knowing and includes personal and impersonal knowledge.

8.79 Metastrategic knowing involves knowledge about cognitive processes including strategy selection, application, effectiveness and limitations in different tasks.

8.80 Metastrategic knowledge consists of two components: knowledge of task objectives or metatask and knowledge of strategies or meta-strategic understanding.

8.81 Knowledge of task objectives involves knowledge, understanding and awareness of the task including its nature, structure, goals and objectives.

8.82 Knowledge of task objectives facilitates selection and application of task-specific strategies and task completion.

8.83 Knowledge of strategies is the awareness and understanding of the applicability of strategies for a particular task which address task objectives.

8.84 The relationship between metacognitive and metastrategic knowing is influenced by the specific task.

8.85 Epistemological meta-knowing (epistemological or epistemic understanding) is a component of metacognitive or declarative knowing and is important for metacognitive development.

Figure 8.8 is an amplification of Kuhn's theory of meta-knowing. It draws from assertions 8.72–8.85.

Conclusion

Flavell (1977, 1978, 1979, 1981a, 1987) and Brown (1978, 1981, 1987; Brown and Campione, 1981; Brown and Palincsar, 1982) contributed to research on memory and metamemory which subsequently led to the identification of different categories or clusters of metacognition. Flavell identified metacognition as knowledge about variables related to person, task, and strategy. He used the term cognitive monitoring to describe the interaction between metacognitive knowledge, metacognitive experiences, cognitive goals or tasks, and cognitive actions or strategies. It involves reflective awareness of knowledge and the monitoring, control and regulation of this knowledge, facilitating task performance and completion. Similarly, Kuhn used the broad term of meta-knowing to also describe the same reflective awareness related to knowledge of cognition, its processes and the influence of monitoring and control.

Brown also identified knowledge of cognition as the primary cluster or categorisation of metacognition as well as regulation of cognition or executive cognition as the secondary category, which includes planning, monitoring and control of cognitive processes. These two contributions are drawn together to categorise metacognition as knowledge about cognition and processes, and regulation, executive functioning and the monitoring and control of metacognition (Bendixen and Hartley, 2003; Borkowski,

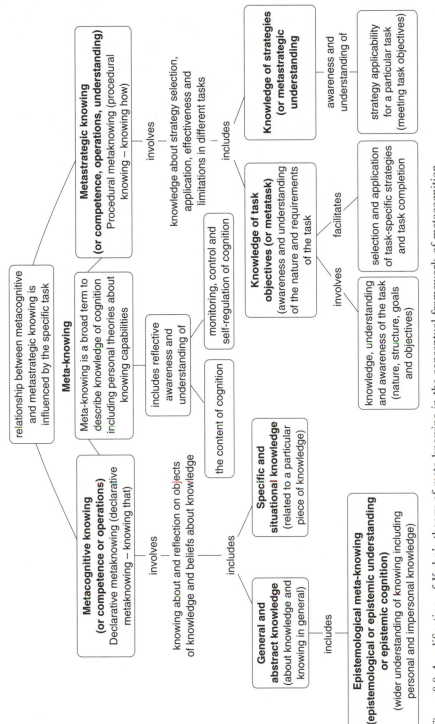

Figure 8.8 Amplification of meta-knowing in the conceptual framework of metacognition

1985; Brown *et al.*, 1983; Davidson and Sternberg, 1998; Hacker, 1998; Jacobs and Paris, 1987; Kluwe, 1982; Kluwe and Friedrichsen, 1985; Lawson, 1984; Meichenbaum, 1986; Nelson and Narens, 1990; Nisbet and Shucksmith, 1984; Paris and Winograd, 1990; Pintrich *et al.*, 2000; Schraw, 1998; Schraw and Dennison, 1994; Schraw and Moshman, 1995; Sternberg, 1998; Weed *et al.*, 1990; Wellman, 1983, 1985b). Jacobs and Paris (1987) identify like categories but use the terms 'self-appraisal of cognition and self-management of thinking' to label knowledge of cognition and regulation of cognition (p. 259). Contributions to both clusters or categories of metacognition have also been drawn from the developmental psychology work of Piaget and information processing theories of executive control (Brown, 1987; Cheng, 1999; Langrehr and Palmer, 1998).

9 The categorisation of the taxonomy of metacognition

This chapter builds upon previous chapters to describe the foundations of the *conceptual framework of metacognition* and the *taxonomy of metacognition*.

Knowledge of cognition or metacognitive knowledge: Declarative, procedural and conditional knowledge

Knowledge of cognition or metacognitive knowledge is defined as the knowledge individuals have about and of their own cognition and cognition in general (Pintrich, 2002; Schraw and Moshman, 1995). This includes knowledge of learning strengths and weaknesses and knowledge about strategies and their appropriate application, especially in complex problems (Kluwe, 1982). Essentially, it is the 'knowledge about when, how, and why to engage in various cognitive activities' (Baker, 1991, p. 2) and includes person, task and strategy knowledge (Boekaerts, 1997, 1999a; Efklides, 2001, 2003; Flavell, 1977, 1978, 1979, 1981a; Flavell and Wellman, 1977).

It also involves self-awareness relying upon self-knowledge and self-appraisal through reflectivity (Baker, 1991; Bobrow, 1975; Brown, 1977, 1978, 1981, 1987; Brown and Campione, 1981; Brown and Palincsar, 1982; Brown and Smiley, 1977; Cavanaugh and Perlmutter, 1982; Cornoldi, 1998; Hartman, 2001a; Jacobs and Paris, 1987; Paris and Winograd, 1990).

Knowledge of cognition involves and is influenced by personal theories or beliefs about knowing capabilities and abilities (Schoenfeld, 1983, 1985, 1987; Wellman, 1985b). These influences include self-system components such as self-esteem, attributional beliefs, self-appraisal or self-reflection and self-efficacy (Paris and Winograd, 1990). Self-appraisal involves the reflective, static assessment of one's knowledge, ability, task, context or strategy applicability (Jacobs and Paris, 1987).

Knowledge of cognition includes declarative and procedural knowledge (Kluwe, 1982; Kuhn, 1999a, 1999b, 2000a, 2000b; Kuhn et al., 1995; Kuhn and Udell, 2001; Ryle, 1949; Schraw, 2001, 2009; Schraw and Moshman, 1995). Introduced by Paris et al. (1983), an extended categorisation of metacognitive knowledge includes conditional or contextual knowledge

(Garner, 1987; Hartman, 2001a; Jacobs and Paris, 1987; Paris, 2002; Paris and Winograd, 1990; Pintrich *et al.*, 2000; Schneider, 1998; Schneider and Lockl, 2002; Schraw, 2001; Schraw and Moshman, 1995). Declarative, procedural and conditional knowledge involve knowledge and processes related to person, task and strategy variables and are essential metacognition processes. These variables are influenced by sensitivities which affect the problem outcome.

This book synthesises the categorisation of knowledge of cognition or metacognitive knowledge to also include Flavell and Wellman's variables of person, task and strategy.

The following assertions are identified from the above discussion. A number of these are identified as higher-order assertions (HOA). The numbering of the HOAs continues from previous chapters:

9.1   Knowledge of cognition or metacognitive knowledge is the knowledge or personal theories or beliefs individuals have about and of their own cognition (HOA.24).

9.2   Knowledge of cognition or metacognitive knowledge includes declarative, procedural and conditional or contextual knowledge (HOA.25).

9.3   Declarative, procedural and conditional knowledge involve knowledge and processes related to person, task and strategy variables. These variables are influenced by sensitivities (HOA.26).

9.4   Knowledge of cognition involves self-awareness relying upon self-knowledge and self-appraisal through reflectivity (HOA.27).

9.5   Person metacognitive knowledge influences include self-system components such as self-esteem, attributional beliefs, self-appraisal or self-reflection and self-efficacy.

9.6   Self-appraisal involves the reflective, static assessment or evaluation of one's knowledge, ability, task, context or strategy applicability.

Figure 9.1 synthesises theories of knowledge of cognition or metacognitive knowledge to depict its main categories and the interaction between these categories. It draws from assertions 9.1–9.6.

Declarative, procedural and conditional knowledge are discussed in detail in the following sections.

Declarative knowledge

Declarative knowledge is stable, familiar, constant, established long-term knowledge which involves self-knowledge, self-awareness and a sensitivity to and evaluation of this knowledge (Jonassen and Tessmer, 1996/1997; Kluwe, 1982). It also includes knowledge of oneself and others as cognitive beings, of tasks and task demands, and of strategies (Garner, 1987; Schraw, 1998, 2001; Schraw and Moshman, 1995). Kluwe (1982) describes two forms

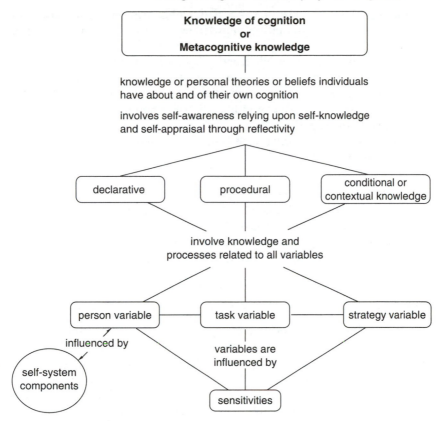

Figure 9.1 Amplification of knowledge of cognition in the conceptual framework of metacognition

of declarative knowledge: 'domain knowledge' and 'cognitive knowledge' (p. 203). He describes domain knowledge as 'an individual's stored information about the domains of reality' (ibid.). Cognitive knowledge refers to 'an individual's stored assumptions, hypotheses, and beliefs about thinking' (ibid.). Kluwe's description of cognitive knowledge is similar to Jacobs and Paris' (1987) description of declarative knowledge as 'propositional manner' (p. 259) and Anderson's (1982) 'propositional knowledge' (p. 370). Shuell (1990) describes it as 'knowledge about something' (p. 537).

Essentially, declarative knowledge is knowing when and what you know and do not know, including what you need to know, knowledge of strategy applicability and effectiveness and knowledge of what type of information is needed to meet task demands. Reliant upon reflection and verbalisation, it can be statable but it can also be fallible as facts known about cognition can be incorrect. Feeling and knowing phenomena also inform declarative knowledge.

Cornoldi (1998) also introduces a new categorisation of metacognitive knowledge labelled 'connotative knowledge' (p. 141), which relies upon declarative knowledge to make connotations between information. Cornoldi explains that it is ill-structured in that it does not necessarily involve static knowledge but involves associations made between one object and another. For example, 'cats are pleasant animals and we could probably estimate how much we would like all other mammals in the same way (connotative knowledge)' (p. 141).

The following higher-order assertions (HOA) are identified from the above discussion:

9.7   Declarative knowledge includes two forms: domain (knowledge of reality domains) and cognitive knowledge (beliefs about thinking or propositional manner) (HOA.28).

9.8   Connotative knowledge relies upon declarative knowledge to facilitate associations made between objects (HOA.29).

Person (knowledge of self and others)

Knowledge of oneself or self-knowledge and knowledge of others as cognitive beings are categorised as the person subcategory of declarative knowledge or person metacognitive knowledge. It includes intra-individual and inter-individual differences and universals of cognition. Intra-individual differences are beliefs about oneself as a learner, inter-individual differences are beliefs of others and their ability as learners compared with oneself, and universal cognitions relate to beliefs and intuitions, understandings, misunderstandings, perceptions and conceptions regarding general abilities, properties and processes of oneself and others (Flavell, 1979, 1981a, 1981b; Pintrich, 2002). Self-knowledge involves self-awareness and is essential to metacognitive knowledge (Eteläpelto, 1993; Pintrich, 2002). It involves knowledge of one's strengths and weaknesses, knowledge of when one knows and when one does not know and knowledge of a range of strategies and their applicability in different contexts (Pintrich, 2002). Pintrich also points out that it is essential to develop self-awareness and self-knowledge about one's own motivations. This includes beliefs about motivation which involve self-efficacy judgments, task goals, and the significance and importance of the task. Accurate self-knowledge enables adjustments to be made to processes applied during problem solving (Pintrich, 2002).

The following assertions are identified from the above discussion. A number of these are identified as higher-order assertions (HOA):

9.9   Knowledge of oneself or self-knowledge and knowledge of others as cognitive beings is categorised as the person subcategory of declarative knowledge or person metacognitive knowledge (HOA.30).

9.10 Self-knowledge involves self-awareness, knowledge of strengths and weaknesses, knowledge of when one knows and does not know, knowledge of strategies and applicability in different contexts (HOA.31).

9.11 Self-knowledge is essential for knowledge and beliefs about one's motivations (HOA.32).

9.12 Beliefs about motivation are affected by self-efficacy judgments, task goals and task importance.

Task (knowledge of task and context including sensitivity)

Task metacognitive knowledge includes two subcategories: task information and task demands. Knowledge of task and context including sensitivity to task is categorised as the task subcategory of declarative knowledge or task metacognitive knowledge. Task information includes all available information provided by the task including its context and solution requirements. Task demands include knowledge of task complexity and characteristics and the management of these demands. It also involves awareness of the influence of task demands on strategy selection and application. This knowledge develops through experience and involves awareness of progress, success or failure. Sensitivity to task demands and information supports the identification of strategies that match task information, facilitating task completion and success. Task knowledge and sensitivity are supported by reflectivity. Reflection enables awareness of task complexity, learner limitations and cognitive processes, and facilitates planning to address task demands (Flavell, 1979, 1981a, 1981b). These are important processes necessary for successful complex problem solving.

The following assertion and higher-order assertion (HOA) are identified from the above discussion:

9.13 Knowledge of task and context including sensitivity to task is categorised as the task subcategory of declarative knowledge or task metacognitive knowledge (HOA.33).

9.14 Task knowledge and sensitivity is supported by reflection. It enables awareness of task complexity, learner limitations and cognitive processes, and facilitates planning to meet task demands.

Strategy (knowledge of cognitive strategies)

Metacognitive knowledge of strategies involves knowledge of strategy attributes, applicability and effectiveness in meeting task demands to achieve successful outcomes. It relies upon understanding, reflection and awareness of the value and transferability of different strategies in various contexts and tasks. Monitoring and control processes support the development of knowledge regarding the selection, application and revision of particular strategies in different task situations. It helps inform knowledge of the outcomes or goals of using particular strategies in certain types of tasks. This knowledge also develops through the interaction between person and task variables and is influenced by metacognitive experiences and the self-system. There are a number of different types of strategies including rehearsal, elaboration, organisation and repair. Knowledge of strategies supports regulatory processes such as planning, monitoring and control (Paris *et al.*, 1983; Pintrich, 2002). Strategy knowledge is essential for the solving of complex problems (Pintrich, 2002).

The following assertions and higher-order assertions (HOA) are identified from the above discussion:

9.15 Strategy knowledge relies upon understanding, reflection and aware-ness of the value and transferability of different strategies in various contexts and tasks. It is especially important for complex problem solving.

9.16 Monitoring and control facilitate the development of strategy knowl-edge, specifically their selection, application and revision in different task contexts.

9.17 Strategy knowledge develops through the interaction between person and task variables and is influenced by metacognitive experiences and the self-system (HOA.34).

9.18 Strategy knowledge supports regulation such as planning, monitoring and control (HOA.35).

Figure 9.2 is a depiction of declarative knowledge including knowledge of oneself or knowledge of self, knowledge of task and context, and knowl-edge of strategy. It draws from assertions 9.7–9.18.

Procedural knowledge

Procedural knowledge refers to knowledge of processes and actions or essentially knowing how (Schraw, 1998, 2001; Schraw and Moshman, 1995). It is also labelled as metastrategic knowing – knowledge and aware-ness of the processes or how to meet task demands or task objectives – and involves metastrategic understanding or procedural strategy knowledge of the application of strategies or procedures which facilitate the realisation of cognitive goals or objectives of a problem (Chi, 1987; Jacobs and Paris, 1987; Kluwe, 1982; Kuhn, 1999a, 1999b, 2000a, 2000b; Paris *et al.*, 1983). Developed through application and experience, procedural knowledge can become unconscious, automatic processes or refined strategies or skills initiated in familiar problem-solving situations (Garner, 1987; Hartman, 2001a; Paris, 1988; Schraw and Moshman, 1995; Slusarz and Sun, 2001). Implicit processes are necessary in skill development and learning (Slusarz and Sun, 2001). These automatic and implicit processes are considered by

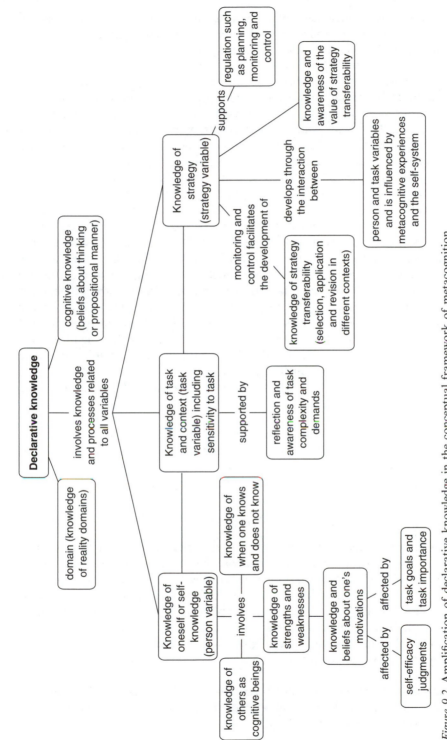

Figure 9.2 Amplification of declarative knowledge in the conceptual framework of metacognition

some not to be metacognitive; it is also thought that metacognition can actually hinder the application of refined, automatic strategies and processes (Jacobs and Paris, 1987; Sternberg, 1998).

There is substantial debate as to whether these processes are considered metacognitive once they become automatic and implicit. Adding to the complexity of metacognition, conscious and unconscious processes have implications for providing a clear definition of metacognition (Chambres *et al.*, 2002). This is an issue as some researchers consider that not all cognitions about cognitions, such as implicit and unconscious thoughts and processes, should be considered metacognition (Jacobs and Paris, 1987; Paris, 2002), whereas others believe metacognition involves both conscious and unconscious or explicit and implicit processes (Cary and Reder, 2002; Koriat, 2000; Sun and Mathews, 2002). Cary and Reder contend that there are many unconscious or automatic strategy selections and that they should also be considered metacognitive. Although Darling *et al.* (1998) state that 'metacognition is essentially a conscious activity', they also state that 'the gap between implicit and conscious functions may not be so great as has generally been supposed' (p. 89). Explicit knowledge prompts implicit representations and vice versa (Dienes and Perner, 2002). This debate is current and will generate substantial future discussion and research. It is evident that a new field of research is developing under the title of implicit metacognition thus drawing philosophers into the discussion to determine what constitutes implicit metacognition.

The following assertion and higher-order assertion (HOA) are identified from the above discussion:

9.19 Through experience procedural knowledge can become implicit, automatic refined strategies or skills initiated in familiar problems (HOA.36).

9.20 Explicit knowledge prompts implicit representations and vice versa.

Person (knowledge of self and others)

Positive or negative self-concept as a problem solver, self-efficacy and intrinsic motivation can affect strategy selection, application and transferability. One's self-system influences strategy selection and monitoring of strategy application and helps to develop an understanding of the importance of strategy knowledge. Strategy application and transferability, especially in novel complex problems, can be affected by one's self-system.

The following assertions and higher-order assertion (HOA) are identified from the above discussion:

9.21 Positive or negative self-concept as a problem solver, self-efficacy and intrinsic motivation can affect strategy selection, application and transferability (HOA.37).

9.22 The self-system influences strategy selection and monitoring of strategy application and facilitates understanding the importance of strategy knowledge especially in complex, novel problems.

Task (sensitivity to task)

Procedural task knowledge essentially involves knowledge of task objectives including awareness of the cognitive goals or tasks and subgoals or tasks, and their nature and structure. It relies upon declarative task knowledge to help determine the appropriate strategy or strategies. This is supported by knowledge of task goals and subgoals which influence and facilitate the selection and application of task-specific strategies to match cognitive goals to support task completion. The flexible application of strategies in different complex contexts reflects a developed knowledge and understanding of the strategies and the awareness of the possible outcomes of their application. Beliefs about task difficulty can positively or negatively influence the identification and successful application of strategies.

The following assertions and higher-order assertion (HOA) are identified from the above discussion:

9.23 Procedural task knowledge relies upon knowledge of task objectives and the nature and structure of cognitive goals and subgoals.
9.24 Procedural task knowledge facilitates the selection and flexible application of task-specific strategies to match cognitive goals supporting task completion (HOA.38).
9.25 Beliefs about task difficulty can positively or negatively influence the identification and successful application of strategies.

Strategy (sensitivity to strategy application)

Strategy application is influenced by the level of sensitivity to the task itself and the identification of appropriate and applicable strategies. Regulatory processes such as monitoring and control support the selection, application and adaptation of strategies to different learning contexts. This supports trans-situational strategy application.

The following higher-order assertion (HOA) is identified from the above discussion:

9.26 Task sensitivity influences the identification of appropriate and applicable strategies and subsequent strategy application (HOA.39).

Figure 9.3 is a depiction of procedural knowledge including knowledge of oneself or knowledge of self, knowledge of task and context, and knowledge of strategy. It draws from assertions 9.19–9.26.

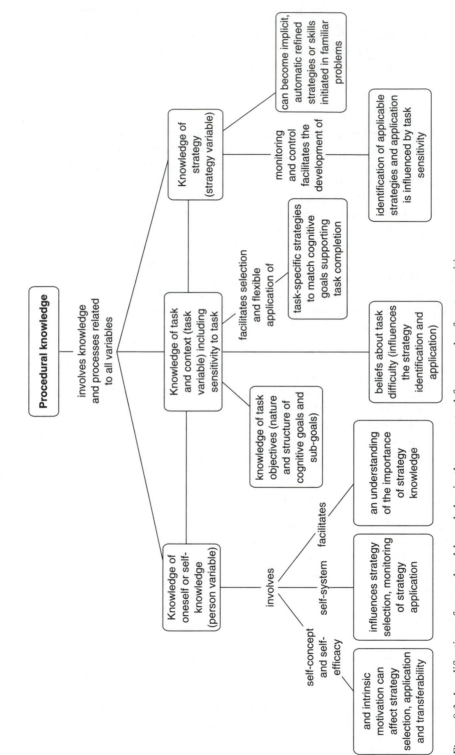

Figure 9.3 Amplification of procedural knowledge in the conceptual framework of metacognition

Conditional knowledge

Conditional knowledge involves 'knowing when and why to use declarative and procedural knowledge' (Schraw, 1998, p. 114). It is discussed mainly in terms of declarative and procedural strategy knowledge, application and effectiveness in various task situations (Jacobs and Paris, 1987; Paris *et al.*, 1983; Schraw, 1998, 2001; Schraw and Moshman, 1995). It specifically refers to knowledge and awareness of the 'conditions which affect learning such as "*why* strategies are effective, *when* they should be applied and *when* they are appropriate"' (Jacobs and Paris, 1987, p. 259).

The following higher-order assertion (HOA) is identified from the above discussion:

9.27 Relying upon declarative and procedural knowledge, conditional knowledge determines why, when and where to use this knowledge (especially strategy knowledge) (HOA.40).

Task: Conditional (when) and contextual knowledge (sensitivity to task)

Conditional knowledge supports awareness and knowledge of task type, demands and context and is also needed to support both declarative and procedural knowledge. Both would be ineffective if it were not for conditional knowledge of when and why to apply knowledge and processes (Jacobs and Paris, 1987; Paris *et al.*, 1983; Pintrich, 2002; Schneider, 1998; Schneider and Lockl, 2002; Schraw, 1998, 2001).

The following assertions are identified from the above discussion:

9.28 Conditional knowledge supports awareness and knowledge of task type, demands and context.
9.29 Conditional knowledge supports the adaptive application and transfer of strategies in unfamiliar, complex problems and contexts.
9.30 Conditional knowledge can be inhibited by inadequate domain knowledge, weak cognitive monitoring, ineffective strategies and lack of awareness of task demands.

Strategy (sensitivity to strategy initiation)

Conditional knowledge supports the adaptive application and transfer of strategies in unfamiliar, complex problems and contexts (Desoete *et al.*, 2001; Garner, 1990; Hartman, 2001a; Paris *et al.*, 1983). This can be inhibited by inadequate domain knowledge, weak cognitive monitoring, ineffective strategies and lack of awareness of task demands and goals (Garner, 1990; Hartman, 2001a). Context influences strategy use, transfer and regulation of cognition. As strategies are driven by task goals and affected by task complexity and demands, they are also strongly influenced by context and changes in context (Garner, 1990; Pintrich, 2002). Additionally, novel, complex problems require the identification of applicable, effective strategies (Pintrich, 2002; Zimmerman, 1995) and these task demands require not only monitoring and regulation of strategic processes, but also knowledge about 'contextual conditions' or conditional knowledge and self-efficacy when dealing with multiple pathways which bring complexity, uncertainty and limited or vague feedback. Conditional knowledge involves sensitivity to the task or contextual awareness as well as sensitivity to strategy initiation that is influenced by the task context.

The following assertion is identified from the above discussion:

9.31   Context and contextual conditions influence strategy use, transfer and regulation.

Figure 9.4 is a depiction of conditional knowledge including knowledge of oneself or knowledge of self, knowledge of task and context, and knowledge of strategy. It draws from assertions 9.27–9.30.

Regulation of cognition, metacognitive skills or metacognitive regulation

Regulation of cognition, metacognitive skills or metacognitive regulation is the secondary process of metacognition (Brown, 1978) and is also labelled as executive control or functioning (Kluwe and Friedrichsen, 1985; Neisser, 1967; Schoenfeld, 1987). It involves metacognitive processes that facilitate and support the evaluation and control of the learning process and is especially important to facilitate problem solving. These processes include predicting, planning, cognitive monitoring, diagnosing, regulating, checking and evaluating learning processes, difficulties and outcomes in problem-solving situations (Borkowski *et al.*, 2000; Brown, 1978; Brown and DeLoache, 1978; Efklides, 2003; Hacker, 1998; Nisbet and Shucksmith, 1984; Paris and Lindauer, 1977; Schraw and Moshman, 1995; Vermunt, 1996; Wellman, 1983). They are also referred to as 'self-management' of cognition involving reflective 'self-appraisal' (Jacobs and Paris, 1987; Paris and Winograd, 1990; Weed *et al.*, 1990) and support the awareness of metacognitive experiences, especially during problem solving (Boekaerts, 1997, 1999a). Marzano (2001) identifies goal specification, process monitoring, monitoring clarity and monitoring accuracy as regulatory processes. Goal specification involves planning goals in relation to one's knowledge, process monitoring is the monitoring of that knowledge, monitoring clarity is the awareness of the extent of the clarity of that knowledge, and monitoring accuracy is the determination of the degree of accuracy about that knowledge.

The following assertions are identified from the above discussion:

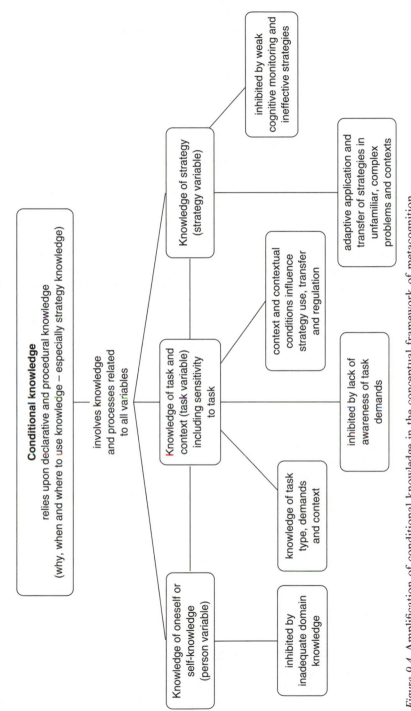

Figure 9.4 Amplification of conditional knowledge in the conceptual framework of metacognition

9.32   Regulatory strategies support the awareness of metacognitive experiences especially during problem solving.

9.33   Goal specification involves planning goals related to one's knowledge, process monitoring is monitoring planning goals, monitoring clarity is awareness of the extent of clarity of that knowledge, and monitoring accuracy is determination of the degree of accuracy of knowledge.

Self-regulation

Metacognition is a key subprocess of and is vital to effective self-regulation (Gourgey, 1998; Zimmerman, 1989b). It can be argued that the metacognitive aspects of self-regulation are a subprocess of metacognition, specifically regulation of cognition. Self-regulation involves processes such as control, monitoring and regulation of learning processes, planning, organising, self-instruction, self-monitoring and self-evaluation (Baumeister and Vohs, 2004; Boekaerts, 1999b; Corno, 1986; Ellis and Zimmerman, 2001; Paris and Paris, 2001; Zimmerman, 1986, 1989b; Zimmerman and Schunk, 2001). Zimmerman (1989b) defines metacognition in relation to self-regulation as 'decision-making processes that regulate the selection and the use of various forms of knowledge' (p. 329). Although metacognition is an important subprocess of self-regulation, alone it is insufficient to enable successful self-regulated learning. Self-regulated learners are metacognitively, motivationally and behaviourally committed, independent and active learners (Wolters, 1998, 2003; Zimmerman, 1986, 1989b), focused, goal-orientated, persistent in their learning, and aware of their knowledge, beliefs and volition (Butler and Winne, 1995; Corno, 1986; Zimmerman, 1989b). They are also highly motivated and use regulatory processes to monitor and control their motivation to meet task demands (Wolters, 2003). A high level of self-regulated learning is reliant upon a strong sense of self, including self-control, self-efficacy, self-esteem, self-attainment and self-actualisation (McCombs, 1986; Zimmerman, 1989b, 1995, 2000). Generally, self-regulated learners initiate their own learning strategies to attain desired learning goals and monitor the effectiveness of these strategies (Corno, 1986; Purdie *et al.*, 1996; Wolters, 1998; Zimmerman, 1989b). They are goal-orientated and apply a number of metacognitive strategies to attain these goals. They are aware of the importance of efficiently monitoring strategy applications and modifying strategies to meet task demands to achieve task goals (Wolters, 1998). The important interaction between metacognition and self-regulation is the regulation, monitoring and control of metacognitive strategies. These include processes such as determining plans and actions, identifying task demands, task goals and subgoals, and reviewing and monitoring strategies, especially in complex problems. Self-competence beliefs can affect motivation and application, impacting on the problem-solving process (Winne, 1995; Zimmerman, 1986). Personal expectations of achievement and the need for attainment facilitate the development of self-regulatory skills to help meet these goals. Students' perceptions of their self-regulatory learning abilities are influenced by a combination of internal and external comparisons which can directly affect self-regulatory processes (Butler and Winne, 1995; Miller, 2000). Volitional control is an important self-regulatory process which is important for the 'control and regulation of motivation, emotion, and environment' (Corno, 1986; Pintrich *et al.*, 2000, p. 46). Internal verbalisation which is directed towards oneself can include personal beliefs and learning strategies for goal attainment which influence the development of self-regulation (Schunk, 1986; Vygotsky, 1978).

Knowledge domains and contexts affect self-regulation including the monitoring and control of strategies (Hartman, 2001a; Wolters and Pintrich, 2001; Zimmerman, 1995). Zimmerman (1995) explains that self-regulation goes 'beyond metacognitive knowledge and skill to other issues, especially students' underlying sense of self-efficacy and personal agency' (p. 220). Self-awareness, self-judgments, self-concept and self-efficacy are important factors affecting self-regulation (Bandura, 1997; McCombs, 1986; Zimmerman, 1989a, 1995).

Self-doubt and low perceptions of self-efficacy or 'inefficacious thinking' can influence the effectiveness of problem-solving processes especially during the solving of complex problems (Bandura, 1989, p. 729; Bandura and Locke, 2003; Bouffard *et al.*, 2005; Zimmerman, 1995). Although these are considered separate processes to metacognition, they may arise during the application of metacognitive processes, especially during problem solving (Bandura, 1989; Boekaerts, 1995; Bouffard *et al.*, 2005). Emotions arising during problem solving are labelled in the literature as hot cognitions, not cold cognitions and although they influence metacognition, they are treated as separate to metacognitive processes (Brown *et al.*, 1983; Flavell, 1963; Pintrich *et al.*, 2000; Zajorc, 1980).

Planning and goals that affect learning processes, volitional control, use of learning strategies, self-efficacy and a task-focused approach are considered motivational elements that contribute to effective self-regulation (Howard-Rose and Winne, 1993; Mayer, 1998, 2001; Paris and Paris, 2001; Pintrich, 2000; Zimmerman, 1989a). Self-regulated learners have a repertoire of strategies to help achieve task goals which are facilitated or hindered by self-efficacy perceptions and dedication to achieving them, especially in complex, demanding tasks (Bandura, 1997; Mayer, 1998, 2001; Zimmerman, 1986, 1989b).

The following assertions and higher-order assertions (HOA) are identified from the above discussion:

9.34 Metacognition is an important subprocess of self-regulation but solely insufficient for successful self-regulation.

9.35 Metacognition and self-regulation's main interaction is control, monitoring and regulation of strategies to meet task demands and goals (HOA.41).

9.36 Self-regulation involves planning, organising, self-instruction, self-monitoring and self-evaluation (HOA.42).

9.37 Self-regulated learners are highly metacognitive, motivated, goal-orientated and behaviourally committed, independent and active learners (HOA.43).

9.38 Self-regulated learners are aware of their knowledge, beliefs and volition (HOA.44).

9.39 Self-regulation involves self-efficacy and personal agency (HOA.45).

9.40 Self-regulated learners self-initiate strategies and monitor and control them and their motivation to address task demands and attain desired goals (HOA.46).

9.41 Personal expectations of achievement and attainment facilitate the development of self-regulation.

9.42 Perception of self-regulation ability is influenced by internal and external comparisons and self-competence beliefs.

9.43 Internal verbalisation can include personal beliefs and influences the development of self-regulation.

9.44 Self-awareness, self-judgments, self-concept, self-efficacy and self-doubt affect self-regulation and can influence problem solving especially in complex problems.

Figure 9.5 is a depiction of regulation of cognition or metacognitive skills. It draws from assertions 9.32–9.44.

Metacognitive experiences

Knowledge of cognition or metacognitive knowledge, including its three main forms – declarative, procedural and conditional – is the essential ingredient or basis for the effective functioning of metacognitive skills or regulation and for metacognitive experiences to occur (Efklides, 2003; Efklides and Vauras, 1999; Garner, 1994). These three forms also comprise person, task and strategy variables or knowledge (Flavell, 1979, 1981a; Flavell and Wellman, 1977).

Chapter 5 discussed different forms of metamemory feeling and knowing phenomena such as feeling of knowing, judgments of learning or knowing, ease-of-learning judgments, judgment of confidence and feeling-of-warmth. These phenomena can also be categorised as metacognitive experiences although some feeling and knowing phenomena such as tip-of-the-tongue and feeling of knowing are experienced during memory monitoring (Garner, 1994). Metacognitive experiences are those instigated during the monitoring of cognitive, problem-solving or task situations and not all forms are directly related to memory monitoring. Efklides (2001) states that:

> Metacognitive experiences are influenced by a number of factors; namely: (a) task factors such as task complexity, performance, and

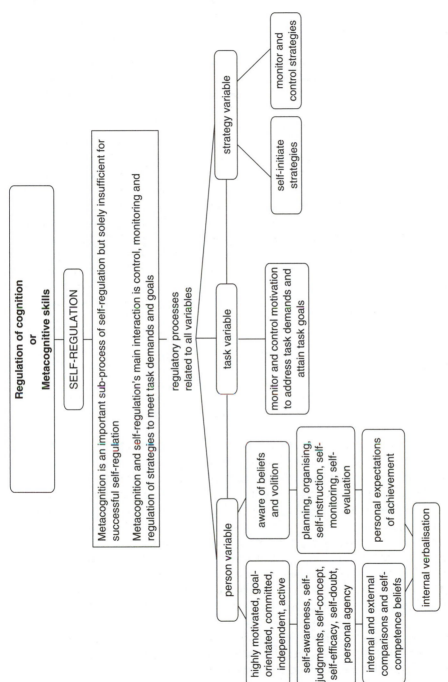

Figure 9.5 Amplification of regulation of cognition including self-regulation in the conceptual framework of metacognition

previous experiences with the same or related tasks; (b) personal factors such as cognitive ability, personality, and self-concept, and (c) meta-cognitive factors such as metacognitive knowledge.

(p. 308)

Metacognitive experiences are not exactly the same as affect or emotions but they do involve metacognitive judgments, feelings or experiences during problem solving and tend to be person-generated or related, whereas metacognitive knowledge can be generated by oneself and with others (Efklides, 2001, 2003; Efklides and Volet, 2005). They are considered to be feelings, judgments, reactions and experiences which occur during a cognitive task or problem solving (Efklides, 2001, 2006; Efklides and Tsiora, 2002; Efklides and Vauras, 1999; Flavell, 1979, 1981a; Metallidou and Efklides, 2001; Paris and Winograd, 1990). They are also important for and are involved in monitoring to promote successful problem solving (Efklides, 2003; Efklides and Tsiora, 2002; Garner, 1994). Metacognitive experiences occur within and provide an 'intrinsic context' which is both influenced by and influences person, task and strategy variables, especially during problem solving (Efklides, 2003). Efklides considers they are 'products of the person–task interaction' (p. 304). Essentially, metacognitive experiences are influenced by person characteristics including beliefs regarding ability to meet the task demands in light of difficulty, complexity and context (Efklides, 2001, 2003; Flavell, 1979, 1981a). Therefore, sensitivity to the task, including its variables, demands and context, both familiar and unfamiliar, influence metacognitive experiences and the interaction between person and task variables is fundamental to them (Efklides, 2001, 2003). In essence, metacognitive experiences monitor the interaction between task and person variables and are also products of these interactions (Efklides, 2001). Context therefore can exert a number of influences including substantial or subtle context changes, task or problem familiarity or unfamiliarity, task complexity related to the knowledge domain but also involving multiple contexts. This would be especially evident in complex problems.

Metacognitive experiences are described as 'online monitoring of cognition' or 'online metacognition' or 'online awareness' which occur during problem solving or a cognitive task. Online monitoring suggests that metacognitive experiences are directly involved in the monitoring of metacognitive processes and are generated through the interaction between monitoring and the more general, static metacognitive knowledge (Efklides, 2001, 2002). Metacognitive knowledge involves a broader knowledge, awareness and understanding of person, task and strategy variables, whereas metacognitive experiences involve very specific feelings, judgments, realisations and reactions related to these variables (Efklides, 2001, 2002; Flavell, 1979, 1981a; Garner, 1994). The interaction between metacognitive knowledge and metacognitive experiences is fundamental to metacognitive processes. Metacognitive experiences of task or strategy application rely upon metacognitive task and strategy knowledge and are influenced by person cognitive knowledge and beliefs (Efklides, 2001, 2003; Flavell, 1979, 1981a). Flavell's (1979, 1981a) model provides a detailed description of the interaction between metacognitive knowledge and experiences. Metacognitive knowledge, including self-knowledge, awareness and the integration of different forms of knowledge, is essential for metacognitive experiences to occur (Efklides, 2001). They are influenced by task attributes and monitor the process of task completion, and inform, influence and prompt control and self-regulation (Efklides, 2001, 2003; Efklides *et al.*, 2002; Nelson and Narens, 1990, 1994).

Through monitoring processes, metacognitive experiences, especially metacognitive feelings, provide feedback on the process of problem solving and stimulate control and strategy processes (Efklides, 2003); they can be both implicit and explicit. During task monitoring, implicit metacognitive experiences, especially metacognitive feelings, can be quickly generated without specific, explicit awareness of their activation (Efklides, 2001, 2003). Awareness of metacognitive experiences or explicit metacognitive experiences such as judgments or estimates of learning and solution correctness consciously inform strategy selection, application and control processes. Not only do both implicit and explicit metacognitive experience situations prompt control processes, but they also interact with meta-cognitive knowledge to draw from previous experiences and also inform knowledge about new experiences (Efklides, 2003). The learning situation and task provide a context for the generation of metacognitive experiences. Therefore collaborative problem-solving situations, complex problems and multiple contexts such as complex problems can initiate different forms of metacognitive experiences.

Self-concept is influenced by and influences metacognitive experiences (Efklides, 2003; Efklides and Tsiora, 2002). Academic self-concept affects the development of strategy knowledge, strategy selection and application in problem-solving situations (Efklides, 2001, 2003). It can affect both monitoring and control and therefore influences the types of metacognitive experiences experienced. Control processes are activated by metacognitive experiences and inform self-regulation which is also affected by self-concept and self-efficacy. Therefore, metacognitive experiences are instigated in problem-solving situations but are also informed by and influence self-concept, affect attributions and control processes (Efklides, 2001, 2003; Efklides and Tsiora, 2002). They interact with metacognitive knowledge and evolve from and inform monitoring and control processes and in doing so support self-regulation (Efklides, 2001, 2002, 2006; Efklides and Tsiora, 2002; Efklides and Vauras, 1999). In addition and importantly, Efklides (2003) considers that they 'also provide input to self-reflection and long-term motivation' (p. 18). Efklides' (2001) research has discovered that academic self-concept, especially self-efficacy and self-perception, influence metacognitive experiences and also inform metacognitive knowledge. Her research found, for example, that self-efficacy influences judgments or estimations of solution correctness and self-perception influences feeling of difficulty. One's strategy knowledge or reported strategy knowledge is influenced by the perceptions of others (Efklides, 2001, 2003).

The main forms of metacognitive experiences – both metacognitive judgments and metacognitive feelings – investigated by Efklides and colleagues include feeling of familiarity, feeling of difficulty, feeling of confidence, feeling of satisfaction, estimate of effort expenditure, and estimate of solution correctness (Efklides, 2001, 2002, 2003; Efklides and Tsiora, 2002). Feeling of familiarity is the monitoring of knowledge, fluency and the possible task success based upon the familiarity of the task, context and the applicability of current knowledge during problem solving (Efklides, 2002, 2003).

Feeling of difficulty involves awareness and monitoring of task difficulty and impediments to problem solving, and facilitates the identification of correction strategies or the need to develop new strategies. Task difficulty cannot be solely identified in terms of feeling of difficulty – feeling of difficulty monitors task difficulty but does not fully reflect it. In other words, task context, complexity, familiarity or sensitivity to task difficulty influence whether the task is perceived as difficult or not. This generally occurs at the beginning of problem solving and as it progresses, the feeling of difficulty changes or is updated (Efklides, 2002, 2003). Efklides (2003) explains that it is important that teachers expose students not only to well-structured tasks or familiar tasks but to complex problems as these require students to apply focused, continued effort. Also, an expert in a problem-solving task may have a very low feeling of difficulty and therefore may not be sufficiently aware of any difficulties to warrant their analysis. Novice problem solvers may have high levels of feeling of difficulty which interrupt progress of problem solving. Lack of experience in analysing difficulties combined with task unfamiliarity can lead to novice problem solvers encountering problems without actually pinpointing and explaining exactly what the difficulties are. This would then affect the ability to identify and apply corrective strategies to continue problem solving. This would be especially evident in novel, complex problems.

Feeling of satisfaction involves monitoring problem solutions to assess whether they meet personal standards of achievement or outcomes (Efklides, 2002, 2003). Both are retrospective metacognitive feelings (Efklides, 2002). Feeling of confidence is influenced by task complexity, lack of domain knowledge and lack of strategic task-specific knowledge. Other metacognitive experiences can provide information regarding progress of problem solving and affect feeling of confidence experiences – these include feeling of difficulty and feeling of knowing (Efklides, 2001, 2002, 2003).

Judgment or estimate of solution correctness, judgment of learning, feeling of confidence and feeling of satisfaction provide information via monitoring of progress of problem solving and outcomes (Efklides, 2003). Judgment or estimate of solution correctness is related to feeling of confidence in regard to task variables. Both judgment of solution correctness and feeling of confidence are influenced by the person variable, including beliefs about cognitive ability and self-concept (Efklides, 2001, 2003).

Essentially metacognitive feelings 'make the person aware of the fluency (or interruption) of cognitive processing and of the match or mismatch between the goal set and the outcome achieved' (Efklides and Tsiora, 2002, p. 225). They are related to perceptions of the task and one's ability to meet task demands and also provide information regarding cognitive processing such as facilitation or impediments to problem solving (Efklides, 2001, 2002). They can occur implicitly or explicitly. This means that they can occur with or without reflection and interaction with metacognitive knowledge. Efklides explains that enduring metacognitive feelings can begin to become conscious, leading to explicit control during problem solving (Efklides, 2001, 2003).

Metacognitive experiences provide feedback regarding self-concept including ability, attributions, confidence and difficulty related to the knowledge domain, context and task (Efklides, 2003; Efklides and Tsiora, 2002). Feeling of confidence relates to the outcome of problem solving, including whether the solution is correct, and can involve levels of confidence, including under- and over-confidence.

The following assertions and higher-order assertions (HOA) are identified from the above discussion:

9.45 Metacognitive experiences are not the same as affect or emotions but are feelings, judgments, reactions and experiences instigated during the monitoring of cognitive and task situations (HOA.47).

9.46 Metacognitive experiences monitor the interaction of metacognitive knowledge task and person variables and are products of these interactions (HOA.48).

9.47 Metacognitive experiences are influenced by person characteristics including self-concept, self-knowledge, self-awareness and beliefs regarding ability to meet the task demands.

9.48 Sensitivity to the task and its variables, task perceptions, demands and context, including context familiarity and unfamiliarity, influence metacognitive experiences.

9.49 Metacognitive experiences are described as 'online monitoring of cognition' or 'online metacognition' or 'online awareness' which occurs during problem solving or a cognitive task.

9.50 Metacognitive experiences inform, influence and prompt control and self-regulation.

9.51 Metacognitive experiences provide feedback regarding self-concept, including ability, attributions, confidence and difficulty related to the knowledge domain, context and task.

9.52 Self-concept can affect both monitoring and control and influence and is influenced by metacognitive experiences.

9.53 Academic self-concept affects the development of strategy knowledge, selection and application.

9.54 Academic self-concept, especially self-efficacy and self-perception, influences metacognitive experiences and informs metacognitive knowledge (HOA.49).

9.55 Metacognitive experiences (metacognitive judgments and metacognitive feelings) include feeling of familiarity, feeling of difficulty, feeling of confidence, feeling of satisfaction, judgment or estimate of effort expenditure, and judgment or estimate of solution correctness (HOA.50).

9.56 Metacognitive experiences such as judgments or estimates of learning and solution correctness consciously inform strategy selection, application and control.

9.57 Metacognitive feelings facilitate the awareness of 'fluency or interruption' in cognitive processing and the connection or disparity between the task goals and actual outcome (HOA.51).

9.58 Self-efficacy influences judgment or estimate of solution correctness and self-perception influences feeling of difficulty.

9.59 Feeling of familiarity involves the monitoring of task familiarity and context, and the applicability of current knowledge.

9.60 Feeling of difficulty involves awareness and monitoring of task difficulty and impediments to problem solving.

9.61 Feeling of difficulty facilitates the identification of correction strategies or the need to develop new strategies.

9.62 Feeling of satisfaction involves monitoring problem solutions as to whether they meet personal standards of achievement or outcomes.

9.63 Feeling of confidence relates to the outcome of problem solving including whether the solution is correct; it can involve levels of confidence including under- and over-confidence.

9.64 Judgment of solution correctness and feeling of confidence are influenced by the person variable including beliefs about cognitive ability and self-concept.

9.65 Feeling of confidence is influenced by task complexity, lack of domain knowledge and lack of strategic task-specific knowledge.

Figures 9.6, 9.7 and 9.8 (see pp. 177–179) are depictions of metacognitive experiences including metacognitive judgments and metacognitive feelings. They draw from assertions 9.45–9.65.

Other metacognition: Metacognition and affective beliefs

There is a strong link between affect and metacognition (Gourgey, 1998, 2001; Hartman, 2001c; Hartman and Sternberg, 1993; Schoenfeld, 1983, 1987). Some researchers consider that beliefs directly affect metacognitive processes, but are not necessarily a specific element of metacognition (e.g.

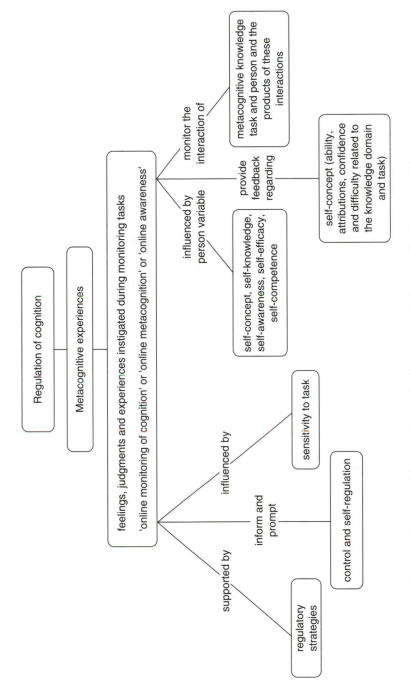

Figure 9.6 Amplification of metacognitive experiences in the conceptual framework of metacognition

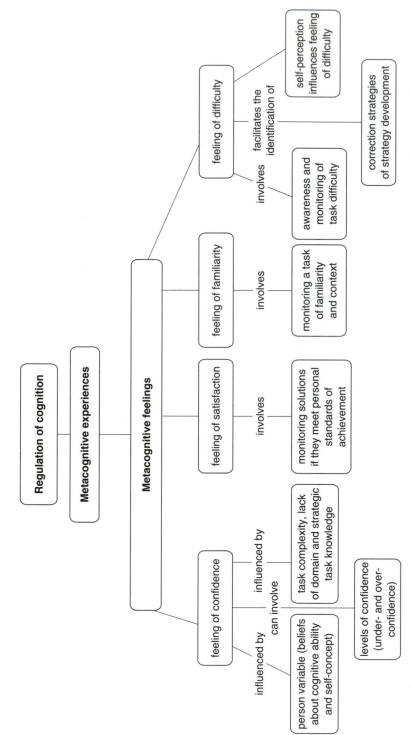

Figure 9.7 Amplification of metacognitive experiences, including metacognitive feelings, in the conceptual framework of metacognition

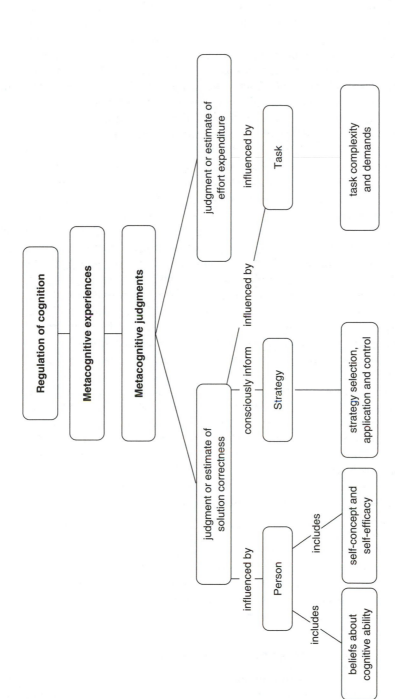

Figure 9.8 Amplification of metacognitive experiences, including metacognitive judgments, in the conceptual framework of metacognition

Desoete *et al.*, 2001; Hartman, 2001c; Hartman and Sternberg, 1993; Schraw, 2001; Vermunt, 1996). Others consider beliefs are another element of metacognition (e.g. Schoenfeld, 1987; Simons, 1996; Tsai, 2001; Wells, 2000). Metacognition is considered to include not only knowledge of cognition, but also the beliefs and knowledge about which strategies would be most effective in solving a particular task, including knowledge of any obstacles (Antonietti *et al.*, 2000). Metacognitive beliefs – beliefs about cognition involving understandings, views and interpretations of one's own cognition and that of others – are considered integral to metacognitive processes such as self-regulation, monitoring and control of learning processes (Schoenfeld, 1987; Simons, 1996; Weed *et al.*, 1990; Wells, 2000).

Affective elements directly influence metacognitive processes and are also identified as metacognitive beliefs. These include attributional beliefs, attitudinal, emotions, conative, motivation and self-esteem (Borkowski *et al.*, 1990; Borkowski *et al.*, 2000; Hartman, 2001a; Hartman and Sternberg, 1993; Paris and Winograd, 1990; Sinkavich, 1994; Turner *et al.*, 1996; Wells, 2000). Both metacognitive knowledge and metacognitive control and monitoring are affected by beliefs and emotions (Cullen, 1985; Flavell *et al.*, 1993; Wells, 2000). Wells (2000) discusses beliefs about thinking as part of self-knowledge which is an element of metacognitive knowledge. He explains that metacognitive knowledge includes explicit and implicit processes. There can be implicit processes such as 'implicit plans that guide processing and operate largely outside of conscious awareness' (p. 19).

Problem solving requires a number of affective dispositions, especially self-confidence, beliefs and biases, and is affected by strong emotions either facilitating or impeding the process, even breaking mental sets (Meacham and Emont, 1989; Zajorc, 1980; Zajorc and Markus, 1984). Affective elements, such as emotions and attitudes, can inhibit successful utilisation and selection of effective metacognitive strategies (Garner and Alexander, 1989; Zan, 2000). There is a strong relationship between the affect of beliefs and the problem-solving process, especially in the solving of complex problems (Meacham and Emont, 1989; Sinnott, 1989).

The following assertion and higher-order assertion (HOA) are identified from the above discussion:

9.66 Metacognitive knowledge and metacognitive control and monitoring are affected by beliefs and emotions (HOA.52).
9.67 Affective elements, such as emotions and attitudes, can inhibit successful utilisation and selection of effective metacognitive strategies, especially in complex problems.

Metacomprehension: An offshoot of metacognition

Comprehension monitoring or metacomprehension entails reflection, self-regulation and monitoring to ensure ongoing successful comprehension when reading and listening (Baker, 1979; Baker and Brown, 1984a; Garner and Alexander, 1989; Gourgey, 1998; Wagoner, 1983). Effective meta-comprehension is the ability to 'know when they understand, when they don't understand, and when they partially understand' (Baker, 1979, p. 365). Ineffective metacomprehension is the failure to monitor comprehension or to invoke repair strategies consciously during reading and problem solving (Baker, 1979; Garner and Alexander, 1989; Osman and Hannafin, 1992).

Metacomprehension involves knowing about and knowing how to com-prehend. Knowing how to comprehend involves awareness or recognition of comprehension success and failure and involves an awareness of the strategies necessary to enable comprehension when there is failure to comprehend (Wagoner, 1983). Successful metacomprehension involves the ability to apply executive control or self-regulatory processes during the interaction of four metacognitive variables: text, task, strategies and learner characteristics (Brown *et al.*, 1986).

The following assertion and higher-order assertion (HOA) are identified from the above discussion:

9.68 Metacomprehension involves knowing about and how to comprehend (HOA.53).
9.69 Metacomprehension involves reflection, self-regulation and monitor-ing to ensure ongoing successful comprehension.

Conclusion

This chapter has presented a detailed discussion of the theoretical contri-butions to metacognition and included the conceptual analysis of the major models of metacognition, providing the foundation for analysing and iden-tifying categories, supercategories, subcategories, key elements and elements of metacognition. This provided the final structure for the *taxonomy of metacognition*. The *conceptual framework of metacognition* depicts the categ-orisation of metacognition reflected in the *taxonomy of metacognition*. Both will be depicted in Chapter 10. Further discussion of the categorisations of metacognition in relation to the taxonomy will be discussed in Chapter 10.

10 The taxonomy of metacognition

This chapter illustrates and represents the analysis of the major models of metacognition and the main theoretical contributions described in previous chapters. The *conceptual framework of metacognition* has been constructed throughout the book and reflects the *taxonomy of metacognition*.

Analysis of higher-order assertions

The higher-order assertions contribute succinct and specific statements which reflect the advanced level of abstraction applied in the analysis of the data. This section represents a concluding analysis of these assertions providing a summary which links the categorisations in the final *taxonomy of metacognition* (Table 10.1) and the *conceptual framework of metacognition* (Figures 10.1–10.5). Specific links to the HOAs are made in the Part III discussion.

Contributions to the taxonomy of metacognition from Part I – Reflection: The quintessence of metacognition

The types of knowledge of cognition identified in the analysis of the literature related to reflection and metacognition show a stronger connection with declarative person (specifically knowledge of self) and strategy knowledge than declarative task knowledge (specifically knowledge of task demands) and procedural knowledge. An analysis of Part I assertions also demonstrated that reflective processes have greater influence on the regulation of self-knowledge and strategy knowledge than the regulation of task knowledge. It has shown a strong interrelationship between reflection, metacognition and regulation of intra-individual person knowledge; however, it has not demonstrated a strong relationship between reflection and self-regulation of task knowledge and strategy knowledge. This does not necessarily signify that reflective metacognitive processes do not influence self-regulation of task demands and strategy and applicability but that self-regulation has a greater influence on the regulation of intra-individual person knowledge. It does indicate that there is a lack of discussion and research regarding the role that reflective metacognitive processes play in facilitating knowledge of task demands, regulation of task knowledge, and self-regulation of task and strategy knowledge. It is important to note that Part I does not provide a comprehensive analysis of all the specific categorisations of the construct of metacognition but provides an in-depth analysis of the connection between metacognition and reflection.

An analysis of the higher-order assertions in Part I reinforces a number of specific connections which have been established between metacognition and reflection, that:

(a) reflection is essential to facilitate metacognition;
(b) self-knowledge is developed through reflection, introspection and consciousness;
(c) self-knowledge and self-awareness are fundamental to critical reflection and metacognition;
(d) critical reflection and critical thinking rely upon purposeful reflection to support metacognition;
(e) self-knowledge is labelled as a form of knowledge of cognition; and
(f) self-knowledge is influenced by noncognitive variables and contextual situations.

Contributions to the taxonomy of metacognition from Part II – Metamemory: The foundational construct

Metamemory has been categorised into knowledge of memory and regulation of memory. Knowledge of memory includes declarative metamemory and procedural metamemory. Declarative metamemory involves knowledge of self and others, knowledge of task and knowledge of memory strategies. All of the key elements of these subcategories were identified in the analysis as metamemory processes. However, knowledge of cognitive goals, which is a key element of knowledge of task and context, was not strongly identified in the data as essential to metamemory. This may be due to the term cognitive goals being introduced in the specific metacognition literature by Flavell (1979) in his model of cognitive monitoring, where the term is first used, and it could also be due to the term and similar terms being related to problem-solving processes rather than mnemonic processes.

Procedural metamemory includes knowledge of self and others, knowledge of task and context and knowledge of memory strategies. The key element which emerged as essential to knowledge of self and others was knowledge of intra-individual processes. Knowledge of task and context includes three key elements: knowledge of task objectives, knowledge of task complexity and knowledge of task context. Knowledge of task objectives was not identified in the data as a strong key element of procedural metamemory. This may be linked to the lack of support for declarative metamemory – knowledge of cognitive goals. It can be argued that these two key elements are interrelated and may be co-dependent. Knowledge of memory strategy includes two key elements: knowledge of strategy application and knowledge of strategy appropriateness. The third key element, knowledge of strategy transferability and adaptation, did not have a strong presence in the metamemory literature. Self-regulatory processes supporting metamemory mainly involved the regulation of intra-individual processes but not necessarily regulation of task and strategy knowledge. This could be due to the self being a prominent part of self-regulation. Metamemory experiences are fundamental to metamemory and include judgments and feelings. Metamemory feelings of task did not feature strongly in the data. This may again be related to the lack of task-related variables in declarative and procedural metamemory.

This does not signify that the task variable is not a necessary part of metamemory but it does represent that the person variable is essential in facilitating metamemory and indicates that there is a lack of discussion and research regarding the role that task knowledge plays in metamemory processes.

Analysis of these higher-order assertions highlights core aspects of metamemory. Overall, these establish that metamemory involves:

(a) the application of mnemonic strategy knowledge which relies on monitoring and control;
(b) an awareness of self-knowledge which influences procedural strategy knowledge;
(c) mnemonic self-efficacy and self-concept which influence metamemory ability and capability;
(d) a knowledge of memory which facilitates memory acquisition, storage and retrieval;
(e) strategy selection, adaptivity and application which influence strategy monitoring and control and task performance;
(f) memory monitoring and control which regulates strategy efficiency and supports strategy development;
(g) memory monitoring and control which involves self-awareness, reflection and introspection;
(h) memory monitoring which includes feeling and knowing phenomena;
(i) task complexity which increases the demands upon the interaction between the metamemory variables of person, task and strategy; and
(j) situational knowledge and task complexity which influence metamemory.

Part III – Metacognition: The taxonomy

Knowledge of cognition or metacognitive knowledge

Knowledge of cognition or metacognitive knowledge includes declarative, procedural and conditional or contextual knowledge. Relying upon declarative and procedural knowledge, conditional knowledge determines why, when and where to use this knowledge (HOA.40). Knowledge of cognition involves knowledge, personal theories or beliefs one has about one's own cognition which influences and interacts with planning, strategy selection and application and task knowledge (HOA.11, HOA.24, HOA.25, HOA.28).

KNOWLEDGE OF SELF AND OTHERS (PERSON METACOGNITIVE KNOWLEDGE)

Knowledge of oneself (self-knowledge) and of others as cognitive beings is categorised as the person subcategory of declarative knowledge or person metacognitive knowledge (HOA.7, HOA.30). Self-awareness, self-knowledge and personal cognitive attributes (strengths and weaknesses) are influenced by self-efficacy, self-concept and beliefs regarding ability and capability. Reflection, introspection and self-appraisal facilitate the development of self-knowledge and self-awareness (HOA.1, HOA.11, HOA.15, HOA.27, HOA.31). Self-knowledge is essential for knowing one's beliefs about motivations and is especially important for knowing when one knows and when one does not know (HOA.31, HOA.32). It is influenced by feelings, beliefs, false beliefs, self-doubt, contexts and challenges which can be instigated during and affect problem-solving processes and developed through the interaction between reflection, introspection and consciousness (HOA.6, HOA.8). Reflection is considered to be critical when it is focused and purposeful and involves critical thinking and reflective judgment. Both critical reflection and thinking rely upon critically knowing oneself, relying on self-knowledge (HOA.3, HOA.4). Self-knowledge influences and is influenced by task and strategy variables and is affected by beliefs and emotions. It also develops in, and is affected by, complex problem-solving situations (HOA.7, HOA.31, HOA.37, HOA.52).

KNOWLEDGE OF TASK AND CONTEXT (TASK METACOGNITIVE KNOWLEDGE)

Knowledge of task and context, including sensitivity to task, is categorised as a subcategory of declarative knowledge (HOA.33). Situational knowledge and task complexity increase knowledge of and demands upon the interaction between the person and strategy variables. Task complexity also influences reconstruction of schemata, connotative knowledge, strategy knowledge and application in problem-solving situations (HOA.14, HOA.17, HOA.29). Reflection on task knowledge and task sensitivity supports the development of problem representation(s), facilitating decomposition and encoding. This supports the identification of appropriate task-specific strategies and their flexible application to match cognitive goals and facilitate task completion (HOA.38, HOA.39).

KNOWLEDGE OF STRATEGY (STRATEGY METACOGNITIVE KNOWLEDGE)

Critical reflection, including verbalisation, supports strategy development, selection and application in complex problems. This level of reflection supports conscious, purposeful strategy application or procedural knowledge although through experience procedural knowledge can become implicit and refined strategies can become automatic in familiar situations. Strategy selection, application and transferability in different contexts is influenced by self-knowledge, self-concept as a problem solver, self-efficacy and intrinsic motivation (HOA.1, HOA.4, HOA.7, HOA.12, HOA.31, HOA.36, HOA.37). Strategy knowledge, knowing how, develops through the interaction between person and task variables and is influenced by metacognitive experiences and supported by monitoring and control. Strategy knowledge involves adaptivity, selection, execution and solution procedures which support task analysis and performance (HOA.13, HOA.16, HOA.18, HOA.34, HOA.35, HOA.53).

Regulation of cognition

Regulation of cognition, including frontal lobe functioning or executive functioning, involves the monitoring, control and awareness of knowledge and processes (HOA.19, HOA.23).

MONITORING AND CONTROL

Monitoring and control interact with metacognitive knowledge and reflective processes, including verbalisation, to instigate and facilitate strategy application, problem decomposition, subgoaling and subproblem development. Monitoring and control promote strategy efficiency and development which facilitate performance in novel, complex tasks (HOA.1, HOA.9, HOA.21, HOA.22).

SELF-REGULATION

Metacognition and self-regulation's main interaction is control, monitoring and regulation of strategies to meet task demands and goals. Self-regulation involves planning, organising, self-instruction, self-monitoring, self-evaluation, self-efficacy and personal agency (HOA.41, HOA.42, HOA.45). Self-regulated learners are highly metacognitive, including awareness of beliefs and volition. They are motivated, goal orientated and behaviourally committed, independent and active learners who self-initiate strategies and monitor and control them and their motivation to address task demands and goals (HOA.43, HOA.44, HOA.46).

METACOGNITIVE EXPERIENCES

Metacognitive experiences (metacognitive judgments and feelings labelled as feeling and knowing phenomena) facilitate the retrieval and application of knowledge through feelings, judgments, reactions and experiences instigated during the monitoring of cognitive and task situations. They monitor processes through evaluations, intuitions and unconscious feelings and facilitate the awareness of 'fluency or interruption' in cognitive processing. They also monitor interaction and are the product of the interaction between person, task and strategy variables (HOA.10, HOA.20, HOA.47, HOA.48, HOA.50, HOA.51). Academic self-concept, especially self-efficacy and self-perception, influence metacognitive experiences and inform metacognitive knowledge (HOA.49).

Conceptual framework of metacognition

The *conceptual framework of metacognition* (see Figures 10.1–10.5) was informed by the amplification diagrams and is reflective of the *taxonomy of metacognition*. The development of the *conceptual framework of metacognition* supported and facilitated the development of the *taxonomy of metacognition*. The framework and amplification diagrams are models representing specific conceptual interactions which can be used by researchers as a basis to discuss the conceptual relationships. This is supported by Moseley *et al.* (2005) who consider that:

> Although a taxonomy alone is a descriptive framework, when it is shaped by a *model*, it can become a theoretical framework that explains and predicts. An explanatory model is a construct that behaves in some way like the phenomenon it represents.
>
> (p. 40)

The *conceptual framework of metacognition* (Figures 10.1–10.5, see pp. 188–192) reflects the final *taxonomy of metacognition* (Table 10.1). The framework represents the two core-components of metacognition – knowledge of cognition and regulation of cognition – and links these to the categories, supercategories, subcategories, key elements and elements of the construct. It illustrates connections between the components, subcomponents, categories, supercategories, subcategories and key elements of metacognition.

Taxonomy of metacognition

The final *taxonomy of metacognition* (Table 10.1) represents a framework, continuum and 'comprehensive research and development system'

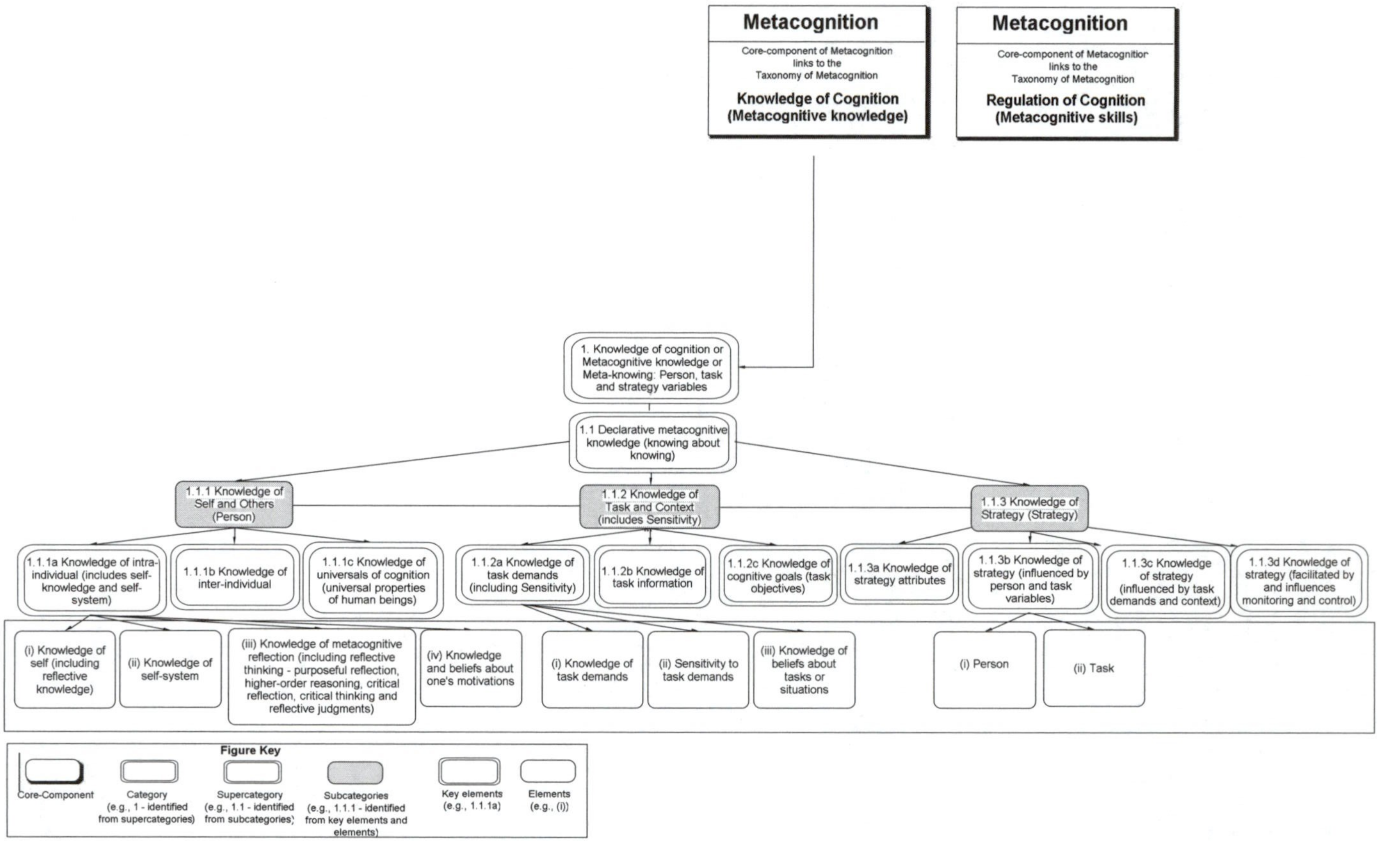

Figure 10.1 The conceptual framework of metacognition – reflecting declarative knowledge in the final taxonomy of metacognition (Table 10.1)

This diagram can be viewed online at www.psypress.com/the-taxonomy-of-metacognition-9781841698694

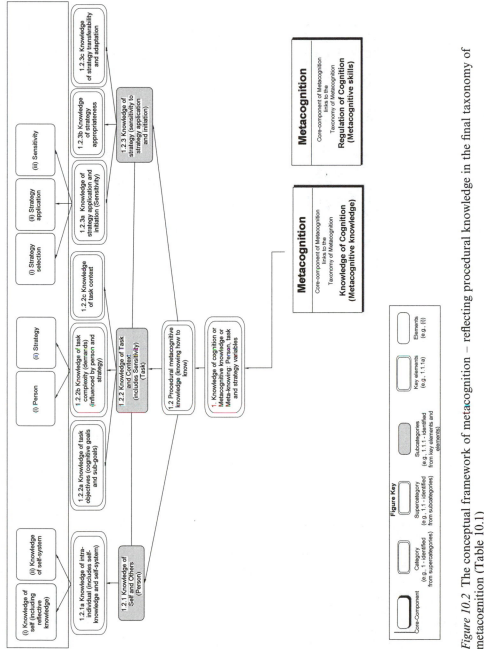

Figure 10.2 The conceptual framework of metacognition – reflecting procedural knowledge in the final taxonomy of metacognition (Table 10.1)
This diagram can be viewed online at www.psypress.com/the-taxonomy-of-metacognition-9781841698694

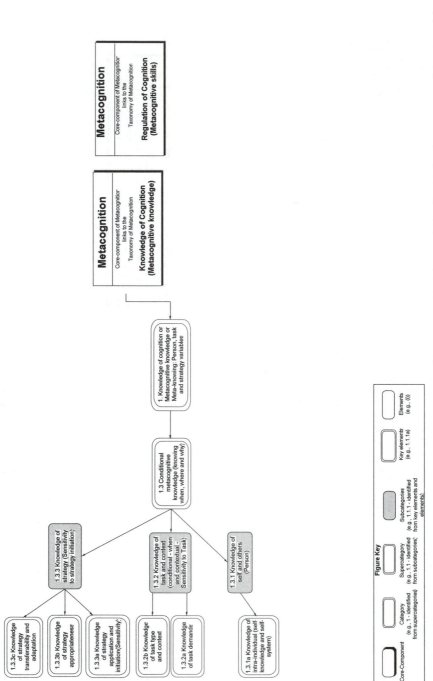

Figure 10.3 The conceptual framework of metacognition – reflecting conditional knowledge in the final taxonomy of metacognition (Table 10.1)

This diagram can be viewed online at www.psypress.com/the-taxonomy-of-metacognition-9781841698694

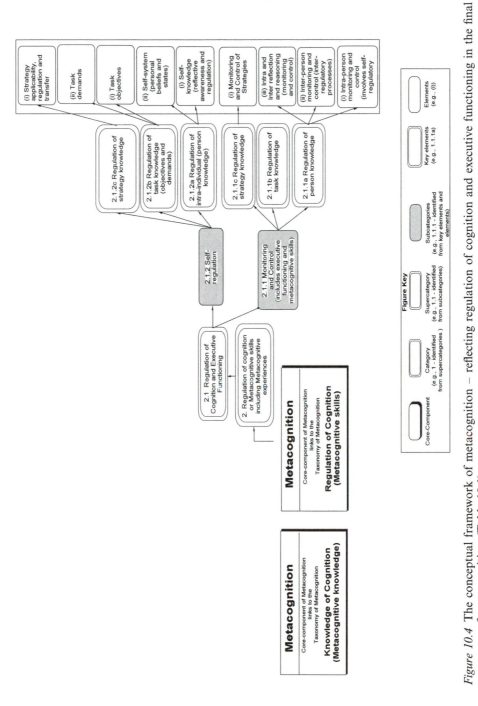

Figure 10.4 The conceptual framework of metacognition – reflecting regulation of cognition and executive functioning in the final taxonomy of metacognition (Table 10.1)

This diagram can be viewed online at www.psypress.com/the-taxonomy-of-metacognition-9781841698694

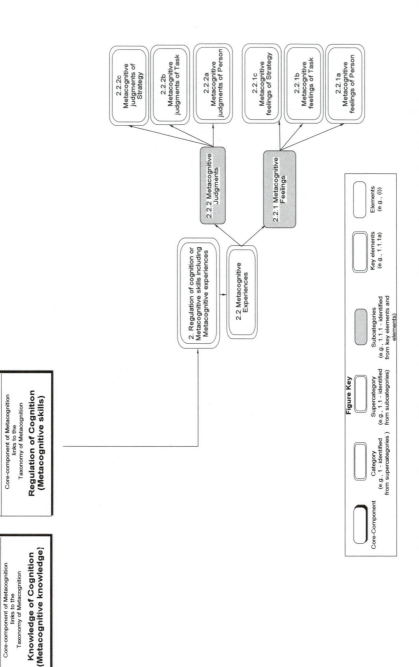

Figure 10.5 The conceptual framework of metacognition – reflecting metacognitive experiences in the final taxonomy of metacognition (Table 10.1)

This diagram can be viewed online at www.psypress.com/the-taxonomy-of-metacognition-9781841698694

(Anderson and Krathwohl, 2001; Jonassen and Tessmer, 1996/1997, p. 23; Martin and Briggs, 1986). It provides a detailed and comprehensive representation and categorisation of the categories, supercategories, sub-categories, key elements and elements of metacognition.

Taxonomies are often (but not always) hierarchical (as in family, genus, species) and evolutionary (Bailey, 1994, p. 6). As suggested by Lipman (1987), 'virtually any taxonomic approach to cognitive skills is bound to be problematical . . . it is advisable to avoid hierarchical approaches – one of the more obvious difficulties with Bloom's taxonomy' (p. 157). In addition, Hauenstein (1998) explains that a hierarchical approach 'presumes that a lower-order class is a prerequisite to a higher-order class' (p. 2). It is not the intention that the *taxonomy of metacognition* is read as a definitive hierarchical framework classified into higher-order and lower-order processes. Although the taxonomy has levels (e.g. 1.1, 1.2 etc) which are grouped with the aid of labels such as categories, supercategories and subcategories, this classification reflects the structure of the construct. The levels help depict the relationships between the categories and are not intended to provide a hierarchical representation of the construct like many scientific taxonomies.

The analysis of the construct informed the development, representation and categorisations in the taxonomy and not vice versa. The categorisations were developed throughout the analysis of both theoretical and empirical research and are grouped in terms of their similarities; however, the groups are also interactive. Essentially, what the taxonomy represents, supported by the *conceptual framework of metacognition*, is that metacognitive processes are interactive. This means that although specific categories of metacognition have been classified and grouped, providing a framework for detailed research on these categorisations, it is important to acknowledge that the construct is interactive and therefore the processes are interactive. The taxonomy, therefore, provides researchers with a rich and detailed source of information for specific studies on isolated variables of metacognition and also for studies investigating the interaction between particular variables.

Successful taxonomies rely upon theorisation and classification as they enable the researcher to determine a comprehensive and even definitive number of taxa. This reduces the complexity of theoretical data to achieve metaprocedural reorganisation and simplification, but not oversimplification, providing a rich and valuable conceptualised source which can be used by researchers and teachers. This book labels this type of taxonomy as a construct taxonomy.

The final *taxonomy of metacognition* (Table 10.1) is depicted by the final *conceptual framework of metacognition* (Figures 10.1–10.5). Tables 10.1.1– 10.1.7 provide the elaborations for the entries in the final *taxonomy of metacognition*. These are specific elaborations that can be used for the basis of future research.

Table 10.1 Taxonomy of metacognition (see Tables 10.1.1–10.1.7 for elaborations)

CATEGORY OF METACOGNITION
1. Knowledge of cognition or Metacognitive knowledge or Meta-knowing: Person, task and strategy variables

SUPERCATEGORY OF METACOGNITION
1.1 Declarative Metacognitive Knowledge (knowing about knowing)

Subcategories of 1.1 Declarative Metacognitive Knowledge	*Key Elements and Elements*
1.1.1 Knowledge of self and others (Person)	1.1.1a Knowledge of intra-individual (includes self-knowledge and self-system)
	(i) Knowledge of self (including reflective knowledge)
	(ii) Knowledge of self-system
	(iii) Knowledge of metacognitive reflection (including reflective thinking – purposeful reflection, higher-order reasoning, critical reflection, critical thinking and reflective judgments)
	(iv) Knowledge and beliefs about one's motivations
	1.1.1b Knowledge of inter-individual
	1.1.1c Knowledge of universals of cognition (universal properties of human beings)
1.1.2 Knowledge of task and context (including Sensitivity) (Task)	1.1.2a Knowledge of task demands (including Sensitivity)
	(i) Knowledge of task demands
	(ii) Sensitivity to task demands
	(iii) Knowledge of beliefs about tasks or situations
	1.1.2b Knowledge of task information
	1.1.2c Knowledge of cognitive goals (task objectives)
1.1.3 Knowledge of strategy (Strategy)	1.1.3a Knowledge of strategy attributes
	1.1.3b Knowledge of strategy (influenced by person and task variables)
	(i) Person
	(ii) Task
	1.1.3c Knowledge of strategy (influenced by task demands and context)
	1.1.3d Knowledge of strategy (facilitated by and influences monitoring and control)

continues

Table 10.1 (continued)

SUPERCATEGORY OF METACOGNITION	
1.2 Procedural Metacognitive Knowledge (knowing how to know)	
Subcategories of 1.2 Procedural Metacognitive Knowledge	*Key Elements and Elements*
1.2.1 Knowledge of self and others (Person)	1.2.1a Knowledge of intra-individual (self-knowledge and self-system) (i) Knowledge of self (including reflective knowledge) (ii) Knowledge of self-system
1.2.2 Knowledge of task and context (including Sensitivity) (Task)	1.2.2a Knowledge of task objectives (cognitive goals and subgoals) 1.2.2b Knowledge of task complexity (demands) (influenced by person and strategy) (i) Person (ii) Strategy 1.2.2c Knowledge of task context
1.2.3 Knowledge of strategy (sensitivity to strategy application and initiation)	1.2.3a Knowledge of strategy application and initiation (Sensitivity) (i) Strategy selection (ii) Strategy application (iii) Sensitivity 1.2.3b Knowledge of strategy appropriateness 1.2.3c Knowledge of strategy transferability and adaptation

SUPERCATEGORY OF METACOGNITION	
1.3 Conditional Metacognitive Knowledge (knowing when, where and why)	
Subcategories of 1.3 Conditional Metacognitive Knowledge (knowing when, where, and why)	*Key Elements and Elements*
1.3.1 Knowledge of self and others (Person)	1.3.1a Knowledge of intra-individual (self-knowledge and self-system)
1.3.2 Knowledge of task and context (conditional – when and contextual – Sensitivity to Task)	1.3.2a Knowledge of task demands 1.3.2b Knowledge of task type and context
1.3.3 Knowledge of strategy (sensitivity to strategy initiation)	1.3.3a Knowledge of strategy application and initiation (Sensitivity) 1.3.3b Knowledge of strategy appropriateness 1.3.3c Knowledge of strategy transferability and adaptation

continues

Table 10.1 (continued)

CATEGORY OF METACOGNITION
2. Regulation of cognition or Metacognitive skills including Metacognitive experiences

SUPERCATEGORY OF METACOGNITION
2.1 Regulation of Cognition or Metacognitive Skills and Executive Functioning

Subcategories of 2.1 Regulation of Cognition and Executive Functioning	*Key Elements and Elements*
2.1.1 Monitoring and Control (includes executive functioning and metacognitive skills)	2.1.1a Regulation of person knowledge (i) Intra-person monitoring and control (involves self-regulatory processes) (ii) Inter-person monitoring and control (inter-regulatory processes) (iii) Intra- and Inter-reflection and reasoning (monitoring and control) 2.1.1b Regulation of task knowledge 2.1.1c Regulation of strategy knowledge (i) Monitoring and Control of Strategies
2.1.2 Self-regulation	2.1.2a Regulation of intra-individual (person knowledge) (i) Self-knowledge (reflective awareness and regulation) (ii) Self-system (personal beliefs and states) 2.1.2b Regulation of task knowledge (i) Task objectives (ii) Task demands 2.1.2c Regulation of strategy knowledge (i) Strategy applicability, regulation and transfer

SUPERCATEGORY OF METACOGNITION
2.2 Metacognitive Experiences

Subcategories of 2.2 Metacognitive Experiences	*Key Elements and Elements*
2.2.1 Metacognitive Feelings	2.2.1a Metacognitive feelings of Person 2.2.1b Metacognitive feelings of Task 2.2.1c Metacognitive feelings of Strategy
2.2.2 Metacognitive Judgments	2.2.2a Metacognitive judgments of Person 2.2.2b Metacognitive judgments of Task 2.2.2c Metacognitive judgments of Strategy

Table 10.1.1 Taxonomy of metacognition: 1. Knowledge of cognition

CATEGORY OF METACOGNITION: 1. Knowledge of Cognition or Metacognitive Knowledge or Meta-knowing: Person, task and strategy variables

Knowledge of cognition or meta-knowing includes declarative (knowing that), procedural (knowing how) and conditional knowledge (knowing when, where and why)

(i) Knowledge of Cognition	*(ii) Reflective Awareness of Knowledge of Cognition*
• knowledge of cognition involves explicit or implicit knowledge • knowledge of cognition involves rich structural or semantic knowledge • knowledge of the interaction of memory/cognitive variables (person, task and strategy) • knowledge facilitates recall and reconstruction of information and processes • knowledge is influenced by developmental, learning and task experiences • knowledge is important for memory development, performance and problem solving • sensitivity to knowledge (influences person, task and strategy variables) • inferential reasoning and judgments	• knowledge of cognition involves reflective awareness of knowledge (known and not known) • knowledge of cognition involves reflective awareness of strategies and skills and processes • reflection on knowledge of cognition supports the interpretation of metacognitive experiences • reflection on knowledge of cognition supports the interpretation of strategies • reflective awareness of the influence of monitoring, control and self-regulation on cognition

Table 10.1.2 Taxonomy of metacognition: 1.1 Declarative metacognitive knowledge

SUPERCATEGORY OF METACOGNITION – 1. KNOWLEDGE OF COGNITION

1.1 Declarative Metacognitive Knowledge (knowing about knowing)

Declarative knowledge (metacognitive knowing or competence or operations) includes person, task and strategy variables

Declarative Knowledge	Types of Declarative Knowledge
• factual, explicit, truthful and conscious knowledge about memory • factual, explicit, truthful and conscious knowledge about cognition • stable, familiar, constant and statable knowledge (involving reflection and communication) • fallible: facts known about cognition can be untrue or incorrect • informed by metacognitive experiences (feeling and knowing phenomena) • informed by reasoning • facilitates connotative knowledge	• 'domain knowledge' (knowledge of reality domains) includes knowing about objects of knowledge and reflection on objects of knowledge • 'cognitive knowledge' (beliefs about thinking or propositional manner) • 'specific and situational' knowledge • 'general and abstract' knowledge (includes epistemological meta-knowing or epistemic cognition) • epistemological meta-knowing (epistemological or epistemic understanding) includes personal and impersonal knowledge

SUBCATEGORY OF 1.1 DECLARATIVE METACOGNITIVE KNOWLEDGE
1.1.1 Knowledge of self and others (Person)

KEY ELEMENTS AND ELEMENTS

1.1.1a Knowledge of intra-individual (includes self-knowledge and self-system)

(i) Knowledge of self (including reflective knowledge)
- knowledge of self as a cognitive being
- knowledge of person theories, attributes (including memory), capabilities, characteristics and abilities
- self-knowledge
- self-awareness
- self-awareness of cognition
- self-appraisal of cognition
- self-discovery
- self-understanding
- knowledge of strengths and weaknesses
- person cognitive characteristics and attributes
- person cognitive abilities and capabilities
- reflection supports awareness of limitations and strengths

- awareness of prior knowledge, skills and experiences
- knowing what and when you do and do not know, what you need to know
- beliefs about self-knowledge
- beliefs about memory ability, capability and effectiveness

(ii) Knowledge of self-system
- self-esteem
- attributional beliefs
- emotions
- self-efficacy (including memory self-efficacy)
- self-concept
- self-appraisal or self-reflection
- self-beliefs as mnemonic or cognitive beings (ability and nature of oneself)
- self-appraisal involves reflective evaluation of one's knowledge, ability, task, context and strategy applicability

continues

Table 10.1.2 (continued)

(iii) Knowledge of metacognitive reflection (including reflective thinking – purposeful reflection, higher-order reasoning, critical reflection, critical thinking and reflective judgments)
Purposeful reflection
o involves higher-order thinking, complex thinking
o identifying and reflecting on prejudice and emotions
Reflective judgments
• reflective judgments involves reflective thinking
Higher-order reasoning
• knowledge promotes new knowledge development
• applicability of inferences
• knowledge facilitates connections through inference and reasoning
• knowledge and inferences move from one judgment or belief to another
• knowledge of affect of epistemic assumptions
• knowledge of affect of epistemological judgments
Critical reflection
• critical knowing
• complex thinking

• justification of ideas
• judgment of rationality
• reflective interpretation
• reflective judgments of beliefs and experiences, values, assumptions, knowledge, inferences
• knowledge of epistemological commitments
• identifying and reflecting on beliefs
• introspective knowledge
Critical thinking
• judgments and analytical judgments
• judgment of credibility
• evaluative, reflective reasoning
• knowledge of and about beliefs
• justification of beliefs
• critical evaluation of bias and assumptions which form the basis of beliefs

(iv) Knowledge and beliefs about one's motivations
• beliefs about motivation
• beliefs about motivation are affected by self-efficacy, motivation and judgments
• beliefs about motivation are affected by task goals and task importance

---

1.1.1b Knowledge of inter-individual

• inter-individual
• knowledge of others as cognitive beings
• beliefs of others as mnemonic or cognitive beings

• beliefs regarding the cognitive ability and nature of others
• beliefs regarding the ability of others compared with oneself

---

1.1.1c Knowledge of universals of cognition (universal properties of human beings)

• knowledge of and about beliefs
• beliefs and intuitions regarding general abilities of oneself and others
• knowledge of general abilities, properties and processes of oneself and others involves awareness of
o beliefs and intuitions (including beliefs about performance
o understandings and misunderstandings regarding information
o perceptions, conceptions, impressions

o current understandings may not be predictors of future understandings
o cognitive differences and similarities within, between and among people
• knowledge of various levels and types of understanding including focus, attention, communication, memory, problem solving
• intangible/tacit knowledge regarding what and how well you know a cognitive object

---

continues

Table 10.1.2 (continued)

SUBCATEGORY OF 1.1 DECLARATIVE METACOGNITIVE KNOWLEDGE
1.1.2 Knowledge of task and context (including Sensitivity) (Task)

KEY ELEMENTS AND ELEMENTS

1.1.2a Knowledge of task demands (including Sensitivity)

(i) Knowledge of task demands
- knowledge of task characteristics
- knowledge of task complexity
- knowledge of task difficulty
- knowledge of task context, specifically its demands
- knowledge of task complexity influences strategy knowledge
- reflection of task demands

(ii) Sensitivity to task demands
- reflection supports task sensitivity
- sensitivity to matching strategies to task demands

(iii) Knowledge of beliefs about tasks or situations
- beliefs affect monitoring in complex, demanding memory task or problem-solving situations
- beliefs promote and inhibit task engagement
- beliefs about task difficulty influences strategy identification

---

1.1.2b Knowledge of task information

- knowledge of task type and terms
- knowledge of task variety
- knowledge of task similarity
- knowledge of task context, specifically related to task information
- knowledge of task information is needed to meet task demands
- knowledge of task information influences strategy knowledge

- reflection supports knowledge of task information
- comprehension and meaning reconstruction and analysis

1.1.2c Knowledge of cognitive goals (task objectives)

- knowledge of the difference types of cognitive/task goals
- cognitive goals (tasks) and subgoals (subtasks) are implicit or explicit objectives
- goal clarification and goal setting
- knowledge about tasks or situations
- task objectives or goals are self-determined
- task objectives are identified through social interaction
- task objectives are identified by task

- identification and elaboration of problem elements and possible solutions
- task goals are influenced by task experiences
- knowledge of task objectives or goals influences strategies or cognitive actions

---

continues

Table 10.1.2 (*continued*)

SUBCATEGORY OF 1.1 DECLARATIVE METACOGNITIVE KNOWLEDGE
1.1.3 Knowledge of strategy (Strategy)

KEY ELEMENTS AND ELEMENTS

1.1.3a Knowledge of strategy attributes

- knowledge of and about specific strategies (prior strategy knowledge)
- knowledge of strategy attributes facilitates procedural strategy knowledge
- knowledge and development of various mnemonic (acquisition, storage and retrieval) and cognitive strategies
  - o strategy training facilitates memory performance
  - o guidance in developing and stimulating strategies (children)
  - o knowledge of sophisticated acquisition and retrieval strategies (adults)

- knowledge of strategy goals and effectiveness (informed strategy knowledge)
- knowledge and identification of appropriate strategies or knowledge of strategy selection
- knowledge of strategy attributes facilitates knowing when, where and how to use and apply strategies (facilitates knowledge of strategy applicability)
- knowledge of strategy attributes facilitates strategy refinement

---

1.1.3b Knowledge of strategy (influenced by person and task variables)

- knowledge of strategy develops through the interaction of person and task knowledge and prior experiences
- person and task knowledge influence strategic processes and the problem solution
- knowledge of strategy is also known as metastrategic skill
(i) Person
- self-knowledge and self-awareness influence strategy knowledge
- self concept influences strategy knowledge development
- mental imagery influences strategy knowledge
- skilful thinking influences strategy knowledge
- analysis of arguments
- applicability of inferences facilitating problem-solving strategies and solutions
- beliefs about strategy knowledge

- beliefs affect memory retrieval and strategy application
- beliefs promote and inhibit memory performance and strategy selection
- general strategy knowledge involves awareness of the value of being strategic, that it develops and is transferable
- general strategy knowledge involves development of higher-order skills
- knowledge of strategic ability involves reflection
- self-appraisal involves reflective evaluation of strategy applicability
- strategy reflection facilitates strategy searching and development
(ii) Task
- general strategy knowledge involves selection of appropriate strategies for tasks
- task and prior experiences influence strategy development

---

continues

Table 10.1.2 (continued)

1.1.3c Knowledge of strategy (influenced by task demands and context)

- task demands and context influence strategic processes
- task demands and context facilitate or impede the problem solution
- knowledge of task context and complexity influence strategy knowledge
- knowledge of strategy applicability and appropriateness in different contexts
- 'knowledge about specific strategies' involves awareness of the influence of task demands on strategy selection and application

- knowledge of strategy effectiveness facilitates meeting task demands
- knowledge of strategy effectiveness facilitates different task contexts or situations (also influenced by person variable)
- knowledge of strategy effectiveness facilitates task completion
- knowledge of strategies facilitates strategy adaptation to different tasks
- knowledge of strategies facilitates strategy adaptation and transfer to different tasks

1.1.3d Knowledge of strategy (facilitated by and influences monitoring and control)

- knowledge of strategy facilitates and supports planning, monitoring and control
- development of strategy knowledge is facilitated by monitoring and control
- knowledge of strategy is influenced by metacognitive experiences

- knowledge of strategy facilitates strategy monitoring and control
- review of strategies and awareness of strategy effectiveness is facilitated by monitoring and control

Table 10.1.3 Taxonomy of metacognition: 1.2 Procedural metacognitive knowledge

SUPERCATEGORY OF METACOGNITION: 1.2 Procedural metacognitive knowledge (knowing how to know)

Procedural knowledge (metastrategic knowing or competence, operations, understanding) includes person, task and strategy variables

Procedural Knowledge	Types of Procedural Knowledge
• influences planning • involves strategy selection and application • explicit knowledge prompts implicit knowledge (automatic refined strategies or skills)	• knowledge of strategies or metastrategic understanding of cognitive actions/strategies facilitate realisation of cognitive goals • knowledge about strategy selection and application • knowledge of task objectives or metatask

SUBCATEGORY OF 1.2 PROCEDURAL METACOGNITIVE KNOWLEDGE
1.2.1 Knowledge of self and others (Person)

KEY ELEMENTS AND ELEMENTS

1.2.1a Knowledge of intra-individual (self-knowledge and self-system)

(i) Knowledge of self (including reflective knowledge)
• self-knowledge facilitates understanding of the importance of procedural strategy knowledge
• self-knowledge facilitates strategy monitoring
• self-knowledge influences strategy selection, transferability and application
• self-awareness

(ii) Knowledge of self-system
• self-system facilitates understanding the importance of strategy knowledge
• self-system facilitates strategy monitoring
• self-system influences strategy selection, transferability and application
• self-system influences metacognitive experiences
• self-concept (positive or negative) as a problem solver
• self-efficacy
• affected by beliefs and ability
• intrinsic motivation

continues

Table 10.1.3 (*continued*)

SUBCATEGORY OF 1.2 PROCEDURAL METACOGNITIVE KNOWLEDGE
1.2.2 Knowledge of task and context (including Sensitivity) (Task)

KEY ELEMENTS AND ELEMENTS

1.2.2a Knowledge of task objectives (cognitive goals and subgoals)

- procedural knowledge of task objectives (goals) and strategies/ actions interact with declarative metacognitive knowledge
- procedural knowledge of task objectives (goals) and strategies/ actions involves and instigates metacognitive experiences
- knowing how to address task objectives or goals involves knowledge of task objectives or metatask
- knowledge of task objectives or goals facilitates selection and flexible application of task-specific strategies

- knowing how to address task objectives or goals involves knowledge of task aims, cognitive goals and subgoals
- knowing how to address task objectives or goals involves knowledge of task structure
- knowing how to address task objectives or goals facilitates task completion
- procedural task knowledge facilitates executive functioning

1.2.2b Knowledge of task complexity (demands) (influenced by person and strategy)

(i) Person
- beliefs about task difficulty influences strategy application
- beliefs about task difficulty influences strategy identification
- beliefs about task difficulty influences strategy transferability
- positive or negative self-concept is affected by task difficulty
- self-efficacy and intrinsic motivation is affected by task difficulty

(ii) Strategy
- knowing how to address task demands
- procedural task knowledge facilitates variable interaction which influences strategy selection, application and adaptation
- knowledge of task complexity influences strategy selection
- knowledge of task complexity influences strategy application
- application of strategies to aid performance
- task complexity involves variable interaction which affects strategy selection

1.2.2c Knowledge of task context

- knowledge of task nature
- procedural task knowledge facilitates knowledge of strategy task adaptability
- procedural task knowledge facilitates knowledge about strategy effectiveness and limitations in different tasks and contexts

- procedural knowledge of strategy application in different tasks and contexts
- involves variable interaction which affects trans-situational strategy selection and application
- task context influences strategic processes by either facilitating or impeding the problem solution

continues

Table 10.1.3 (*continued*)

SUBCATEGORY OF 1.2 PROCEDURAL METACOGNITIVE KNOWLEDGE
1.2.3 Knowledge of strategy (sensitivity to strategy application and initiation)

KEY ELEMENTS AND ELEMENTS

1.2.3a Knowledge of strategy application and initiation (Sensitivity)

(i) Strategy selection
- declarative (general) strategy knowledge facilitates effective strategy selection for specific tasks
- knowledge of mnemonic strategies facilitates acquisition, storage and retrieval
- planning facilitates effective strategy selection
- variable interaction (person [ability and interest] and task knowledge) affects strategy selection
- beliefs influence and facilitate strategy selection
- strategy selection is supported by verbalisation (children)
- self-concept influences strategy selection

(ii) Strategy application
- knowledge of strategy execution or action
- beliefs influence and facilitate strategy application
- self-concept influences strategy application

- strategy application is supported by verbalisation (children)
- planning facilitates effective strategy application
- application of various strategies aids performance
- task knowledge facilitates knowledge of strategy application
- purposeful/conscious/explicit strategy and plan application
- actively knowing when to use deliberate, goal orientated strategies
- actively knowing when to allow spontaneous, implicit use of strategies
- implicit application of learned strategies, systems and plans
- strategy application involves executive function

(iii) Sensitivity
- sensitivity to deliberate strategy use
- sensitivity to allowing spontaneous strategies
- sensitivity to task influences the identification of appropriate strategies
- sensitivity to task influences subsequent strategy application

---

1.2.3b Knowledge of strategy appropriateness

- knowledge of strategy appropriateness
- knowledge of strategy benefits
- knowledge of strategy use (most appropriate and effective strategy to use) is facilitated by knowledge of strategy attributes

- awareness and understanding of strategy applicability or appropriateness (address task objectives)
- identification of appropriate strategies and subsequent strategy application

---

1.2.3c Knowledge of strategy transferability and adaptation

- strategy transfer and maintenance
- knowledge of strategy transferability (governed by different tasks and contexts)
- knowledge of strategy application in different task contexts

- supported and facilitated by monitoring and control (essential for trans-situational application)
- awareness of the benefits and applications of various strategies in different contexts

---

Table 10.1.4 Taxonomy of metacognition: 1.3 Conditional metacognitive knowledge

---

SUPERCATEGORY OF METACOGNITION: 1.3 Conditional metacognitive knowledge (knowing when, where and why)

Conditional knowledge (knowing when, where and why) conditional or contextual knowledge (includes person, task and strategy variables)

Conditional Knowledge
- why, when and where to use declarative knowledge (especially strategy knowledge)
- why, when and where to use procedural knowledge (especially strategy knowledge)

SUBCATEGORY OF 1.3 CONDITIONAL METACOGNITIVE KNOWLEDGE: 1.3.1 Knowledge of self and others (Person)

KEY ELEMENTS AND ELEMENTS

1.3.1a Knowledge of intra-individual (self-knowledge and self-system)
- self-system influences development of specific strategy and general strategy knowledge

---

SUBCATEGORY OF 1.3 CONDITIONAL METACOGNITIVE KNOWLEDGE: 1.3.2 Knowledge of task and context (conditional – when and contextual – Sensitivity to Task)

KEY ELEMENTS AND ELEMENTS

1.3.2a Knowledge of task demands	**1.3.2b Knowledge of task type and context**
• knowledge of task demands and complexity	• knowledge of task type
• knowledge of interaction between context and task demands	• sensitivity to task
	• task and context influence the interaction between declarative and procedural knowledge (metacognitive and metastrategic knowing)

SUBCATEGORY OF 1.3 CONDITIONAL METACOGNITIVE KNOWLEDGE: 1.3.3 Knowledge of strategy (sensitivity to strategy initiation)

KEY ELEMENTS AND ELEMENTS

1.3.3a Knowledge of strategy application and initiation (Sensitivity)	**1.3.3c Knowledge of strategy transferability and adaptation**
• context influences specific strategy knowledge	• facilitates strategy adaptation
• context influences strategy use	• context influences strategy transfer and regulation
1.3.3b Knowledge of strategy appropriateness	
• facilitates strategy transfer	

Table 10.1.5 Taxonomy of metacognition: 2. Regulation of cognition

CATEGORY OF METACOGNITION: 2. Regulation of cognition or Metacognitive skills including Metacognitive experiences

Regulation of cognition or Metacognitive skills includes monitoring and control, executive functioning and metacognitive experiences

2.1 Regulation of Cognition or Metacognitive skills and Executive Functioning	2.2 Metacognitive experiences
• secondary 'cluster' or categorisation of metacognition • labelled as metacognitive skills or regulation of skills • described as executive control, functioning or cognition • 'unstable', rarely 'statable' and late developing • awareness, predicting, planning, revising, checking, reality testing, evaluating, coordinating, monitoring and control • cognitive monitoring and control involves reflective awareness of knowledge • reflective awareness of monitoring, control and regulation	• Metacognitive feelings (person, task and strategy) • Metacognitive judgments (person, task and strategy)

Table 10.1.6 Taxonomy of metacognition: 2.1 Regulation of cognition and Executive functioning

SUPERCATEGORY OF METACOGNITION – 2. REGULATION OF COGNITION OR METACOGNITIVE SKILLS INCLUDING METACOGNITIVE EXPERIENCES
2.1 Regulation of Cognition or Metacognitive Skills and Executive Functioning

Regulation of cognition or Metacognitive skills and Executive functioning involves monitoring and control and self-regulation

2.1.1 Monitoring and Control (includes executive functioning, metacognitive skills)	2.1.2 Self-regulation
• frontal lobe/executive functioning involves regulation, control, planning and organisation of information or memory knowledge and processes • frontal lobe/executive functioning involves goal setting • frontal lobe/executive functioning involves integration of information • monitoring and control are interactive processes • process monitoring (monitoring planning goals) • monitoring clarity (awareness of the extent of clarity of that knowledge) • monitoring accuracy (determining the degree of accuracy of knowledge) • control processes can be explicit or implicit • control processes are modifiable and adaptable • control processes are stimulated by past control experiences	• Metacognition is a subprocess of self-regulation (solely it is insufficient for successful self-regulation) • Self-regulatory processes influence and interact with metacognitive processes • Many self-regulation factors are metacognitive, such as self-knowledge and self-system and their components

SUBCATEGORY OF 2.1 REGULATION OF COGNITION OR METACOGNITIVE SKILLS AND EXECUTIVE FUNCTIONING
2.1.1 Monitoring and Control (includes executive functioning and metacognitive skills)

KEY ELEMENTS AND ELEMENTS

2.1.1a Regulation of person knowledge
(i) Intra-person monitoring and control (involves self-regulatory processes)
• regulation is influenced by self-system components (self-knowledge, personal and motivational states, attributional beliefs, emotions)
• self-knowledge supports self-regulation
• self-awareness supports self-regulation
• frontal lobe/executive functioning involves self-awareness
• self-regulation

• self-monitoring
• self-control
• self-correction
• self-evaluation
• internal verbalisation to critique knowledge
• reflection is essential facilitator of regulation (self-review, self-regulation, self-interrogation, self-instruction, self-monitoring, self-evaluation)

continues

Table 10.1.6 (continued)

(ii) Inter-person monitoring and control (inter-regulatory processes) • argumentation and external verbalisation in collaborative, cooperative situations • critical assessment and evaluation of knowledge **(iii) Intra- and Inter-reflection and reasoning (monitoring and control)** • critical reflection and purposeful reflection	• frontal lobe/executive functioning involves reflection and introspection • reflective abstraction • evaluative, reflective reasoning including of assertions • propositional reasoning and axiomatisation and formalisation • monitoring and control of inferences via reasoning • control of beliefs • decision making and justification of actions
2.1.1b Regulation of task knowledge • interacts with awareness of task demands to determine strategy applicability • control processes are stimulated in complex, demanding tasks • regulatory processes are task dependent	• monitoring and control facilitates memory performance in memory tasks • cognitive/task goal specification (planning goals related to one's knowledge) • regulation facilitates the awareness of failure or success in complex problems
2.1.1c Regulation of strategy knowledge **(i) Monitoring and Control of Strategies** • interpreting, guiding, directing, orchestrating, supervising, overseeing, managing, predicting, planning, scheduling, selecting options, checking, tracking, evaluating, revising, monitoring, controlling and regulating strategies • planning and review of strategies • instigating, starting and concluding strategies and processes by monitoring progress	• monitoring and control of strategies or cognitive monitoring • control processes facilitate strategic processes • monitoring and control processes are stimulated by strategy novelty • control processes are stimulated by complex strategy sequencing and execution • regulatory strategies support the awareness of metacognitive experiences

SUBCATEGORY OF 2.1 REGULATION OF COGNITION AND EXECUTIVE FUNCTIONING
2.1.2 Self-regulation

KEY ELEMENTS AND ELEMENTS

2.1.2a Regulation of intra-individual (person knowledge)
• self-regulation
• planning, organising and allocation of cognitive resources
• self-regulated learners are highly
  o metacognitive learners
  o motivated
  o goal orientated
  o behaviourally committed
	o independent and active learners
	o aware of their knowledge, beliefs, volition
	• regulation is influenced by self-system and self-knowledge (including personal and motivational states, attributional beliefs, emotions)

continues

Table 10.1.6 (continued)

(i) Self-knowledge (reflective awareness and regulation)	(ii) Self-system (personal beliefs and states)

• reflection is essential facilitator of self-regulation
• self-regulation involves and is influenced by
  o self-knowledge
  o self-awareness
  o self-monitoring
  o self-control
  o self-correction
  o self-judgments
  o self-evaluation
  o self-review
  o self-interrogation
  o self-instruction
	• self-regulation involves and is influenced by
	  o self-competence beliefs
	  o personal beliefs (self-beliefs)
	  o personal agency
	  o perceptions of self-regulation ability
	  o internal and external comparisons
	  o self-efficacy
	  o self-concept
	  o self-doubt
	  o regulation of motivation
	• self-regulation development is facilitated by
	  o personal expectations of achievement
	  o internal verbalisation

2.1.2b Regulation of task knowledge (objectives and demands)

(i) Task objectives	(ii) Task demands

• regulation of cognition and executive functioning facilitate
  o attainment of task goals/objectives
  o clarifying and identifying task elements
  o mental representations of task components
	• regulation of cognition and executive functioning facilitate
	  o determining and understanding task demands
	  o addressing task demands

2.1.2c Regulation of strategy knowledge

(i) Strategy applicability, regulation and transfer	

• regulation of cognition and executive functioning facilitates and involves
  o planning, organising and scheduling of appropriate and applicable strategies
  o self-regulation and strategy self-initiation
  o tracking, reviewing and monitoring strategy effectiveness
  o strategy selection, application and transfer
  o control, monitoring and regulation of strategies
	• metacognitive skills or 'metacognitive acquisition procedures'
	  o necessary for strategy evaluation, generalisation and trans-situational application
	  o involve judgments regarding strategy applicability

Table 10.1.7 Taxonomy of metacognition: 2.2 Metacognitive experiences

CATEGORY OF METACOGNITION: 2. REGULATION OF COGNITION OR METACOGNITIVE SKILLS INCLUDING METACOGNITIVE EXPERIENCES

SUPERCATEGORY OF METACOGNITION: 2.2 METACOGNITIVE EXPERIENCES

Metacognitive Experiences	**Types of Metacognitive Experiences**
• are described as 'online monitoring of cognition' or 'online metacognition' or 'online awareness' • are derived from and inform metacognitive knowledge through monitoring and experiences related to person, task or strategies • are instigated during monitoring and facilitate memory and cognitive monitoring • inform, influence and prompt control and self-regulation • are implicit or explicit • include retrospective and prospective monitoring	• Metacognitive feelings (person, task and strategy) • Metacognitive judgments (person, task and strategy)

SUBCATEGORY OF METACOGNITION 2.2.1 METACOGNITIVE FEELINGS

KEY ELEMENTS AND ELEMENTS

2.2.1a Metacognitive feelings of Person
- feeling and knowing phenomena rely upon reflection and reflective assessment
- metacognitive feelings (not the same as emotions or affect)
- metacognitive feelings involve awareness and unexpected awareness
- metacognitive feelings related to person include feeling of confidence and feeling of satisfaction
- feeling of confidence involves levels of confidence including under- and over-confidence
- feeling of satisfaction involves monitoring outcomes in regard to personal achievement standards
- metacognitive feelings are influenced by person characteristics including
  o self-knowledge
  o self-awareness
  o self-perception

- o self-efficacy (influences feeling of difficulty)
- o self-concept
- o beliefs about ability
- o beliefs regarding ability to meet the task demands
- o beliefs (positive and negative) about capabilities affect monitoring
- o beliefs about successful memory/ task performance affect monitoring
- o emotions
- o personality
- o thoughts and reactions
- o intuitions
- o perceptions
- metacognitive feelings provide feedback regarding
  o self-concept
  o ability
  o attributions
  o confidence

continues

Table 10.1.7 (continued)

2.2.1b Metacognitive feelings of Task

- metacognitive feelings involve awareness of the connection or disparity between the task goals and outcome
- metacognitive feelings which are more related to task include
  - o feeling of familiarity
  - o feeling of difficulty
  - o feeling of satisfaction – involves monitoring task solutions in regard to achievement standards
- feeling of difficulty involves
  - o awareness of task difficulty
  - o monitoring of task difficulty
  - o monitoring of task familiarity and context
  - o awareness of the applicability of current knowledge to specific task

- feeling of confidence is influenced by
  - o task complexity
  - o lack of domain knowledge
  - o lack of strategic task specific knowledge
  - o the task solution
- feeling of satisfaction involves monitoring task solutions
- metacognitive feelings are influenced by
  - o task demands
  - o sensitivity to task and its components
  - o task perceptions
  - o task context
  - o task context familiarity and unfamiliarity

2.2.1c Metacognitive feelings of Strategy

- feeling and knowing phenomena instigate strategy selection and application
- accurate assessment of feeling and knowing phenomena leads to effective monitoring, control and strategy selection and evaluation

- metacognitive feelings support effective monitoring, control and strategy selection
- metacognitive feelings involve the awareness of fluency of interruption in processing
- feeling of difficulty facilitates the
  - o identification of correction strategies
  - o need to develop new strategies

SUBCATEGORY OF METACOGNITION 2.2.2 METACOGNITIVE JUDGMENTS

KEY ELEMENTS AND ELEMENTS

2.2.2a Metacognitive judgments of Person

- metacognitive judgments include judgment or estimate of learning/ feeling-of-knowing judgments
- metamemory judgments of memory accuracy
- self-system influences metacognitive experiences (monitoring and interpreting mnemonic/cognitive experiences)
- feeling and knowing phenomena (metamemory/metacognitive judgments) rely upon reflective assessment and reflective judgments

- metacognitive judgments are influenced by person characteristics including
  - o self-knowledge
  - o self-awareness
  - o self-perception
  - o self-efficacy (influences judgment/ estimate of solution correctness)
  - o self-concept (influences judgment/ estimate of solution correctness)
  - o self-concept (influences monitoring and control of metacognitive judgments and informs metacognitive knowledge)

continues

Table 10.1.7 (continued)

o beliefs about ability (influences judgment or estimate of solution correctness)
o beliefs regarding ability to meet the task demands
o beliefs (positive and negative) about capabilities, which affect monitoring
o beliefs about successful memory/ task performance, which affect monitoring
o emotions
o intuitions
o personality
o thoughts and reactions

• metacognitive judgments provide feedback regarding
o self-concept
o ability
o attributions
o confidence
• judgments of memory accuracy
• judgments facilitate memory retrieval and allocation to a context

2.2.2b Metacognitive judgments of Task

• metacognitive judgments include judgment or estimate of solution correctness
• metacognitive judgments provide feedback regarding difficulty related to the knowledge domain, context and task
• metacognitive judgments are influenced by
o task demands
o sensitivity to task and its components

o task perceptions
o task context familiarity and unfamiliarity
o beliefs regarding ability to meet the task demands
o beliefs about successful memory/ task performance
o beliefs which affect monitoring in complex, demanding memory or cognitive tasks
• judgments facilitate memory retrieval and allocation to a context

2.2.2c Metacognitive judgments of Strategy

• metacognitive judgments: judgment or estimate of effort expenditure
• metamemory/metacognitive judgments instigate strategy identification, selection and application
• metamemory/metacognitive judgments monitor and instigate strategy control
• judgment or estimate of learning informs strategy selection, application and control
• judgment or estimate of solution correctness informs strategy, selection, application and control

• metacognitive judgments of strategy is influenced by
o self-concept, which informs strategy knowledge development
o self-concept, which informs strategy selection and application
o self-awareness, which informs strategy monitoring and control
o self-awareness, which facilitates problem solution(s)
o confidence in knowing, retrieving and using strategies
• metamemory/metacognitive judgments via monitoring influence
o development of new strategies, selection and application of learned strategies, strategy efficiency

Conclusion

This chapter has presented a detailed discussion of the theoretical contributions to metacognition and included the conceptual analysis of the major models of metacognition which provided the foundation for analysing and identifying categories, supercategories, subcategories, key elements and elements of metacognition, the final structure for the *taxonomy of metacognition*. The *conceptual framework of metacognition* depicts the categorisation of it reflected in the *taxonomy of metacognition*.

11 Future directions in research and conclusion

The research suggestions in this chapter are not intended to be exhaustive but provide evidence of the depth and extent of the possibilities of future research.

Research possibilities

Metacognition and reflection

Reflection and metacognition research can form stronger connections between psychology and philosophy, especially in the areas of implicit metacognition, consciousness and introspection. This research can be a small step towards revitalising the roots of philosophy in developmental, cognitive and educational psychology (Alexander, 2006).

Little research has taken place with regard to reviewing and testing a variety of identified critical reflection and critical thinking techniques. Although there is a strong connection in the literature regarding metacognition and these higher-order forms of reflection, scant research is available in this field. Specifically, how does critical reflection inform metacognition? How does metacognition support reflection becoming critical? This is where the interaction between knowledge of cognition and regulation of cognition is essential, but it would be fruitful to understand how critical reflection can be facilitated during complex problem solving through the support of metacognition. The role that critical thinking takes in supporting metacognition during complex problem solving would provide an initial framework for further investigation of how reflective reasoning facilitates critical thinking and metacognition. Research on the influence of feelings, understandings and beliefs and their affect on the effectiveness of reflection would provide some understanding of how reflection can be influenced by other factors.

Self-knowledge unites reflection and metacognition, and therefore would provide a rich theoretical framework to investigate how self-knowledge supports metacognition and how reflection interacts with both metacognition and self-knowledge to facilitate decision making. Connections between judgment and critical thinking or critical judgment, and judgment and creative judgment is another possible, unexplored area of research.

Continued research on reasoning, metalogical understanding and the development of epistemic cognition in complex problem solving would provide an insight into their role in these contexts. Moshman's (2004, 2009a 2009b, 2011) work provides detailed theoretical discussions of reasoning, inferences, rationality, metalogical understanding, metacognition, epistemic cognition and cognitive development. Higher-order thinking is considered to be inherently ambiguous (Lipman, 1991) and therefore a clarification would help to determine its relationship to metacognition, although the literature does recognise and establish, to some extent, this relationship (e.g. Resnick, 1987; Vockell and van Deusen, 1989). Future theoretical analysis of this relationship would be a contribution to this field.

The research possibilities (RP) related to metacognition and reflection provide rich areas of potential research (see Table 11.1).

Table 11.1 Metacognition and reflection research possibilities

RP.1	What is the relationship between reflective reasoning, metacognitive monitoring and control of inferences, and how do they facilitate critical thinking?
RP.2	What are the relationships between metacognitive processes, critical thinking and epistemological commitments?
RP.3	How does reflection become critical? Reflection becomes critical when self-correction is involved although this may not be metacognitive unless there is purposeful reflection or a 'higher level' of metacognition identified as complex thinking or higher-order thinking.
RP.4	What is the relationship between critical thinking and metacognition, especially related to Hartman and Sternberg's (1993) BACEIS model?
RP.5	How are Kuhn's (1999a) three categories of metacognition or meta-knowing – metacognitive, metastrategic, and epistemological – fundamental to critical thinking?
RP.6	What effect does reflection have on specific metacognitive components such as metamemory, metacomprehension and metaattention?
RP.7	What are the possible links between metamentation or mental reflexivity, metacognition and reflection?
RP.8	What are the relationships between metacognitive reflection and metacognitive knowledge of beliefs during complex problem solving?
RP.9	What is the effect during problem solving on metacognitive judgments or the conceptualisation of a problem, and problem-solving processes, including specific strategy knowledge?
RP.10	What is the effect of reflection on metacognitive attitudes towards the problem, including problem-solving effort, perseverance, and self-perception of problem solving ability?

Metamemory

Metamemory research has predominately investigated feeling and knowing phenomena. There is still potential in this field, especially in identifying what relationship exists between reflection and feeling and knowing phenomena. Any interrelationship would provide an insight into how each may support the other and what types of interactions may occur. Another possible area of research is identifying how context influences metamemory and what metamemory processes are more prevalent in different types of memory tasks.

There are many rich areas of potential research of metamemory, especially feeling and knowing phenomena. Many of these involve investigating the relationships between knowledge of memory and regulation of memory. They draw attention to the need to explore relationships and the influences of task complexity and beliefs on knowledge and regulation of memory.

The research possibilities (RP) related to metamemory provide other rich areas of potential research (see Table 11.2).

Table 11.2 Metamemory research possibilities

RP.11	What is the relationship between feeling and knowing phenomena and reflection?
RP.12	What are the effects of and interaction between various types of feeling and knowing phenomena, (e.g. judgment of uncertainty, feeling-of-warmth, confidence, and ease-of-learning judgments) and complex cognitive tasks?
RP.13	What is the relationship between various feeling and knowing phenomena and specific elements of metamemory? This would help to identify the connections between the action and theory.
RP.14	What is the relationship between Nelson and Narens' (1990) model or an adaptation of that model and monitoring and control processes, such as feeling and knowing phenomena and complex problem-solving contexts?
RP.15	What are the effect of beliefs on metamemorial processes such as feeling and knowing judgments, especially in complex tasks?
RP.16	What are the specific types of mnemonic strategies, including acquisition and retrieval strategies, used by adults and adolescents in complex tasks?
RP.17	What is the specific role that reflection and introspection play in regard to knowledge of memory and knowledge of regulation?
RP.18	What are the contextual or situational task influences on knowledge of memory and knowledge of regulation?
RP.19	What are the specific interactions between declarative metamemory and procedural metamemory?
RP.20	How does procedural metamemory interact with monitoring and control processes and how do these processes support the application of strategy?
RP.21	What are the influences of schematic and contextual knowledge in promoting or inhibiting memory performance and task solution success?
RP.22	In what ways do complex, novel task situations instigate the development and application of novel strategies?
RP.23	How do beliefs influence knowledge of memory and regulation of memory in complex, novel task situations?

Metacognition

There is a lack of research on the specific interactions between the person, task and strategy variables, especially in the context of complex problem solving. Not enough research has been carried out, specifically on Flavell's components of metacognition. Although there are theorists who have taken the construct a step further, a number have neglected this significant underpinning of the construct. This in itself has created a number of variations of the components or elements of metacognition. The *taxonomy of metacognition* resolves the component issue but there is a need for research on the interrelationships between the main categories of metacognition.

Pressley (2005) argues that 'skilled teaching is heavily metacognitive' (p. 394). Pressley is referring to teaching as reliant upon highly developed metacognitive processes which are applied to developing teaching strategies that are focused on creating learning opportunities that promote the development of metacognition in students. Are we training our teachers to teach metacognitively? Are we providing opportunities for teachers to create teaching strategies that are specifically focused on promoting learning in any context? Schunk (2008) explains that there is a need to investigate how to facilitate metacognition at different stages of development and how this research can translate into educational practice and teacher education. The *taxonomy of metacognition* could be used as a source of information about metacognition in preservice and inservice teacher education to develop teachers' understanding of what metacognition is, how it is immersed in pedagogy, and therefore how to teach metacognitively. Improved metacognitive knowledge and skills would greatly improve teaching and learning outcomes.

The amplification diagrams and the *conceptual framework of metacognition* could also be used as visual cognitive teaching tools to depict relationships between different concepts related to metacognition. Students and teachers can use the diagrams as a source of visual information to support discussions regarding the relationships between concepts. This could be very useful in cognitive, developmental and educational psychology classes.

The research possibilities (RP) related to metacognition within the context of complex problem solving provide other rich areas of potential research (see Table 11.3).

Other areas of research

The following is a list of other possible areas of research on metacognition. It is not intended to be exhaustive. Research could be both theoretical and empirical. This list does not imply that no research exists in these areas but they are in need of further investigation. In-depth theoretical analysis and investigation are needed of the relationship between:

- implicit metacognition and consciousness including how implicit metacognition informs explicit metacognition and vice versa;
- metacognition and motivation;

- other areas of self-regulation including conation, volition, self-efficacy, attribution and their relationship to metacognition;
- metacognition and affect;
- metacognition and epistemic cognition and how metacognition informs epistemic development;
- metacognition and agency;
- metamemory and neuroscience;
- metacognitive control and neuroimaging;
- metacognition and creativity;
- metacognition and transfer;
- metacognition and calibration;
- social metacognition and co-regulation;
- metacognition and the improvement of teacher education;
- metacognition and the improvement of pedagogical outcomes;
- metacognition and teacher beliefs;
- metacognition and self-system during complex problem solving; and
- metacognition and learned helplessness.

Table 11.3 Metacognition research possibilities

RP.24	What are the interrelationships between the person, task and strategy variables and the sensitivity category?
RP.25	What specific teaching strategies can be used to improve students' application of metacognitive knowledge and skills during complex problem solving?
RP.26	How does the self-system affect metacognition during complex problem solving?
RP.27	How do specific forms of metacognitive experiences interact with self-system beliefs during complex problem solving?
RP.28	How can purposeful self-reflexivity and awareness be improved in novice problem solvers to facilitate problem solving complex problems?
RP.29	How can we improve knowledge of task demands and complexity and the awareness of strategy development to meet these demands during complex problem solving?
RP.30	How can argumentation and justification be used to facilitate the development of specific metacognitive variables e.g. person, task and strategy?
RP.31	How does knowledge of self affect conditional knowledge? (There is scarce information regarding their connection.)

Conclusion

The *taxonomy of metacognition* and *conceptual framework of metacognition* intend to meet the needs of research and teaching communities by providing a comprehensive view and detailed depiction of the conceptual relationships which comprise the construct of metacognition. The main implications of this contribution are to:

- clarify the construct, enabling a more informed understanding of metacognition by teachers and researchers who are novices in the field;
- provide a detailed, reliable source for expert academics which can be used to extend their current research on metacognition;
- inform the development of curriculum in schools and higher education to improve learning outcomes for students;
- provide a detailed source of information which can be used develop metacognitively informed pedagogy;
- provide a clear framework and a source of information to form the theoretical basis of new and exciting empirical studies;
- provide a source for identifying the conceptual connections between categories of metacognition and therefore instigate original theoretical research on metacognition;
- reaffirm the theoretical roots of the construct from Brown, and Flavell and Wellman;
- identify gaps in theory and research and instigate further research;
- add significant value to theoretical discussions of metacognition and link the major theoretical contributions extending the theory;
- represent the interactions between the categories of metacognition, providing a more informed understanding of metacognition by teachers and researchers who are novices in the field; and
- reaffirm the status and importance of theoretical research as a foundation for reliable empirical studies.

This book has moved metacognition through what Brown *et al.* (1983) described as the third stage of theorisation, enabling a comprehensive understanding of the construct represented in the contributions demonstrated in the *taxonomy of metacognition* and *conceptual framework of metacognition.*

References

Abell, S. (2009). Thinking about thinking in science class. *Science and Children*, *46*(6), 56–57.

Ach, N. (1905). *Über die Willenstätigkeit und das Denken*. Göttingen: Vanderhoeck & Ruprecht.

Alexander, P. A. (2006). Evolution of a learning theory: A case study. *Educational Psychologist*, *41*(4), 257–264.

Anderson, J. R. (1982). Acquisition of cognitive skills. *Psychological Review*, *89*(4), 369–406.

Anderson, L. W., & Krathwohl, D. R. (Eds.) (2001). *A Taxonomy for Learning, Teaching and Assessing: A Revision of Bloom's Taxonomy of Educational Objectives*. New York: Addison Wesley Longman, Inc.

Andreassen, C., & Waters, H. S. (1989). Organization during study: Relationships between metamemory, strategy use, and performance. *Journal of Educational Psychology*, *81*(June), 190–195.

Antaki, C., & Lewis, C. (1986). Mental mirrors: Metacognition in social knowledge. In C. Antaki, & C. Lewis (Eds.), *Mental Mirrors: Metacognition in Social Knowledge and Communication* (pp. 1–10). London: Sage Publications Ltd.

Antonietti, A., Ignazi, S., & Perego, P. (2000). Metacognitive knowledge about problem-solving methods. *British Journal of Educational Psychology*, *70*, 1–16.

Appel, L. P., Cooper, R. G., McCarrell, N., Sims-Knight, J., Yussen, S. R., & Flavell, J. H. (1972). The development of the distinction between perceiving and memorizing. *Child Development*, *43*, 1365–1381.

Astington, J., Harris, P. L., & Olson, D. (Eds.) (1988). *Developing Theories of Mind*. Cambridge and New York: Cambridge University Press.

Augustine. (1991). *The Works of Saint Augustine: A Translation for the 21st Century* (E. Hill, Trans. Vol. 5: The Trinity, Part I – Books). Brooklyn, NY: New City Press.

Babbs, P., & Moe, A. (1983). Metacognition: A key for independent learning from text. *The Reading Teacher*, *35*, 422–426.

Babkie, A. M., & Provost, M. C. (2002). Select, write, and use metacognitive strategies in the classroom. *Intervention in School and Clinic*, *37*(3), 173–177.

Bailey, K. D. (1994). *Typologies and Taxonomies: An Introduction to Classification Techniques*. Thousand Oaks, CA: Sage Publications.

Baker, L. (1979). Comprehension monitoring: Identifying and coping with text confusions. *Journal of Reading Behavior*, *XI*(4), 365–374.

Baker, L. (1991). Metacognition, reading, and science education. In C. Santa, & D.

Alvermann (Eds.), *Science Learning: Processes and Applications* (pp. 2–13). Newark, DE: International Reading Association.

Baker, L., & Brown, A. L. (1984a). Cognitive monitoring in reading. In J. Flood (Ed.), *Understanding Reading Comprehension: Cognition, Language and the Structure of Prose* (pp. 21–44). Newark, DE: International Reading Association.

Baker, L., & Brown, A. L. (1984b). Metacognitive skills and reading. In P. D. Pearson, R. Barr, M. L. Kamil, & P. Mosenthal (Eds.), *Handbook of Reading Research* (pp. 353–394). New York: Longman.

Bakracevic Vukman, K. (2005). Developmental differences in metacognition and their connections with cognitive development in adulthood. *Journal of Adult Development, 12*(4), 211–221.

Baldwin, M. J. (1909). How children study. *Archives of Psychology, 12*, 65–70.

Bandura, A. (1989). Regulation of cognitive processes through perceived self-efficacy. *Developmental Psychology, 25*(5), 729–735.

Bandura, A. (1997). *Self-Efficacy: The Exercise of Control.* New York: Freeman.

Bandura, A., & Locke, E. A. (2003). Negative self-efficacy and goal effects revisited. *Journal of Applied Psychology, 88*(1), 87–99.

Baumeister, R. F., & Vohs, K. D. (2004). *Handbook of Self-Regulation: Research, Theory, and Applications.* New York and London: Guilford Press.

Beare, J. I. (1906). *Greek Theories of Elementary Cognition: From Alcmaeon to Aristotle.* Oxford: Clarendon Press.

Bellezza, F. S. (1996). Mnemonic methods to enhance storage and retrieval. In E. L. Bjork, & R. A. Bjork (Eds.), *Memory* (pp. 345–380). San Diego, CA: Academic Press, Inc.

Belmont, J. M., & Butterfield, E. C. (1969). The relations of short-term memory to development and intelligence. In L. C. Lipsitt, & H. W. Reese (Eds.), *Advances in Child Development and Behavior* (Vol. 4, pp. 29–82). New York: Academic Press, Inc.

Bendixen, L. D., & Hartley, K. (2003). Successful learning with hypermedia: The role of epistemological beliefs and metacognitive awareness. *Journal of Educational Computing Research, 28*(1), 15–30.

Berry, J. M. (1989). Cognitive efficacy across the life span: Introduction to the special series. *Developmental Psychology, 25*(5), 683–686.

Best, J. (1986). *Cognitive Psychology.* St Paul, MN: West Publishing Company.

Biggs, J. B. (1985). The role of metalearning in study processes. *British Journal of Educational Psychology, 55*, 185–212.

Binet, A. (1903). *L'Etude experimentale de l'intelligence.* Paris: Schleicher.

Binet, A. (1910). *Les idees modernes sur les enfants.* Paris: Ernest Flamarion.

Birenbaum, M., & Amdur, L. (1999). Reflective active learning in a graduate course on assessment. *Higher Education Research and Development, 18*(2), 201–218.

Blasi, A. (1983). The self and cognition: The roles of self in the acquisition of knowledge. In B. Lee, & G. Noam (Eds.), *Developmental Psychologies of the Self* (pp. 189–213). New York: Plenum Press.

Blasi, A., & Hoeffel, E. C. (1974). Adolescence and formal operations. *Human Development, 17*(5), 344–363.

Bloom, B. S. (1956). *Taxonomy of Educational Objectives: The Classification of Educational Goals. Handbook I: Cognitive Domain.* New York: Longman.

Bobrow, D. G. (1975). Dimensions for representation. In D. G. Bobrow, & A.

Collins (Eds.), *Representation and Understanding: Studies in Cognitive Science* (pp. 1–34). New York: Academic Press, Inc.

Boekaerts, M. (1995). Self-regulated learning: Bridging the gap between meta-cognitive and metamotivation theories. *Educational Psychologist, 30*(4), 195–200.

Boekaerts, M. (1997). Self-regulated learning: A new concept embraced by researchers, policy makers, educators, teachers, and students. *Learning and Instruction, 7*, 161–186.

Boekaerts, M. (1999a). Metacognitive experiences and motivational state as aspects of self-awareness: Review and discussion. *European Journal of Psychology of Education, XIV*(4), 571–584.

Boekaerts, M. (1999b). Self-regulated learning: Where we are today. *International Journal of Educational Research, 31*(6), 445–457.

Bogdan, R. J. (2000). *Minding Minds: Evolving a Flexive Mind by Interpreting Others*. Cambridge, MA: The MIT Press.

Boraas, J. (1924). *Teaching to Think*. New York: The Macmillian Company.

Borkowski, J. G. (1985). Signs of intelligence: Strategy generalization and meta-cognition. In S. R. Yussen (Ed.), *The Growth of Reflection in Children* (pp. 105–148). Orlando, FL: Academic Press, Inc.

Borkowski, J. G. (1996). Metacognition: Theory or chapter heading? *Learning and Individual Differences, 8*(4), 391–402.

Borkowski, J. G., & Cavanaugh, J. C. (1981). Metacognition and intelligence theory. In M. P. Friedman, J. P. Das, & N. O'Connor (Eds.), *Intelligence and Learning* (pp. 253–258). New York: Plenum Press.

Borkowski, J. G., & Turner, L. A. (1989). Transsituational characteristics of metacognition. In W. Schneider, & F. E. Weinert (Eds.), *Interactions Among Aptitude, Strategies and Knowledge in Cognitive Performance* (pp. 159–176). New York: Springer-Verlag.

Borkowski, J. G., & Muthukrishna, N. (1992). Moving metacognition into the classroom: 'Working Models' and effective strategy teaching. In M. Pressley, K. R. Harris, & J. T. Guthrie (Eds.), *Promoting Academic Competence and Literacy in School* (pp. 477–501). San Diego, CA: Academic Press, Inc.

Borkowski, J. G., Carr, M., & Pressley, M. (1987). 'Spontaneous' strategy use: Perspectives from metacognitive theory. *Intelligence, 11*, 61–75.

Borkowski, J. G., Johnston, M. B., & Reid, M. K. (1987). Metacognition, moti-vation, and the transfer of controlled performance. In S. J. Ceci (Ed.), *Handbook of Cognitive, Social, and Neuropsychological Aspects of Learning Disabilities* (pp. 147–174). Hillsdale, NJ: Lawrence Erlbaum Associates.

Borkowski, J. G., Milstead, M., & Hale, C. (1988). Components of children's metamemory: Implications of strategy generalization. In F. E. Weinert, & M. Perlmutter (Eds.), *Memory Development: Universal Changes and Individual Differences* (pp. 73–100). Hillsdale, NJ: Lawrence Erlbaum Associates.

Borkowski, J. G., Estrada, M. T., Milstead, M., & Hale, C. (1989). General problem-solving skills: Relations between metacognition and strategic processing. *Learning Disability Quarterly, 12*(Winter), 57–70.

Borkowski, J. G., Carr, M., Rellinger, E., & Pressley, M. (1990). Self-regulated cognition: Interdependence of metacognition, attributions, and self-esteem. In B. F. Jones, & L. Idol (Eds.), *Dimensions of Thinking and Cognitive Instruction* (pp. 53–92). Hillsdale, NJ: Lawrence Erlbaum Associates.

Borkowski, J. G., Chan, L. K. S., & Muthukrishna, N. (2000). A process-oriented model of metacognition: Links between motivation and executive functioning. In G. Schraw, & J. C. Impara (Eds.), *Issues in the Measurement of Metacognition* (pp. 1–43). Lincoln, NE: Buros Institute of Mental Measurements.

Boud, D., Keogh, R., & Walker, D. (1985a). Promoting reflection in learning: A model. In D. Boud, R. Keogh, & D. Walker (Eds.), *Reflection: Turning Experience into Learning* (pp. 18–40). London: Kogan Page.

Boud, D., Keogh, R., & Walker, D. (1985b). *Reflection: Turning Experience into Learning*. London: Kogan Page.

Bouffard, T., Bouchard, M., Goulet, G., Denoncourt, I., & Courture, N. (2005). Influence of achievement goals and self-efficacy on students' self-regulation and performance. *International Journal of Psychology*, *40*(6), 373–384.

Bowne, B. P. (1886). *Introduction to Psychological Theory*. New York: American.

Bowne, B. P. (1897). *Theory of Thought and Knowledge*. New York: Harper & Brothers.

Boylor, A. L. (2002). Expanding preservice teachers' metacognitive awareness of instructional planning through pedagogical agents. *Educational Technology Research and Development*, *50*(2), 5–22.

Braten, I. (1991a). Vygotsky as precursor to metacognitive theory: The concept of metacognition and its roots. *Scandinavian Journal of Educational Research*, *35*(3), 179.

Braten, I. (1991b). Vygotsky as precursor to metacognitive theory: II. Vygotsky as metacognitivist. *Scandinavian Journal of Educational Research*, *35*(4), 305–320.

Braten, I. (1992). Vygotsky as precursor to metacognitive theory: III. Recent metacognitive research within a Vygotskian framework. *Scandinavian Journal of Educational Research*, *36*(1), 3–19.

Bray, N. W., Huffman, L. F., & Fletcher, K. L. (1999). Developmental and intellectual differences in self-report and strategy use. *Developmental Psychology*, *35*(5), 1223–1236.

Brookfield, S. (1987). *Developing Critical Thinkers: Challenging Adults to Explore Alternative Ways of Thinking and Acting*. Buckingham, England: Open University Press.

Brookfield, S. (1990). Using critical incidents to explore learners' assumptions. In J. Mezirow (Ed.), *Fostering Critical Reflection in Adulthood: A Guide to Transformative and Emancipatory Learning* (pp. 177–193). San Francisco, CA: Jossey-Bass.

Brookfield, S. (1998). Critical thinking techniques. In M. W. Galbraith (Ed.), *Adult Learning Methods: A Guide for Effective Instruction* (pp. 317–336). Malabar, FL: Krieger Publishing Company.

Brown, A. L. (1974). The role of strategic behavior in retardate memory. In N. R. Ellis (Ed.), *International Review of Research in Mental Retardation* (Vol. 7, pp. 55–111). New York: Academic Press, Inc.

Brown, A. L. (1975). The development of memory: Knowing, knowing about knowing, and knowing how to know. In H. W. Reese (Ed.), *Advances in Child Development and Behavior* (Vol. 10, pp. 104–152). New York: Academic Press, Inc.

Brown, A. L. (1977). Development, schooling, and the acquisition of knowledge about knowledge. In R. C. Anderson, R. J. Spiro, & W. E. Montague (Eds.), *Schooling and the Acquisition of Knowledge* (pp. 241–253). Hillsdale, NJ: Lawrence Erlbaum Associates.

Brown, A. L. (1978). Knowing when, where and how to remember: A problem of metacognition. In R. Glaser (Ed.), *Advances in Instructional Psychology* (pp. 77–165). New York: Halsted Press.

Brown, A. L. (1980). Metacognitive development and reading. In R. J. Spiro, B. Bruce, & W. Brewer (Eds.), *Theoretical Issues in Reading Comprehension: Perspectives from Cognitive Psychology, Linguistics, Artificial Intelligence, and Education* (pp. 453–481). Hillsdale, NJ: Lawrence Erlbaum Associates.

Brown, A. L. (1981). Metacognition: The development of selective attention strategies for learning from texts. In M. L. Kamil (Ed.), *Directions in Reading: Research and Instruction* (pp. 21–43). Washington, DC: National Reading Conference.

Brown, A. L. (1987). Metacognition, executive control, self-regulation, and other more mysterious mechanisms. In F. E. Weinert, & R. H. Kluwe (Eds.), *Metacognition, Motivation and Understanding* (pp. 65–116). Hillsdale, NJ: Lawrence Erlbaum Associates.

Brown, A. L. (1997). Transforming schools into communities of thinking and learning about serious matters. *American Psychologist, 52*(4), 399–413.

Brown, A. L., & Barclay, C. R. (1976). The effects of training-specific mnemonics on the metamnemonic efficiency of retarded children. *Child Development, 47*, 71–80.

Brown, A. L., & Campione, J. C. (1977). Training strategic study time apportionment in educable retarded children. *Intelligence, 1*, 94–107.

Brown, A. L., & Lawton, S. C. (1977). The feeling of knowing experience in educable retarded children. *Developmental Psychology, 13*, 364–370.

Brown, A. L., & Smiley, S. S. (1977). Rating the importance of structural units of prose strategies: A problem of metacognitive development. *Child Development, 48*, 1–8.

Brown, A. L., & DeLoache, J. S. (1978). Skills, plans, and self-regulation. In R. S. Siegler (Ed.), *Children's Thinking: What Develops?* (pp. 3–35). Hillsdale, NJ: Lawrence Erlbaum Associates.

Brown, A. L., & Campione, J. C. (1981). Inducing flexible thinking: The problem of access. In M. P. Friedman, & N. O'Connor (Eds.), *Intelligence and Learning* (pp. 515–529). New York: Plenum Press.

Brown, A. L., & Palincsar, A. S. (1982). Inducing strategic learning from texts by means of informed, self-control training. *Topics in Learning and Learning Disabilities, 7*(2), 1–17.

Brown, A. L., & Campione, J. C. (1986). Psychological theory and the study of learning disabilities. *American Psychologist, 14*(10), 1059–1068.

Brown, A. L., & Palincsar, A. S. (1989). Guided, cooperative learning and individual knowledge acquisition. In L. B. Resnick (Ed.), *Knowing, Learning, and Instruction: Essays in Honor of Robert Glaser* (pp. 393–451). Hillsdale, NJ: Lawrence Erlbaum Associates.

Brown, A. L., & Campione, J. C. (1996). Psychological learning theory and the design of innovative learning environments: On procedures, principles, and systems. In L. Schauble, & R. Glaser (Eds.), *Innovations in Learning: New Environments for Education* (pp. 289–325). Hillsdale, NJ: Lawrence Erlbaum Associates.

Brown, A. L., Bransford, J. D., Ferrara, R. A., & Campione, J. C. (1983). Learning, remembering, and understanding. In J. H. Flavell, & M. E. Markman (Eds.),

Handbook of Child Psychology (4th ed., Vol. III, Cognitive Development, pp. 77–166). New York: Wiley.

Brown, A. L., Armbruster, B. B., & Baker, L. (1986). The role of metacognition in reading and studying. In J. Orasanu (Ed.), *Reading Comprehension from Research to Practice* (pp. 49–75). Hillsdale, NJ: Lawrence Erlbaum Associates.

Brown, A. L., Ellery, S., & Campione, J. C. (1998). Creating zones of proximal development electronically. In J. G. Greeno, & S. Goldman (Eds.), *Thinking Practices in Mathematics and Science Learning* (pp. 341–367). Hillsdale, NJ: Lawrence Erlbaum Associates.

Brown, C., Hedberg, J., & Harper, B. (1994). Metacognition as a basis for learning support software. *Performance Improvement Quarterly, 7*(2), 3–26.

Brown, R., & McNeil, D. (1966). The 'tip of the tongue' phenomenon. *Journal of Verbal Learning and Verbal Behavior, 5,* 325–337.

Bruner, J. (1964). The course of cognitive growth. *American Psychologist, 19,* 1–15.

Bruner, J. (1985). Vygotsky: A historical and conceptual perspective. In J. V. Wertsch (Ed.), *Culture, Communication, and Cognition: Vygotskian Perspectives* (pp. 21–34). Cambridge: Cambridge University Press.

Bruning, R. H., Schraw, G. J., & Ronning, R. R. (1999). *Cognitive Psychology and Instruction* (3rd ed.). Upper Saddle River, NJ: Merrill.

Bryson, M., & Scardamalia, M. (1996). Fostering reflectivity in the argumentative thinking of students with different learning histories. *Reading and Writing Quarterly: Overcoming Learning Difficulties, 12,* 351–384.

Butler, D. L., & Winne, P. H. (1995). Feedback and self-regulated learning: A theoretical synthesis. *Review of Educational Research, 65*(3), 245–281.

Butterfield, E. C. (1994). Metacognition. In R. J. Sternberg (Ed.), *Encyclopedia of Human Intelligence* (Vol. 2, pp. 725–732). New York: Macmillian Publishing Company.

Butterfield, E. C., Wambold, C., & Belmont, J. M. (1973). On the theory and practice of improving short-term memory. *American Journal of Mental Deficiency, 77,* 654–669.

Butterfield, E. C., Nelson, T. O., & Peck, V. (1988). Developmental aspects of the feeling of knowing. *Developmental Psychology, 24,* 654–663.

Callison, D. (2001). Scaffolding. *School Library Media Activities Monthly, 17*(6), 37–39.

Campione, J. C. (1987). Metacognitive components of instructional research with problem learners. In F. E. Weinert, & R. H. Kluwe (Eds.), *Metacognition Motivation and Understanding* (pp. 117–140). Hillsdale, NJ: Lawrence Erlbaum Associates.

Campione, J. C., & Brown, A. L. (1974). The effects of contextual changes and degree of component mastery of transfer training. In H. W. Reese (Ed.), *Advances in Child Development and Behavior* (Vol. 9, pp. 69–114). New York: Academic Press, Inc.

Campione, J. C., & Brown, A. L. (1977). Memory and metamemory development in educable retarded children. In R. V. Kail, & J. W. Hagen (Eds.), *Perspectives on the Development of Memory and Cognition* (pp. 367–406). Hillsdale, NJ: Lawrence Erlbaum Associates.

Carnap, R. (1934). *Logische Syntax der Sprache.* Vienna: Springer.

Cary, M., & Reder, L. (2002). Metacognition in strategy selection: Giving consciousness too much credit. In P. Chambres, M. Izaute, & P.-J. Marescaux (Eds.),

Metacognition: Process, Function and Use (pp. 63–77). Dordrecht, Boston, London: Kluwer Academic Publishers.

Cavanaugh, J. C. (1996). Memory self-efficacy as a moderator of memory change. In F. Blanchard-Fields, & T. M. Hess (Eds.), *Perspectives on Cognitive Change in Adulthood and Aging* (pp. 488–507). New York: McGraw-Hill.

Cavanaugh, J. C., & Borkowski, J. G. (1979). The metamemory-memory connection: Effects of strategy training and maintenance. *The Journal of General Psychology, 101*, 161–174.

Cavanaugh, J. C., & Borkowski, J. G. (1980). Searching for memory–metamemory connection: Effects of strategy training and maintenance. *Journal of General Psychology, 16*, 441–453.

Cavanaugh, J. C., & Perlmutter, M. (1982). Metamemory: A critical examination. *Child Development, 53*, 11–28.

Chambres, P., Marescaux, P.-J., & Izaute, M. (2002). Preface. In P. Chambres, P.-J. Marescaux, & M. Izaute (Eds.), *Metacognition: Process, Function and Use* (pp. xi–xvi). Boston, MA: Kluwer Academic.

Cheng, P. (1999). Cognition, metacognition, and metacognitive theory: A critical analysis. *The Korean Journal of Thinking and Problem Solving, 9*(1), 85–103.

Chi, M. (1978). Knowledge structures and memory development. In R. S. Siegler (Ed.), *Children's Thinking: What Develops?* (pp. 73–96). Hillsdale, NJ: Lawrence Erlbaum Associates.

Chi, M. (1987). Representing knowledge and metaknowledge: Implications for interpreting metamemory research. In F. E. Weinert, & R. H. Kluwe (Eds.), *Metacognition, Motivation, and Understanding* (pp. 239–266). Hillsdale, NJ: Lawrence Erlbaum Associates.

Cho, K.-L., & Jonassen, D. H. (2002). The effects of argumentation scaffolds on argumentation and problem solving. *Educational Technology Research and Development, 50*(3), 5–22.

Cicognani, A. (2000). Concept mapping as a collaborative tool for enhanced online learning. *Educational Technology and Society, 3*(3), 150–158.

Commons, M. L., Richards, F. A., & Armon, C. (Eds.) (1984). *Beyond Formal Operations: Late Adolescent and Adult Cognitive Development.* New York: Praeger Publishers.

Corno, L. (1986). The metacognitive control components of self-regulated learning. *Contemporary Educational Psychology, 11*, 333–346.

Cornoldi, C. (1998). The impact of metacognitive reflection on cognitive control. In G. Mazzoni, & T. O. Nelson (Eds.), *Metacognition and Cognitive Neuropsychology: Control and Monitoring Processes* (pp. 139–160). Mahwah, NJ: Lawrence Erlbaum Associates.

Cornoldi, C., & Vianello, R. (1992). Metacognitive knowledge, learning disorders and mental retardation. In T. E. Scruggs, & M. Mastropieri (Eds.), *Advances in Learning and Behavioral Disabilities* (Vol. 7, pp. 87–134). Greenwich, CT: JAI Press.

Cornoldi, C., Gobbo, C., & Mazzoni, G. (1991). On metamemory–memory relationship: Strategy availability and training. *International Journal of Behavioral Development, 14*(1), 101–121.

Corsini, D. A. (1971). Memory: Interaction of stimulus and organismic factors. *Human Development, 14*, 227–235.

Cowan, N. (1997). *The Development of Memory in Childhood*. Hove, East Sussex, UK: Psychology Press.

Cullen, J. L. (1985). Children's ability to cope with failure: Implications for a metacognitive approach for the classroom. In D. L. Forrest-Pressley, G. E. MacKinnon, & T. Gary Waller (Eds.), *Metacognition, Cognition and Human Performance: Instructional Practices* (Vol. 2, pp. 269–300). London: Academic Press, Inc.

Cunningham, J. G., & Weaver, S. L. (1989). Young children's knowledge of their memory span: Effects of task and experience. *Journal of Experimental Psychology*, *48*(1), 32–44.

Daley, B. J. (2002). Facilitating learning with adult students through concept mapping. *Journal of Continuing Higher Education*, *50*(1), 21–31.

Darling, S., Della Sala, S., Gray, C., & Trivelli, C. (1998). Putative functions of the prefrontal cortex: Historical perspectives and new horizons. In G. Mazzoni, & T. O. Nelson (Eds.), *Metacognition and Cognitive Neuropsychology: Monitoring and Control* (pp. 53–95): Mahwah, NJ: Lawrence Erlbaum Associates.

Davidson, J. E., & Sternberg, R. J. (1998). Smart problem solving: How meta-cognition helps. In D. J. Hacker, J. Dunlosky, & A. C. Graesser (Eds.), *Metacognition in Educational Theory and Practice* (pp. 47–68). Mahwah, NJ: Lawrence Erlbaum Associates.

Descartes, R. (1986). *Meditations on First Philosophy* (J. Cottingham, R. Stoothoff, D. Murdoch, & A. Kenny, Trans.). Cambridge and New York: Cambridge University Press.

Deshler, D. (1990). Conceptual mapping: Drawing charts of the mind. In J. Mezirow (Ed.), *Fostering Critical Reflection in Adulthood: A Guide to Transformative and Emancipatory Learning* (pp. 336–353). San Francisco, CA: Jossey-Bass.

Desoete, A., Roeyers, H., & Buysse, A. (2001). Metacognition and mathematical problem solving in grade 3. *Journal of Learning Disabilities*, *34*(5), 435–449.

Dewey, J. (1933). *How We Think: A Restatement of the Relation of Reflective Thinking to the Educative Process*. Boston and New York: D. C. Heath and company.

Dienes, Z., & Perner, J. (2002). The metacognitive implications of the implicit–explicit distinction. In P. Chambres, M. Izaute, & P.-J. Marescaux (Eds.), *Metacognition: Process, Function and Use* (pp. 171–189). Dordrecht, Boston, London: Kluwer Academic Publishers.

Digby, G., & Lewis, C. (1986). *Training Children to Use Mnemonic Skills: What Causes Improvements in Memory Performance?* Paper presented at the Conference of the Developmental Psychology Section of the British Psychological Society, Exeter, England (ERIC Document Reproduction Service No. ED 280 568).

Dinsmore, D. L., Alexander, P. A., & Loughlin, S. M. (2008). Focusing the conceptual lens on metacognition, self-regulation, and self-regulated learning. *Educational Psychology Review*, *20*(4), 391–409.

Dixon, R. A., & Hertzog, C. (1988). A functional approach to memory and metamemory development in adulthood. In F. E. Weinert, & M. Perlmutter (Eds.), *Memory Development: Universal Changes and Individual Differences* (pp. 293–330). Hillsdale, NJ: Lawrence Erlbaum Associates.

Dominowski, R. L. (1998). Verbalization and problem solving. In D. J. Hacker, J.

Dunlosky, & A. C. Graesser (Eds.), *Metacognition in Educational Theory and Practice* (pp. 25–45). Mahwah, NJ: Lawrence Erlbaum Associates.

Duffy, T., & Cunningham, D. J. (1996). Constructivism: Implications for the design and delivery of instruction. In D. H. Jonassen (Ed.), *Handbook of Research for Educational Communications and Technology. A Project of the Association for Educational Communications and Technology* (pp. 170–198). New York: Simon & Schuster, Macmillan.

Dunlosky, J. (1998). Epilogue: Linking metacognitive theory to education. In D. J. Hacker, J. Dunlosky, & A. C. Graesser (Eds.), *Metacognition in Educational Theory and Practice* (pp. 367–381). Mahwah, NJ: Lawrence Erlbaum Associates.

Dunlosky, J., & Hertzog, C. (1998). Training programs to improve learning in later adulthood: Helping older adults educate themselves. In D. J. Hacker, J. Dunlosky, & A. C. Graesser (Eds.), *Metacognition in Educational Theory and Practice* (pp. 249–275). Mahwah, NJ: Lawrence Erlbaum Associates.

Dunlosky, J., & Bjork, R. A. (2008a). The integrated nature of metamemory and memory. In J. Dunlosky, & R. A. Bjork (Eds.), *Handbook of Metamemory and Memory* (pp. 11–28). New York, Hove: Psychology Press, Taylor and Francis.

Dunlosky, J., & Bjork, R. A. (Eds.) (2008b). *Handbook of Metamemory and Memory*. New York and Hove: Psychology Press, Taylor and Francis.

Dunlosky, J., & Metcalfe, J. (2009). *Metacognition*. Thousand Oaks, CA: Sage Publications Ltd.

Efklides, A. (2001). Metacognitive experiences in problem solving: Metacognition, motivation, and self-regulation. In A. Efklides, J. Kuhl, & R. M. Sorrentino (Eds.), *Trends and Prospects in Motivation Research* (pp. 297–324). Dordrecht, Netherlands: Kluwer Academic Publishers.

Efklides, A. (2002). The systemic nature of metacognitive experiences. In P. Chambres, M. Izaute, & P.-J. Marescaux (Eds.), *Metacognition: Process, Function and Use* (pp. 19–34). Dordrecht, Netherlands: Kluwer Academic Publishers.

Efklides, A. (2003). *Metacognition and Affect: What Can Metacognitive Experiences Tell Us About the Learning Process?* Paper presented at the 10th European Association for Research on Learning and Instruction, Padova, Italy.

Efklides, A. (2006). Metacognitive experiences: The missing link in the self-regulated learning process. *Educational Psychology Review, 18*(3), 287–291.

Efklides, A. (2008). Metacognition: Defining its facets and levels of functioning in relation to self-regulation and co-regulation. *European Psychologist, 13*(4), 277–287.

Efklides, A., & Vauras, M. (1999). Metacognitive experiences and their role in cognition (special issue). *European Journal of Psychology of Education, XIV*(4), 455–459.

Efklides, A., & Tsiora, A. (2002). Metacognitive experiences, self-concept, and self-regulation. *Psychologia: An International Journal of Psychology in the Orient, 45*, 222–236.

Efklides, A., & Volet, S. E. (2005). Emotional experiences during learning: Multiple, situated and dynamic. *Learning and Instruction, 15*(5), 377–380.

Efklides, A., Demetriou, A., & Metallidou, Y. (1994). The structure and development of propositional reasoning ability: Cognitive and metacognitive aspects. In A. Demetriou, & A. Efklides (Eds.), *Intelligence, Mind, and Reasoning: Structure and Development* (pp. 151–172). Amsterdam: North-Holland.

Efklides, A., Niemivirta, M., & Yamauchi, H. (2002). Introduction: Some issues on self-regulation to consider. *Psychologia: An International Journal of Psychology in the Orient*, *45*, 207–210.

Elder, L., & Paul, R. (2001). Critical thinking: Thinking to some purpose. *Journal of Developmental Education*, *25*(1), 40–41.

Ellis, D., & Zimmerman, B. J. (2001). Enhancing self-monitoring during self-regulated learning of speech. In H. J. Hartman (Ed.), *Metacognition in Learning and Instruction: Theory, Research and Practice* (pp. 205–228). Dordrecht, Netherlands: Kluwer Academic Publishers.

Ennis, R. H. (1987). A taxonomy of critical thinking dispositions and abilities. In J. Boykoff Baron, & R. J. Sternberg (Eds.), *Teaching Thinking Skills: Theory and Practice* (pp. 9–26). New York: W H Freeman & Co.

Ennis, R. H. (1993). Critical thinking assessment. *Theory Into Practice*, *32*(3), 179–186.

Ertmer, P. A., & Newby, T. J. (1996). The expert learner: Strategic, self-regulated, and reflective. *Instructional Science*, *24*(1), 1–24.

Eteläpelto, A. (1993). Metacognition and the expertise of computer program comprehension. *Scandinavian Journal of Educational Research*, *37*(3), 243–254.

Ferry, B., & Brown, C. (1998). The influence of reflective tools on teaching strategies and subject design. In R. M. Corderoy (Ed.), *Proceedings of the 15th Annual Conference of the Australasian Society for Computers in Learning in Tertiary Education* (pp. 231–239). Wollongong, NSW: University of Wollongong.

Fischer, K. W., & Pruyne, E. (2002). Reflective thinking in adulthood: Emergence, development, and variation. In J. Demick, & C. Andreoletti (Eds.), *Handbook of Adult Development* (pp. 169–198). New York: Plenum Press.

Flavell, J. H. (1963). *The Developmental Psychology of Jean Piaget*. Princeton, NJ: Van Nostrand.

Flavell, J. H. (1970). Developmental studies in mediated memory. *Advances in Child Development*, *5*, 182–209.

Flavell, J. H. (1971a). First discussant's comments: What is memory development the development of? *Human Development*, *14*, 272–278.

Flavell, J. H. (1971b). Stage-related properties of cognitive development. *Cognitive Psychology*, *2*, 421–453.

Flavell, J. H. (1976). Metacognitive aspects of problem solving. In L. B. Resnick (Ed.), *The Nature of Intelligence* (pp. 231–235). Hillsdale, NJ: Lawrence Erlbaum Associates.

Flavell, J. H. (1977). *Cognitive Development*. Englewood Cliffs, NJ: Prentice-Hall.

Flavell, J. H. (1978). Metacognitive development. In J. M. Scandura, & C. J. Brainerd (Eds.), *Structural Process Theories of Complex Human Behavior* (pp. 213–245). Alphen aan den Rijn, The Netherlands: Sijthoff and Noordhoff.

Flavell, J. H. (1979). Metacognition and cognitive monitoring – A new area of cognitive–developmental inquiry. *American Psychologist*, *34*(10), 906–911.

Flavell, J. H. (1981a). Cognitive monitoring. In W. P. Dickson (Ed.), *Children's Oral Communication Skills* (pp. 35–60). New York: Academic.

Flavell, J. H. (1981b). Monitoring social cognitive enterprises: Something else that may develop in the area of social cognition. In J. H. Flavell, & L. Ross (Eds.), *Social Cognitive Development: Frontiers and Possible Futures* (pp. 272–287). Cambridge, UK: Cambridge University Press.

Flavell, J. H. (1987). Speculations about the nature and development of metacognition. In F. E. Weinert, & R. H. Kluwe (Eds.), *Metacognition,*

Motivation, and Understanding (pp. 21–29). Hillsdale, NJ: Lawrence Erlbaum Associates.

Flavell, J. H. (1993). Young children's understanding of thinking and consciousness. *Current Directions in Psychological Science, 2*(2, April), 40–43.

Flavell, J. H. (2004). Theory-of-mind development: Retrospect and prospect. *Merrill-Palmer Quarterly, 50*(3), 274–290.

Flavell, J. H., & Wellman, H. M. (1977). Metamemory. In R. V. Kail, & W. Hagen (Eds.), *Perspectives on the Development of Memory and Cognition.* Hillsdale, NJ: Lawrence Erlbaum Associates.

Flavell, J. H., Friedrichs, A. G., & Hoyt, J. D. (1970). Developmental changes in memorization processes. *Cognitive Psychology, 1*, 324–340.

Flavell, J. H., Miller, P. H., & Miller, S. A. (1993). *Cognitive Development* (3rd ed.). Englewood Cliffs, NJ: Prentice-Hall.

Flavell, J. H., Green, F. L., & Flavell, E. R. (2000). Development of children's awareness of their own thoughts. *Journal of Cognition and Development, 1*, 97–112.

Flavell, J. H., Miller, P. H., & Miller, S. A. (2002). *Cognitive Development* (4th ed.). Upper Saddle River, NJ: Prentice-Hall.

Fletcher, P. C., & Henson, R. N. A. (2001). Frontal lobes and human memory: Insights from functional neuroimaging. *Brain, 124*(5), 849–881.

Fox, E., & Riconscente, M. (2008). Metacognition and self-regulation in James, Piaget, and Vygotsky. *Educational Psychology Review, 20*, 373–389.

Freire, P. (1973). *Education for the Critical Consciousness.* New York: The Continuum Publishing Company.

Funnell, M., Metcalfe, J., & Tsapkini, K. (1996). In the mind but not on the tongue: Feeling of knowing in an anomic patient. In L. Reder (Ed.), *Implicit Memory and Metacognition* (pp. 171–193). Mahwah, NJ: Lawrence Erlbaum Associates.

Gage, N. L., & Berliner, D. C. (1984). *Educational Psychology.* Boston, MA: Houghton Mifflin Company.

Gagné, R. M. (1977). *The Conditions of Learning* (3rd ed.). New York: Holt, Rinehart and Winston.

Garner, R. (1987). *Metacomprehension and Reading Comprehension.* Norwood, NJ: Ablex Publishing Corporation.

Garner, R. (1990). When children and adults do not use learning strategies: Toward a theory of settings. *Review of Educational Research, 60*(4), 517–529.

Garner, R. (1994). Metacognition and executive control. In R. B. Ruddell, M. Ruddell, & H. Singer (Eds.), *Theoretical Models and Processes of Reading* (pp. 715–732). Newark, DE: International Reading Association.

Garner, R., & Alexander, P. A. (1989). Metacognition: Answered and unanswered questions. *Educational Psychologist, 24*(2), 143–158.

Gaskins, I. W., Rauch, S., Gensemer, E., Cunicelli, C., O'Hara, C., Six, L., & Scott, T. (1997). Scaffolding the development of intelligence among children who are delayed in learning to read. In K. Hogan, & M. Pressley (Eds.), *Scaffolding: A Powerful Tool in Social Constructivist Classrooms* (pp. 43–73). Cambridge, MA: Brookline Books.

Gathercole, S. E. (1998). The development of memory. *The Journal of Child Psychology and Psychiatry and Allied Disciplines, 39*(Jan), 3–27.

Georghiades, P. (2004). From general to the situated: Three decades of meta-cognition. *International Journal of Science Education, 26*(3), 365–383.

Ghatala, E. S., Levin, J. R., Pressley, M., & Lodico, M. G. (1985). Training cognitive strategy-monitoring in children. *American Educational Research Journal, 22*, 199–215.

Goos, M., Galbraith, P., & Renshaw, P. (2002). Socially mediated metacognition: Creating collaborative zones of proximal development in small group problem solving. *Educational Studies in Mathematics, 49*(2), 193–223.

Gourgey, A. F. (1998). Metacognition in basic skills instruction. *Instructional Science, 26*(1–2), 81–96.

Gourgey, A. F. (2001). Metacognition in basic skills instruction. In H. J. Hartman (Ed.), *Metacognition in Learning and Instruction* (pp. 17–32). Dordrecht, Netherlands: Kluwer Academic Publishers.

Greene, M. (1990). Realizing literature's emancipatory potential. In J. Mezirow and Associates (Eds.), *Fostering Critical Reflection in Adulthood: A Guide to Transformative and Emancipatory Learning* (pp. 251–268). San Francisco, CA: Jossey-Bass Publishers.

Grimes, P. W. (2002). The overconfident principles of economics students: An examination of a metacognitive skill. *The Journal of Economic Education, 33*(1), 15–30.

Habermas, J. (1987). *Knowledge and Human Interests* (J. J. Shapiro, Trans.). Cambridge: Polity.

Hacker, D. J. (1998). Metacognition: Definitions and empirical foundations. In D. J. Hacker, J. Dunlosky, & A. C. Graesser (Eds.), *Metacognition in Educational Theory and Practice* (pp. 1–23). Mahwah, NJ: Lawrence Erlbaum Associates.

Hagen, J. W., & Kingsley, P. R. (1968). Labeling effects in short-term memory. *Child Development, 39*, 113–121.

Hagen, J. W., & Stanovich, K. G. (1977). Memory: Strategies of acquisition. In R. V. Kail, & J. W. Hagen (Eds.), *Perspectives on the Development of Memory and Cognition* (pp. 89–112). Hillsdale, NJ: Lawrence Erlbaum Associates.

Hall, L. K., & Bahrick, H. P. (1998). The validity of metacognitive predictions of widespread learning and long-term retention. In G. Mazzoni, & T. O. Nelson (Eds.), *Metacognition and Cognitive Neuropsychology: Monitoring and Control* (pp. 23–36). Mahwah, NJ: Lawrence Erlbaum Associates.

Hanley, G. L. (1995). Teaching critical thinking: Focusing on metacognitive skills and problem solving. *Teaching of Psychology, 22*(1), 68–72.

Hart, J. T. (1965). Memory and the feeling-of-knowing experience. *Journal of Educational Psychology, 56*, 208–216.

Hart, J. T. (1966). Methodological note on feeling-of-knowing experience. *Journal of Educational Psychology, 56*, 208–216.

Hart, J. T. (1967a). Memory and the memory monitoring process. *Journal of Verbal Learning and Behavior, 6*, 685–691.

Hart, J. T. (1967b). Second-try recall and the memory monitoring process. *Journal of Educational Psychology, 58*, 193–197.

Hartman, H. J. (2001a). Developing students' metacognitive knowledge and skills. In H. J. Hartman (Ed.), *Metacognition in Learning and Instruction: Theory, Research and Practice* (pp. 33–68). Dordrecht, Netherlands: Kluwer Academic Publishers.

Hartman, H. J. (2001b). Metacognition in science teaching and learning. In H. J. Hartman (Ed.), *Metacognition in Learning and Instruction: Theory, Research and Practice* (pp. 173–201). Dordrecht, Netherlands: Kluwer Academic Publishers.

Hartman, H. J. (Ed.) (2001c). *Metacognition in Learning and Instruction: Theory, Research and Practice*. Dordrecht, Netherlands: Kluwer Academic Publishers.

Hartman, H. J., & Sternberg, R. J. (1993). A broad BACEIS for improving thinking. *Instructional Science, 21*, 401–425.

Hatton, N., & Smith, D. (1995). Facilitating reflection: Issues and research. *Forum of Education, 50*(1), 49–65.

Hauenstein, A. D. (1998). *A New Conceptual Framework for Educational Objectives*. Lanham, MD: University Press of America.

Healy, A., & Sinclair, G. P. (1996). The long-term retention of training and instruction. In E. L. Bjork, & R. A. Bjork (Eds.), *Memory* (pp. 525–564). San Diego, CA: Academic Press, Inc.

Hedberg, J., Harper, B., Lockyer, L., Ferry, B., Brown, C., & Wright, R. (1998). Supporting learners to solve ill-structured problems. In R. M. Corderoy (Ed.), *Proceedings of the 15th Annual Conference of the Australasian Society for Computers in Learning in Tertiary Education* (pp. 317–327). Wollongong, NSW: University of Wollongong.

Hertzog, C., & Dixon, R. A. (1994). Metacognitive development in adulthood and old age. In J. Metcalfe, & A. P. Shimamura (Eds.), *Metacognition: Knowing about Knowing* (pp. 227–251). Cambridge: The MIT Press.

Hertzog, C., Hultsch, D. F., & Dixon, R. A. (1989). Evidence for the convergent validity of two self-report metamemory questionnaires. *Developmental Psychology, 25*, 687–700.

Hertzog, C., Dunlosky, J., Robinson, A. E., & Kidder, D. P. (2003). Encoding fluency is a cue used for judgments about learning. *Journal of Experimental Psychology, Learning, Memory and Cognition, 29*(1), 22–34.

Hilbert, D. (1927). Über das Unendliche. *Jahresbericht der Deutschen Mathematiker-Vereinigung, 36*, 201–215.

Hine, A. (2000). *Mirroring Effective Education Through Mentoring, Metacognition and Self-Reflection*. Paper presented at the Australian Association for Research in Education Conference, Sydney, Australia. Retrieved April 16, 2002 from http://www.aare.edu.au/00pap/hin00017.htm

Hine, A., Newman, H., & Peacock, L. (2001). Self reflection strategies for change. *The Korean Journal of Thinking and Problem Solving, 11*(2), 37–48.

Hirst, W. (1982). The amnesic syndrome: Descriptions and explanations. *Psychological Bulletin, 91*, 435–460.

Hofer, B. K., & Pintrich, P. R. (1997). The development of epistemological theories: Beliefs about knowledge and knowing and their relation to learning. *Review of Educational Research, 67*(1), 88–140.

Howard-Rose, D., & Winne, P. H. (1993). Measuring component and sets of cognitive processes in self-regulated learning. *Journal of Educational Psychology, 85*(4), 591–604.

Huberman, A. M., & Miles, M. B. (1998). Data management and analysis methods. In N. K. Denzin, & Y. S. Lincoln (Eds.), *Collecting and Interpreting Qualitative Materials* (pp. 179–210). Thousand Oaks, CA: Sage Publications.

Huet, N., & Marine, C. (1997). Metamemory assessment and memory behavior in a simulated memory professional task. *Contemporary Educational Psychology, 22*(4), 507–520.

Inhelder, B., & Piaget, J. (1958). *The Growth of Logical Thinking from Childhood to*

Adolescence: An Essay on the Construction of Formal Operational Structures (A. Parson & S. Milgram, Trans.). London: Routledge Kegan & Paul.

Iran-Nejad, A., & Gregg, M. (2001). The brain–mind cycle of reflection. *Teachers College Record, 103*(5), 868–895.

Izaute, M., Chambres, P., & Larochelle, S. (2002). Feeling-of-knowing for proper names. *Canadian Journal of Experimental Psychology, 56*(4), 263–272.

Jacob, E. (1992). Culture, context, and cognition. In M. D. LeCompte, W. L. Millroy, & J. Preissle (Eds.), *The Handbook of Qualitative Research in Education* (pp. 293–336). San Diego, CA: Academic Press, Inc.

Jacobs, J. E., & Paris, S. G. (1987). Children's metacognition about reading: Issues in definition, measurement, and instruction. *Educational Psychologist, 22*, 255–278.

James, W. (1890a). *The Principles of Psychology* (Vol. 1). New York: Holt.

James, W. (1890b). *The Principles of Psychology* (Vol. 2). New York: Holt.

James, W. (1892). *The Stream of Consciousness*. Retrieved Sept, 2003, from http://psychclassics.yorku.ca/James/jimmy11.htm

Janowsky, J. S., Shimamura, A. P., & Squire, L. R. (1989). Memory and meta-memory: Comparisons between patients with frontal lobe lesions and amnesic patients. *Psychobiology, 17*(1), 3–11.

Jaušovec, N. (1994a). The influence of metacognition on problem-solving performance. *Review of Psychology, 1*, 21–28.

Jaušovec, N. (1994b). Metacognition in creative problem solving. In M. A. Runco (Ed.), *Problem Finding, Problem Solving, and Creativity* (pp. 77–95). Norwood, NJ: Ablex Publishing Corporation.

Jonassen, D. H. (1996). *Computers in the Classroom: Mindtools for Critical Thinking*. Upper Saddle River, NJ: Merrill.

Jonassen, D. H. (2000). *Computers as Mindtools for Schools: Engaging Critical Thinking* (2nd ed.). Upper Saddle River, NJ: Merrill.

Jonassen, D. H. (2003). Using cognitive tools to represent problems. *Journal of Research on Technology in Education, 35*(3), 362–381.

Jonassen, D. H., & Reeves, T. C. (1996). Learning with technology: Using computers as cognitive tools. In D. H. Jonassen (Ed.), *Handbook of Research on Educational Communications and Technology* (pp. 693–719). New York: Scholastic Press.

Jonassen, D. H., & Tessmer, M. (1996/1997). An outcomes-based taxonomy for instructional systems design, evaluation and research. *Training Research Journal, 2*, 11–46.

Jonassen, D. H., & Wang, S. (2003). Using expert systems to build cognitive simulations. *Journal of Educational Computing Research, 28*(1), 1–13.

Joyner, M. H., & Kurtz-Costes, B. (1997). Metamemory development. In N. Cowan (Ed.), *The Development of Memory in Childhood* (pp. 275–300). Hove, East Sussex, UK: Psychology Press.

Kail, R. V. (1990). *The Development of Memory in Children* (3rd ed.). New York: W. H. Freeman & Co.

Kail, R. V., & Hagen, J. W. (Eds.) (1977). *Perspectives on the Development of Memory and Cognition*. Hillsdale, NJ: Lawrence Erlbaum Associates.

Kant, I. (1933). *Immanuel Kant's Critique of Pure Reason* (N. K. Smith, Trans., 1st ed.). London and New York: Macmillan.

Keeler, M. L., & Swanson, H. L. (2001). Does strategy knowledge influence working memory in children with mathematical disabilities? *Journal of Learning Disabilities*, *34*(5), 418–434.

Kelemen, W. L. (2000). Metamemory cues and monitoring accuracy: Judging what you know and what you will know. *Journal of Educational Psychology*, *92*(4), 800–810.

Kelley, C. M., & Jacoby, L. L. (1996). Memory attributions: Remembering, knowing, and feeling of knowing. In L. Reder (Ed.), *Implicit Memory and Metacognition* (pp. 287–308). Mahwah, NJ: Lawrence Erlbaum Associates.

Kelly, M., Scholnick, E. K., Travers, S. H., & Johnson, J. W. (1976). Relations among memory, memory appraisal, and memory strategies. *Child Development*, *47*, 648–659.

Kemmis, S. (1985). Action research and the politics of reflection. In D. Boud, R. Keogh, & D. Walker (Eds.), *Reflection: Turning Experience into Learning* (pp. 139–164). London: Kogan Page.

King, P. M. (1986). Formal reasoning in adults: A review and critique. In R. A. Mines, & K. S. Kitchener (Eds.), *Adult Cognitive Development: Methods and Models* (pp. 1–21). New York: Praeger.

King, P. M. (1992). How do we know? Why do we believe? Learning to make reflective judgments. *Liberal Education*, *78*(1), 2–9.

King, P. M., & Kitchener, K. S. (1994). *Developing Reflective Judgment: Understanding and Promoting Intellectual Growth and Critical Thinking in Adolescents and Adults*. San Francisco, CA: Jossey-Bass.

King, P. M., & Kitchener, K. S. (2002). The reflective judgment model: Twenty years of research on epistemic cognition. In B. K. Hofer, & P. R. Pintrich (Eds.), *Personal Epistemology: The Psychology of Beliefs About Knowledge and Knowing* (pp. 37–61). Mahwah, NJ: Lawrence Erlbaum Associates.

Kitchener, K. S. (1983). Cognition, metacognition and epistemic cognition: A three-level model of cognitive processing. *Human Development*, *4*, 222–232.

Kitchener, K. S., & King, P. M. (1981). Reflective judgment: Concepts of justification and their relationship to age and education. *Journal of Applied Developmental Psychology*, *2*, 89–116.

Kitchener, K. S., & King, P. M. (1990a). The reflective judgment model: Ten years of research. In M. L. Commons, C. Armon, L. Kohlberg, F. A. Richards, T. A. Grotzer, & J. D. Sinnott (Eds.), *Adult Development: Models and Methods in the Study of Adolescent and Adult Thought* (Vol. 2, pp. 63–146). New York: Praeger.

Kitchener, K. S., & King, P. M. (1990b). The reflective judgment model: Transforming assumptions about knowing. In J. Mezirow (Ed.), *Fostering Critical Reflection in Adulthood: A Guide to Transformative Emancipatory Learning* (pp. 159–176). San Francisco, CA: Jossey-Bass Publishers.

Klausmeier, H. J. (1990). Conceptualizing. In B. F. Jones, & L. Idol (Eds.), *Dimensions of Thinking and Cognitive Instruction* (pp. 93–138). Hillsdale, NJ: Lawrence Erlbaum Associates.

Kluwe, R. H. (1982). Cognitive knowledge and executive control: Metacognition. In D. R. Griffin (Ed.), *Animal Mind – Human Mind* (pp. 201–224). New York: Springer-Verlag.

Kluwe, R. H. (1987). Executive decisions and regulation of problem-solving behavior. In F. E. Weinert, & R. H. Kluwe (Eds.), *Metacognition, Motivation, and Understanding* (pp. 31–64). Hillsdale, NJ: Lawrence Erlbaum Associates.

Kluwe, R. H., & Friedrichsen, G. (1985). Mechanisms of control and regulation in problem solving. In J. Kuhl, & J. Beckmann (Eds.), *Action Control: From Cognition to Behavior* (pp. 183–218). Berlin: Springer-Verlag.

Knopf, M., Körkel, J., Schneider, W., & Weinert, F. E. (1988). Human memory as a faculty versus human memory as a set of specific abilities: Evidence from a life-span approach. In F. E. Weinert & M. Perlmutter (Eds.), *Memory Development: Universal Changes and Individual Differences* (pp. 331–352). Hillsdale, NJ: Lawrence Erlbaum Associates.

Kobasigawa, A. (1977). Retrieval strategies in the development of memory. In R. V. Kail, & J. W. Hagen (Eds.), *Perspectives on the Development of Memory and Cognition* (pp. 177–201). Hillsdale, NJ: Lawrence Erlbaum Associates.

Koriat, A. (1994). Memory's knowledge of its own knowledge: The accessibility account of feeling of knowing. In J. Metcalfe, & A. P. Shimamura (Eds.), *Metacognition: Knowing About Knowing* (pp. 115–136). Cambridge, MA: The MIT Press.

Koriat, A. (1995). Dissociating knowing and the feeling of knowing: Further evidence for the accessibility model. *Journal of Experimental Psychology: General, 124*(3), 311–333.

Koriat, A. (1998). Illusions of knowing: The link between knowledge and metaknowledge. In V. Y. Yzerbyt, G. Lories, & B. Dardenne (Eds.), *Meta-cognition: Cognitive and Social Dimensions* (pp. 16–35). London: Sage Publications Ltd.

Koriat, A. (2000). The feeling of knowing: Some metatheoretical implications for consciousness and control. *Consciousness and Cognition, 9,* 149–171.

Koriat, A., & Goldsmith, M. (1998). The role of metacognitive processes in the regulation of memory performance. In G. Mazzoni, & T. O. Nelson (Eds.), *Metacognition and Cognitive Neuropsychology: Control and Monitoring Processes* (pp. 97–119). Mahwah, NJ: Lawrence Erlbaum Associates.

Koriat, A., & Levy-Sadot, R. (2000). Conscious and unconscious metacognition: A rejoinder. *Consciousness and Cognition, 9,* 193–202.

Koriat, A., & Ackerman, R. (2010). Metacognition and mindreading: Judgments of learning for self and other during self-paced study. *Consciousness and Cognition, 19*(1), 251–264.

Koriat, A., Sheffer, L., & Ma'ayan, H. (2002). Comparing objective and subjective learning curves: Judgments of learning exhibit increased underconfidence with practice. *Journal of Experimental Psychology, 131*(2), 147–162.

Kreutzer, M. A., Leonard, C., & Flavell, J. H. (1975). An interview study of children's knowledge about memory. *Monographs of the Society for Research in Child Development, 40*(1), 1–60.

Kuhlmann, F. (1907). On the analysis of the memory consciousness for pictures of familiar objects. *Journal of Psychology, 18,* 389–420.

Kuhn, D. (1983). On the dual executive and its significance in the development of developmental psychology. In D. Kuhn, & J. A. Meacham (Eds.), *On the Development of Developmental Psychology* (pp. 81–111). Basel: Karger.

Kuhn, D. (1991). *The Skills of Argument.* Cambridge, UK: Cambridge University Press.

Kuhn, D. (1999a). A developmental model of critical thinking. *Educational Researcher, 28*(2), 16–26, 46.

Kuhn, D. (1999b). Metacognitive development. In L. Balter, & C. S. Tamis-

LeMonda (Eds.), *Child Psychology: A Handbook of Contemporary Issues* (pp. 259–286). Philadelphia, PA: Psychology Press.

Kuhn, D. (2000a). Metacognitive development. *Curriculum Direction Psychology Science, 9*, 178–181.

Kuhn, D. (2000b). The theory of mind, metacognition and reasoning: A life-span perspective. In P. Mitchell, & K. J. Riggs (Eds.), *Children's Reasoning and the Mind* (pp. 301–326). Hove: Psychology Press.

Kuhn, D. (2001). How do people know? *Psychological Science, 12*(1), 1–8.

Kuhn, D. (2003). Understanding and valuing knowing as developmental goals. *Liberal Education, 89*(3), 16–21.

Kuhn, D., & Pearsall, S. (1998). Relations between metastrategic knowledge and strategic performance. *Cognitive Development, 13*, 227–247.

Kuhn, D., & Udell, W. (2001). The path to wisdom. *Educational Psychologist, 36*(4), 261–264.

Kuhn, D., & Dean, D. (2004). Metacognition: A bridge between cognitive psychology and educational practice. *Theory into Practice, 43*(4), 268–273.

Kuhn, D., Garcia-Mila, M., Zohar, A., & Andersen, C. (1995). Strategies of knowledge acquisition. *Monographs of the Society for Research in Child Development, 60*(Serial No. 245).

Kuhn, D., Black, J., Keselman, A., & Kaplan, D. (2000). The development of cognitive skills that support inquiry learning. *Cognition and Instruction, 18*(4), 495–543.

Kuiper, R. (2002). Enhancing metacognition through the reflective use of self-regulated learning strategies. *The Journal of Continuing Education in Nursing, 33*(2), 78–87.

Lajoie, S. P. (1993). Computer environments as cognitive tools for enhancing learning. In S. P. Lajoie, & S. J. Derry (Eds.), *Computers as Cognitive Tools* (pp. 261–288). Hillsdale, NJ: Lawrence Erlbaum Associates.

Langford, G. (1986). The philosophical basis of cognition and metacognition. In C. Antaki, & C. Lewis (Eds.), *Mental Mirrors: Metacognition in Social Knowledge and Communication* (pp. 11–26). London: Sage Publications Ltd.

Langrehr, D., & Palmer, B. C. (1998, 7 May). *A Historical Perspective of Metacognition: From Abstraction to Paradigm.* Paper presented at the International Reading Association, Orlando, Florida.

Lawson, M. J. (1984). Being executive about metacognition. In J. R. Kirby (Ed.), *Cognitive Strategies and Educational Performance* (pp. 89–109). New York: Academic Press, Inc.

Leal, L. (1987). Investigation of the relation between metamemory and university students' examination performance. *Journal of Educational Psychology, 79*, 35–40.

Leonesio, R. J., & Nelson, T. O. (1990). Do different metamemory judgments tap the same underlying aspects of memory? *Journal of Experimental Psychology: Learning, Memory, and Cognition, 16*, 464–470.

Light, L. L. (1996). Memory and aging. In E. L. Bjork, & R. A. Bjork (Eds.), *Memory* (pp. 444–490). San Diego, CA: Academic Press, Inc.

Lin, X., Hmelo, C., Kinzer, C. K., & Secules, T. J. (1999). Designing technology to support reflection. *Educational Technology Research and Development, 47*(3), 43–62.

Lindsay, P. H., & Norman, D. A. (1972). *Human Information Processing: An Introduction to Psychology.* New York: Academic Press, Inc.

Linn, M. C., & Siegel, H. (1984). Postformal reasoning: A philosophical model. In M. L. Commons, F. A. Richards, & C. Armon (Eds.), *Beyond Formal Operations: Late Adolescent and Adult Cognitive Development* (pp. 239–257). New York: Praeger Publishers.

Lipman, M. (1987). Some thoughts on the foundations of reflective education. In J. Boykoff Baron, & R. J. Sternberg (Eds.), *Teaching Thinking Skills: Theory and Practice* (pp. 151–161). New York: W H Freeman & Co.

Lipman, M. (1988). Critical thinking – What can it be? *Educational Leadership*, *46*(1), 38–43.

Lipman, M. (1991). *Thinking in Education*. Cambridge and New York: Cambridge University Press.

Lipman, M. (2003). *Thinking in Education* (2nd ed.). New York: Cambridge University Press.

Locke, J. (1947). *An Essay Concerning Human Understanding (1632–1704)* (1st ed.). London: J M Dent & Sons Ltd.

Lockl, K., & Schneider, W. (2002). Developmental trends in children's feeling-of-knowing judgements. *International Journal of Behavioral Development*, *26*(4), 327–333.

Lyons, W. (1986). *The Disappearance of Introspection*. Cambridge, MA: The MIT Press.

McAlpine, L., & Weston, C. B. (2000). Reflection: Issues related to improving professors' teaching and students' learning. *Instructional Science*, *28*, 363–385.

McAlpine, L., Weston, C. B., & Beauchamp, J. (1999). Building a metacognitive model of reflection. *Higher Education*, *37*(2), 105–131.

McCombs, B. L. (1986). The role of the self-system in self-regulated learning. *Contemporary Educational Psychology*, *11*, 314–332.

McCracken, D. J. (1950). *Thinking and Valuing: An Introduction, Partly Historical, to the Study of the Philosophy of Value*. London: Macmillian and Co Limited.

McCrindle, A. R., & Christensen, C. A. (1995). The impact of learning journals on metacognitive and cognitive processes and learning performance. *Learning and Instruction*, *5*(2), 167–185.

McDonald-Miszczak, L., Gould, O. N., & Tychynski, D. (1999). Metamemory predictors of prospective and retrospective memory performance. *The Journal of General Psychology*, *126*(1), 37.

Markman, E. M. (1977). Realizing that you don't understand: A preliminary investigation. *Child Development*, *48*, 986–992.

Marra, R. M., & Jonassen, D. H. (2002). Transfer effects of semantic networks on expert systems: Mindtools at work. *Journal of Educational Computing Research*, *26*(1), 1–23.

Martin, B. L., & Briggs, L. J. (1986). *The Affective and Cognitive Domains: Integration for Instruction and Research*. Englewood Cliffs, NJ: Educational Technology Publications.

Marzano, R. J. (2001). *Designing a New Taxonomy of Educational Objectives*. Thousand Oaks, CA: Corwin Press.

Maule, W. R. (2001). Framework for metacognitive mapping to design metadata for intelligent hypermedia presentations. *Journal of Educational Multimedia and Hypermedia*, *10*(1), 27–45.

Mayer, R. E. (1998). Cognitive, metacognitive, and motivational aspects of problem solving. *Instructional Science*, *28*, 49–63.

Mayer, R. E. (2001). Cognitive, metacognitive, and motivational aspects of problem solving. In H. J. Hartman (Ed.), *Metacognition in Learning and Instruction: Theory, Research and Practice* (pp. 87–101). Dordrecht, Netherlands: Kluwer Academic Publishers.

Meacham, J. A., & Emont, N. C. (1989). The interpersonal basis of everyday problem solving. In J. D. Sinnott (Ed.), *Everyday Problem Solving: Theory and Applications* (pp. 7–23). New York: Praeger.

Meichenbaum, D. (1986). Metacognitive methods of instruction: Current status and future prospects. In M. Schwebel, & C. A. Maher (Eds.), *Facilitating Cognitive Development: International Perspectives, Programs, and Practices* (pp. 23–32). New York: The Haworth Press, Inc.

Metallidou, Y., & Efklides, A. (2001). The effects of general success-related beliefs and specific metacognitive experiences on causal attributions. In A. Efklides, J. Kuhl, & R. M. Sorrentino (Eds.), *Trends and Prospects in Motivation Research* (pp. 325–347). Dordrecht, Netherlands: Kluwer Academic Publishers.

Metcalfe, J. (1986a). Feeling of knowing in memory and problem solving. *Journal of Experimental Psychology: Learning, Memory, and Cognition, 12*(2), 288–294.

Metcalfe, J. (1986b). Premonitions of insight predict impending error. *Journal of Experimental Psychology: Learning, Memory, and Cognition, 12*(4), 623–634.

Metcalfe, J. (1996). Metacognitive processes. In E. L. Bjork, & R. A. Bjork (Eds.), *Memory* (2nd ed., pp. 381–407). San Diego, CA: Academic Press, Inc.

Metcalfe, J. (1998). Insight and metacognition. In G. Mazzoni, & T. O. Nelson (Eds.), *Metacognition and Cognitive Neuropsychology: Control and Monitoring Processes* (pp. 181–198). Mahwah, NJ: Lawrence Erlbaum Associates.

Metcalfe, J. (2000). Metamemory: Theory and data. In E. Tulving, & F. I. M. Craik (Eds.), *The Oxford Handbook of Memory* (pp. 197–214). New York: Oxford University Press.

Metcalfe, J. (2008). Evolution of metacognition. In J. Dunlosky, & R. A. Bjork (Eds.), *Handbook of Metamemory and Memory* (pp. 29–46). New York and Hove: Psychology Press, Taylor and Francis.

Metcalfe, J., & Wiebe, D. (1987). Intuition and insight and noninsight problem solving. *Memory and Cognition, 15*, 238–246.

Metcalfe, J., & Greene, M. J. (2007). Metacognition of agency. *Journal of Experimental Psychology: General, 136*(2), 184–199.

Metcalfe, J., Kornell, N., & Son, L. K. (2007). A cognitive-science based programme to enhance study efficacy in a high and low risk setting. *European Journal of Cognitive Psychology, 19*(4/5), 743–768.

Mezirow, J. (1990). How critical reflection triggers transformative learning. In J. Mezirow, and Associates (Eds.), *Fostering Critical Reflection in Adulthood: A Guide to Transformative and Emancipatory Learning* (pp. 1–20). San Francisco, CA: Jossey-Bass.

Mezirow, J. (1991). *Transformative Dimensions of Adult Learning*. San Francisco, CA: Jossey-Bass.

Mezirow, J. (1997). Transformative learning: Theory to practice. *New Directions for Adult and Continuing Education, 74*, 5–12.

Miles, M. B., & Huberman, A. M. (1994). *An Expanded Sourcebook: Qualitative Data Analysis* (2nd ed.). Thousand Oaks, CA: Sage Publications Ltd.

Miller, J. (2000). Exploring the source of self-regulated learning: The influence of internal and external comparisons. *Journal of Instructional Psychology*, *27*(1), 47–52.

Miner, A. C., & Reder, L. (1994). A new look at feeling of knowing: Its metacognitive role in regulating question answering. In J. Metcalfe, & A. P. Shimamura (Eds.), *Metacognition: Knowing About Knowing* (pp. 47–70). Cambridge, MA: The MIT Press.

Moely, B. E. (1977). Organizational factors in the development of memory. In R. V. Kail, & J. W. Hagen (Eds.), *Perspectives on the Development of Memory and Cognition* (pp. 203–236). Hillsdale, NJ: Lawrence Erlbaum Associates.

Moon, J. A. (1999). *Reflection in Learning and Professional Development: Theory and Practice*. London: Kogan Page.

Moran, D. (1999). Idealism in medieval philosophy: The case of Johannes Scottus Eriugena. *Medieval Philosophy and Theology*, *8*, 53–82.

Moseley, D., Baumfield, V., Elliott, J., Gregson, M., Higgins, S., Miller, J., and Newton, D. (2005). *Frameworks for Thinking: A Handbook for Teaching and Learning*. Cambridge, UK: Cambridge University Press.

Moshman, D. (1982). Exogenous, endogenous, and dialectical constructivism. *Developmental Review*, *2*, 371–384.

Moshman, D. (1990). Rationality as a goal of education. *Educational Psychology Review*, *2*(4), 335–364.

Moshman, D. (1994). Reasoning, metareasoning, and the promotion of rationality. In A. Demetriou, & A. Efklides (Eds.), *Intelligence, Mind, and Reasoning: Structure and Development* (pp. 135–150). Amsterdam: Elsevier.

Moshman, D. (1995). Reasoning as self-constrained thinking. *Human Development*, *38*, 53–64.

Moshman, D. (2004). From inference to reasoning: The construction of rationality. *Thinking and Reasoning*, *10*(2), 221–239.

Moshman, D. (2009a). Adolescence. In U. Mller, J. I. M. Carpendale, & L. Smith (Eds.), *Cambridge Companion to Piaget* (pp. 255–269). Cambridge: Cambridge University Press.

Moshman, D. (2009b). The development of rationality. In H. Siegel (Ed.), *Oxford Handbook of Philosophy of Education* (pp. 145–161). Oxford: Oxford University Press.

Moshman, D. (2011). *Adolescent Rationality and Development: Cognition, Morality, and Identity* (3rd ed.). New York: Psychology Press.

Narens, L., Jameson, K. A., & Lee, V. A. (1994). Subthreshold priming and memory monitoring. In J. Metcalfe, & A. P. Shimamura (Eds.), *Metacognition: Knowing About Knowing* (pp. 71–92). Cambridge, MA: The MIT Press.

Neisser, U. (1967). *Cognitive Psychology*. New York: Meredith Publishing Company.

Nelson, T. O. (Ed.) (1992). *Metacognition: Core Readings*. Needham Heights, MA: Allyn and Bacon.

Nelson, T. O. (1996). Consciousness and metacognition. *American Psychologist*, *51*(2, February), 102–116.

Nelson, T. O. (1998). Foreword: Metacognitive food for thought in educational theory and practice. In D. J. Hacker, J. Dunlosky, & A. C. Graesser (Eds.), *Metacognition in Educational Theory and Practice* (pp. ix-xi). Mahwah, NJ: Lawrence Erlbaum Associates.

Nelson, T. O. (1999). Cognition versus metacognition. In R. J. Sternberg (Ed.), *The Nature of Cognition* (pp. 625–644). Cambridge, MA: The MIT Press.

Nelson, T. O., & Narens, L. (1990). Metamemory: A theoretical framework and new findings. In G. H. Bower (Ed.), *The Psychology of Learning and Motivation* (Vol. 26, pp. 125–173). New York: Academic Press.

Nelson, T. O., & Dunlosky, J. (1991). Does the sensitivity of judgments of learning (JOLs) to the effects of various study activities depend on when the JOLs occur? *Journal of Memory and Language, 33*, 545–565.

Nelson, T. O., & Narens, L. (1994). Why investigate metacognition? In J. Metcalfe, & A. P. Shimamura (Eds.), *Metacognition: Knowing About Knowing* (pp. 1–26). Cambridge, MA: The MIT Press.

Newton, E. V. (1991). Developing metacognitive awareness: The response journal in college composition. *Journal of Reading, 34*(6), 476–478.

Nhouyvanisvong, A., & Reder, L. (1998). Rapid feeling-of-knowing: A strategy selection mechanism. In V. Y. Yzerbyt, G. Lories, & B. Dardenne (Eds.), *Metacognition: Cognitive and Social Dimensions* (pp. 35–53). London: Sage Publications Ltd.

Nisbet, J., & Shucksmith, J. (1984). *The Seventh Sense: Reflections on Learning to Learn* (1st ed.). Edinburgh: Scottish Council for Research in Education.

Nisbett, R. E., & Wilson, T. (1977). Telling more than we can know: Verbal reports on mental processes. *Psychological Review, 84*, 231–259.

Novak, J. (1990). Concept maps and Vee diagrams: Two metacognitive tools to facilitate meaningful learning. *Instructional Science, 19*(1), 29–52.

Olson, D., & Astington, J. (1993). Thinking about thinking: Learning how to take statements and hold beliefs. *Educational Psychologist, 28*(1), 7–23.

Osman, M. E., & Hannafin, M. J. (1992). Metacognition research and theory: Analysis and implications for instructional design. *Educational Technology Research and Development, 40*(2), 83–99.

O'Sullivan, J. T., & Howe, M. L. (1995). Metamemory and memory construction. *Consciousness and Cognition: An International Journal, 4*, 104–110.

O'Sullivan, J. T., & Howe, M. L. (1998). A different view of metamemory with illustrations from children's beliefs about long-term retention. *European Journal of Psychology of Education, 13*(1), 9–28.

Pak, P. G. (2003). *Augustine – De Trinitate*. Retrieved September, 2003, from http://www.op.org/steinkerchner/comps/notes/detrinitate.html

Palincsar, A. S., & Brown, A. L. (1984). Reciprocal teaching and comprehension-fostering and monitoring activities. *Cognition and Instruction, 1*(2), 117–175.

Pallier, G., Wilkinson, R., Danthiir, V., & Kleitman, S. (2002). The role of individual differences in the accuracy of confidence judgments. *The Journal of General Psychology, 129*(3), 257–299.

Paris, S. G. (1988). Models and metaphors about learning strategies. In C. Weinstein, E. T. Goetz, & P. A. Alexander (Eds.), *Learning and Study Strategies: Issues in Assessment, Instruction, and Evaluation* (pp. 299–321). San Diego, CA: Academic Press, Inc.

Paris, S. G. (2002). When is metacognition helpful, debilitating or benign? In P. Chambres, M. Izaute, & P.-J. Marescaux (Eds.), *Metacognition: Process, Function and Use* (pp. 105–120). Dordrecht, Boston, London: Kluwer Academic Publishers.

Paris, S. G., & Lindauer, B. K. (1977). Constructive aspects of children's comprehension and memory. In R. V. Kail, & J. W. Hagen (Eds.), *Perspectives on the Development of Memory and Cognition* (pp. 35–60). Hillsdale, NJ: Lawrence Erlbaum Associates.

Paris, S. G., & Lindauer, B. K. (1982). The development of cognitive skills during childhood. In B. Wolman (Ed.), *Handbook of Developmental Psychology* (pp. 333–349). Englewood Cliffs, NJ: Prentice-Hall.

Paris, S. G., & Winograd, P. (1990). How metacognition can promote academic learning and instruction. In B. F. Jones, & L. Idol (Eds.), *Dimensions of Thinking and Cognitive Instruction* (pp. 15–51). Hillsdale, NJ: Lawrence Erlbaum Associates.

Paris, S. G., & Paris, A. H. (2001). Classroom applications of research on self-regulated learning. *Educational Psychologist, 36*(2), 89–101.

Paris, S. G., Lipson, M., & Wixson, K. (1983). Becoming a strategic reader. *Contemporary Educational Psychology, 8*, 293–316.

Parkin, A. J. (1997). The development of procedural and declarative memory. In N. Cowan (Ed.), *The Development of Memory in Childhood* (pp. 113–138). Hove: Psychology Press.

Paul, R. (1992). *Critical Thinking: What Every Person Needs to Survive in a Rapidly Changing World*. Santa Rosa, CA: The Foundation for Critical Thinking.

Paul, R., & Elder, L. (2002). Critical thinking: Teaching students how to study and learn (part 1). *Journal of Developmental Education, 26*(1), 36–37.

Pearson, M., & Smith, D. (1985). Debriefing in experience-based learning. In D. Boud, R. Keogh, & D. Walker (Eds.), *Reflection: Turning Experience into Learning* (pp. 69–84). London: Kogan Page.

Perfect, T. J. (2004). The role of self-rated ability in the accuracy of confidence judgments in eyewitness memory and general knowledge. *Applied Cognitive Psychology, 18*, 157–168.

Perkins, D., & Salomon, G. (1989). Are cognitive skills context-bound? *Educational Researcher, 18*(1), 16–25.

Perlmutter, M. (1988). Research on memory: Past, present, future. In F. E. Weinert, & M. Perlmutter (Eds.), *Memory Development: Universal Changes and Individual Differences* (pp. 353–380). Hillsdale, NJ: Lawrence Erlbaum Associates.

Perry, W. G. (1970). *Forms of Intellectual and Ethical Development in the College Years: A Scheme*. New York: Holt, Rinehart and Winston.

Phillips, L. J. (2003). When flash cards are not enough. *Teaching Children Mathematics, 9*(6), 358–363.

Piaget, J. (1970). *The Principles of Genetic Epistemology* (W. Mays, Trans.). London: Routledge & Kegan Paul.

Pintrich, P. R. (2000). The role of goal orientation in self-regulated learning. In M. Boekarts, P. R. Pintrich, & M. Zeidner (Eds.), *Handbook of Self-Regulation* (pp. 452–502). New York: Academic Press, Inc.

Pintrich, P. R. (2002). The role of metacognitive knowledge in learning, teaching, and assessing. *Theory into Practice, 41*(4), 219.

Pintrich, P. R., Wolters, C. A., & Baxter, G. P. (2000). Assessing metacognition and self-regulated learning. In G. Schraw, & J. C. Impara (Eds.), *Issues in the Measurement of Metacognition* (pp. 43–97). Lincoln, NE: Buros Institute of Mental Measurements.

Pithers, R. J., & Soden, R. (2000). Critical thinking in education. *Educational Research, 42*(3), 237–249.

Plato (1984). *Great Dialogues of Plato* (W. H. D. Rouse, Trans., 2nd ed.). New York: Mentor, Penguin Books.

Plucker, J. (1998). *History of Influences in the Development of Intelligence Theory.* Retrieved April 2002, from http://www.indiana.edu/~intell/ethorndike.html

Plude, D. J., Nelson, T. O., & Scholnick, E. K. (1998). Analytical research on developmental aspects of metamemory. *European Journal of Psychology of Education, XIII*(1), 29–42.

Polanyi, M. (1969). *Knowing and Being: Essays by Michael Polanyi.* Chicago, IL: University of Chicago.

Pressley, M. (2005). Final reflections: Metacognition in literacy learning: Then, now, and in the future. In S. E. Israel (Ed.), *Metacognition in Literacy Learning: Theory, Assessment, Instruction, and Professional Development* (pp. 391–412). Mahwah, NJ: Lawrence Erlbaum Associates.

Pressley, M., Borkowski, J. G., & O'Sullivan, J. T. (1984). Memory strategy instruction is made of this: Metamemory and durable strategy use. *Educational Psychologist, 19*(2), 94–107.

Pressley, M., Levin, J. R., & Ghatala, E. S. (1984). Memory strategy monitoring in adults and children. *Journal of Verbal Learning and Behavior, 23,* 270–288.

Pressley, M., Borkowski, J. G., & O'Sullivan, J. (1985). Children's metamemory and the teaching of memory strategies. In D. L. Forrest-Pressley, G. E. MacKinnon, & T. Gary Waller (Eds.), *Metacognition, Cognition, and Human Performance: Theoretical Perspectives* (Vol. 1, pp. 111–149). London: Academic Press, Inc.

Pressley, M., Borkowski, J. G., & Schneider, W. (1987). Cognitive strategies: Good strategy users coordinate metacognition and knowledge. In R. Vasta (Ed.), *Annals of Child Development* (Vol. 4, pp. 89–129). Greenwich, CT: JAI Press.

Pugalee, D. K. (2001). Writing, mathematics, and metacognition: Looking for connections through students' work in mathematical problem solving. *School Science and Mathematics, 101*(5), 236–245.

Purdie, N., Hattie, J., & Douglas, G. (1996). Students' conceptions of learning and their use of self-regulated learning strategies: A cross-cultural comparison. *Journal of Educational Psychology, 88*(1), 87–100.

Rebok, G. W., & Balcerak, L. J. (1989). Memory self-efficacy and performance differences in young and old adults: The effect of mnemonic training. *Developmental Psychology, 25*(5), 714–721.

Reder, L., & Schunn, C. D. (1996). Metacognition does not imply awareness: Strategy choice is governed by implicit learning and memory. In L. Reder (Ed.), *Implicit Memory and Metacognition* (pp. 45–78). Mahwah, NJ: Lawrence Erlbaum Associates.

Reeve, R. A., & Brown, A. L. (1984). *Metacognition Reconsidered: Implications for Intervention Research.* Cambridge, MA: Bolt Beranek and Newman Inc.

Reeve, R. A., & Brown, A. L. (1985). Metacognition reconsidered: Implications for intervention research. *Journal of Abnormal Child Psychology, 13,* 343–356.

Resnick, L. B. (1987). *Education and Learning to Think.* Washington, DC: National Academy Press.

Richards, T. J., & Richards, L. (1994). Using computers in qualitative research. In N. K. Denzin, & Y. S. Lincoln (Eds.), *Handbook of Qualitative Research* (pp. 445–462). Thousand Oaks, CA: Sage Publications.

Riefer, D. (2002). Comparing auditory vs visual stimuli in the tip-of-the-tongue phenomenon. *Psychological Reports, 90,* 568–576.

Rimor, R., & Kozminsky, E. (2003). *An Analysis of the Reflections of Students in Online Courses.* Retrieved Sept, 2003, from http://burdacenter.bgu.ac.il/publications/rimor.pdf

Roebers, C. M. (2002). Confidence judgments in children's and adults' event recall and suggestibility. *Developmental Psychology, 38*(6), 1052–1067.

Roehler, L. R., & Cantlon, D. J. (1997). Scaffolding: A powerful tool in social constructivist classrooms. In K. Hogan, & M. Pressley (Eds.), *Scaffolding* (pp. 6–42). Cambridge, MA: Brookline Books.

Rogoff, B., & Wertsch, J. V. (Eds.) (1984). *Children's Learning in the 'Zone of Proximal Development'.* San Francisco, CA: Jossey-Bass.

Romine, C., & Reynolds, C. R. (2004). Sequential memory: A developmental perspective on its relation to frontal lobe functioning. *Neuropsychology Review, 14*(1), 43–64.

Rosenthal, D. M. (1986). Two concepts of consciousness. *Philosophical Studies, 49,* 329–359.

Rosenthal, D. M. (1999). Introspection. In R. A. Wilson, & F. C. Keil (Eds.), *The MIT Encyclopedia of the Cognitive Sciences* (pp. 419–421). Cambridge, MA: The MIT Press.

Rosenthal, D. M. (2000). Introspection and self-interpretation. *Philosophical Topics, 28*(2), 201–333.

Ryle, G. (1949). *The Concept of Mind.* London: Hutchinson.

Salatas, H., & Flavell, J. H. (1976). Behavioral and metamnemonic indicators of strategic behaviors under remember instructions in first grade. *Child Development, 47,* 81–89.

Samuels, M., & Betts, J. (2007). Crossing the threshold from description to deconstruction and reconstruction: Using self-assessment to deepen reflection. *Reflective Practice, 8*(2), 269–283.

Schneider, W. (1985). Developmental trends in the metamemory–memory behavior relationship: An integrative review. In D. L. Forrest-Pressley, G. E. MacKinnon, & T. G. Waller (Eds.), *Metacognition, Cognition, and Human Performance* (Vol. 1: Theoretical Perspectives, pp. 57–109). Orlando, FL: Academic Press, Inc.

Schneider, W. (1998). The development of procedural metamemory in childhood and adolescence. In G. Mazzoni, & T. O. Nelson (Eds.), *Metacognition and Cognitive Neuropsychology: Control and Monitoring Processes* (pp. 1–22). Mahwah, NJ: Lawrence Erlbaum Associates.

Schneider, W., & Pressley, M. (1997). *Memory Development Between Two and Twenty* (2nd ed.). Mahwah, NJ: Lawrence Erlbaum Associates.

Schneider, W., & Lockl, K. (2002). The development of metacognitive knowledge in children and adolescents. In T. J. Perfect, & B. L. Schwartz (Eds.), *Applied Metacognition* (pp. 224–257). Cambridge: Cambridge University Press.

Schneider, W., & Bjorklund, D. (2003). Memory and knowledge development. In J. Valsiner, & K. J. Connolly (Eds.), *Handbook of Developmental Psychology* (pp. 370–403). London: Sage Publications Ltd.

Schoenfeld, A. H. (1983). Beyond the purely cognitive: Beliefs, social cognitions and metacognitions as driving forces in intellectual performance. *Cognitive Science, 7,* 329–363.

Schoenfeld, A. H. (1985). Metacognitive and epistemological issues in mathematical understanding. In E. A. Silver (Ed.), *Teaching and Learning Mathematical*

Problem Solving: Multiple Research Perspectives (pp. 361–379). Hillsdale, NJ: Lawrence Erlbaum Associates.

Schoenfeld, A. H. (1987). What's all the fuss about metacognition? In A. H. Schoenfeld (Ed.), *Cognitive Science and Mathematics Education* (pp. 189–215). Hillsdale, NJ: Lawrence Erlbaum Associates.

Schraw, G. (1998). Promoting general metacognitive awareness. *Instructional Science, 26*, 113–125.

Schraw, G. (2000). Assessing metacognition: Implications of the Buros Symposium. In G. Schraw, & J. C. Impara (Eds.), *Issues in the Measurement of Metacognition* (pp. 297–323). Lincoln, NE: Buros Institute of Mental Measurements.

Schraw, G. (2001). Promoting general metacognitive awareness. In H. J. Hartman (Ed.), *Metacognition in Learning and Instruction: Theory, Research and Practice* (pp. 3–16). Dordrecht, Netherlands: Kluwer Academic Publishers.

Schraw, G. (2009). Measuring metacognitive judgments. In D. J. Hacker, J. Dunlosky, & A. C. Graesser (Eds.), *Handbook of Metacognition in Education* (pp. 415–429). New York: Routledge.

Schraw, G., & Dennison, R. S. (1994). Assessing metacognitive awareness. *Contemporary Educational Psychology, 19*, 460–475.

Schraw, G., & Moshman, D. (1995). Metacognitive theories. *Educational Psychology, 7*(4), 351–371.

Schunk, D. H. (1986). Verbalization and children's self-regulated learning. *Contemporary Educational Psychology, 11*, 347–369.

Schunk, D. H. (2008). Metacognition, self-regulation, and self-regulated learning: Research recommendations. *Educational Psychology Review, 20*(4), 463–467.

Schwartz, B. L. (2002). *Tip-of-the-Tongue States: Phenomenology, Mechanism, and Lexical Retrieval*. Mahwah, NJ: Lawrence Erlbaum Associates.

Schwartz, B. L. (2006). Tip-of-the-tongue states as metacognition. *Metacognition and Learning, 1*(2), 149–158.

Schwartz, B. L., & Perfect, T. J. (2002). Introduction: Toward an applied cognition. In T. J. Perfect, & B. L. Schwartz (Eds.), *Applied Metacognition* (pp. 1–11). Cambridge: Cambridge University Press.

Schwartz, B. L., & Bacon, E. (2008). Metacognitive neuroscience. In J. Dunlosky, & R. A. Bjork (Eds.), *Handbook of Metamemory and Memory* (pp. 355–371). New York and Hove: Psychology Press, Taylor and Francis.

Schwebel, M. (1986). Facilitating cognitive development: A new educational perspective. In M. Schwebel, & C. A. Maher (Eds.), *Facilitating Cognitive Development: International Perspectives, Programs, and Practices* (pp. 3–19). New York: The Haworth Press, Inc.

Shimamura, A. P. (1994). Neuropsychology of metacognition. In J. Metcalfe, & A. P. Shimamura (Eds.), *Metacognition: Knowing About Knowing* (pp. 253–276). Cambridge, MA: The MIT Press.

Shimamura, A. P. (1996). The role of the prefrontal cortex in controlling and monitoring memory processes. In L. Reder (Ed.), *Implicit Memory and Metacognition* (pp. 259–274). Mahwah, NJ: Lawrence Erlbaum Associates.

Shimamura, A. P. (2000). Towards a cognitive neuroscience of metacognition. *Consciousness and Cognition, 9*(2), 313–323.

Shimamura, A. P. (2008). A neurocognitive approach to metacognitive monitoring and control. In J. Dunlosky, & R. A. Bjork (Eds.), *Handbook of Metamemory and*

Memory (pp. 373–390). New York and Hove: Psychology Press, Taylor and Francis.

Shimamura, A. P., & Squire, L. R. (1986). Memory and metamemory: A study of the feeling-of-knowing phenomenon in amnesic patients. *Journal of Experimental Psychology: Learning, Memory, and Cognition, 12*, 452–460.

Short, E. J., Schatschneider, C. W., & Friebert, S. E. (1993). Relationship between memory and metamemory performance: A comparison of specific and general strategy knowledge. *Journal of Educational Psychology, 85*(3), 412–423.

Shuell, T. J. (1990). Phases of meaningful learning. *Review of Educational Research, 60*(4), 531–547.

Siegel, H. (1980). *Critical Thinking as an Educational Ideal.* Paper presented at the 64th Annual Meeting of the American Educational Research Association, Boston (ERIC Document Reproduction Service No. ED 187762).

Siegel, H. (1989). *Why Be Rational? On Thinking Critically About Critical Thinking.* Upper Montclair, NJ: Montclair State College. (ERIC Document Reproduction Service No. ED 352 333).

Simons, P. R. J. (1996). Metacognition. In E. DeCorte, & F. E. Weinert (Eds.), *International Encyclopedia of Developmental and Instructional Psychology* (pp. 436–444). Oxford: Elsevier Science.

Simpson, G. G. (1961). *Principles of Animal Taxonomy.* New York: Columbia University Press.

Sinkavich, F. J. (1994). Metamemory, attributional style, and study strategies: Predicting classroom performance in graduate students. *Journal of Instructional Psychology, 21*(June), 172–182.

Sinkavich, F. J. (1995). Performance and metamemory: Do students know what they don't know? *Journal of Instructional Psychology, 22*(Mar), 77–87.

Sinnott, J. D. (1984). Postformal reasoning: The relativistic stage. In M. L. Commons, F. A. Richards, & C. Armon (Eds.), *Beyond Formal Operations: Late Adolescent and Adult Cognitive Development* (pp. 298–325). New York: Praeger Publishers.

Sinnott, J. D. (1989). A model for solution of ill-structured problems: Implications for everyday and abstract problem solving. In J. D. Sinnott (Ed.), *Everyday Problem Solving* (pp. 72–99). New York: Praeger.

Sitko, B. (1998). Knowing how to write: Metacognition and writing instruction. In D. J. Hacker, J. Dunlosky, & A. C. Graesser (Eds.), *Metacognition in Educational Theory and Practice* (pp. 93–116). Mahwah, NJ: Lawrence Erlbaum Associates.

Slife, B. D., Weiss, J., & Bell, T. (1985). Separability of metacognition and cognition: Problem solving in learning disabled and regular students. *Journal of Educational Psychology, 77*(4), 437–445.

Slusarz, R., & Sun, R. (2001). The interaction of explicit and implicit learning: An integrated model. In J. D. Moore, & K. Stenning (Eds.), *Proceedings of the Twenty-Third Annual Conference of the Cognitive Science Society* (pp. 952–957). Edinburgh: Lawrence Erlbaum Associates.

Smith, S. M. (1994). Frustrated feelings of imminent recall: On the tip of the tongue. In J. Metcalfe, & A. P. Shimamura (Eds.), *Metacognition: Knowing About Knowing* (pp. 26–45). Cambridge, MA: The MIT Press.

Son, L. K., & Schwartz, B. L. (2002). The relation between metacognitive monitoring and control. In T. J. Perfect, & B. L. Schwartz (Eds.), *Applied Metacognition* (pp. 15–38). Cambridge: Cambridge University Press.

Sorabji, R. (1972). *Aristotle on Memory*. London: Gerald Duckworth & Company Limited.

Spearman, C. (1923). *The Nature of Intelligence and the Principles of Cognition*. London: Macmillian.

Spinoza, B. (1930). *Spinoza: Selections*. J. Wild (Ed.), London: Charles Scribner's Sons.

Squire, L. R., & Zouzounis, J. A. (1988). Self-ratings of memory dysfunction: Different findings in depression and amnesia. *Journal of Clinical and Experimental Neuropsychology, 10*, 727–738.

Sternberg, R. J. (1979). The nature of mental abilities. *American Psychologist, 34*, 214–230.

Sternberg, R. J. (1984). Higher-order reasoning in postformal-operational thought. In M. L. Commons, F. A. Richards, & C. Armon (Eds.), *Beyond Formal Operations: Late Adolescent and Adult Cognitive Development* (pp. 74–91). New York: Praeger.

Sternberg, R. J. (1998). Metacognition, abilities, and developing expertise: What makes an expert student? *Instructional Science, 26*(1–2), 127–140.

Sun, R., & Mathews, R. (2002). Explicit and implicit processes of metacognition. In S. P. Shohov (Ed.), *Advances in Psychology Research* (Vol. 18, pp. 3–13). Hauppauge, NY: Nova Science Publishers.

Suzuki Slakter, N. S. (1988). Elaboration and metamemory during adolescence. *Contemporary Educational Psychology, 13*(July), 206–220.

Swindal, J. (1999). *Reflection Revisited: Jurgen Habermas's Discursive Theory of Truth*. New York: Fordham University Press.

Tama, M. C. (1989a). Critical thinking has a place in every classroom. *Journal of Reading, 33*(1), 64–65.

Tama, M. C. (1989b). *Critical Thinking: Promoting it in the Classroom*. Bloomington, IN: ERIC Clearinghouse on Reading and Communication Skills (ERIC Document Reproduction Service No. ED306554).

Tan, S. C., Turgeon, A. J., & Jonassen, D. H. (2001). Develop critical thinking in group problem solving through computer-supported collaborative argumentation: A case study. *Journal of Natural Resources and Life Sciences Education, 30*, 97–103.

Tobias, S., & Everson, H. (2000). Assessing metacognitive knowledge monitoring. In G. Schraw, & J. C. Impara (Eds.), *Issues in the Measurement of Metacognition* (pp. 147–223). Lincoln, NE: Buros Institute of Mental Measurements.

Tobias, S., & Everson, H. (2009). The importance of knowing what you know: A knowledge monitoring framework for studying metacognition in education. In D. J. Hacker, J. Dunlosky, & A. C. Graesser (Eds.), *Handbook of Metacognition in Education* (pp. 107–127). New York: Routledge.

Trepanier, M. L. (1982). *How Do I Remember? Young Children's Understanding of the Memory Process*. Paper presented at the National Association for the Education of Young Children, Washington, DC (ERIC Document Reproduction Service No. ED 226 831).

Tsai, C. (2001). A review and discussion of epistemological commitments, metacognition, and critical thinking with suggestions on their enhancement in internet-assisted chemistry classrooms. *Journal Of Chemical Education, 78*(7), 970–974.

Tulving, E., & Madigan, S. A. (1970). Memory and verbal learning. In P. H.

Mussen, & M. R. Rosenzweig (Eds.), *Annual Review of Psychology* (pp. 437–483). Palo Alto, CA: Annual Review of Psychology.

Turner, L. A., Hale, C., & Borkowski, J. G. (1996). Influence of intelligence on memory development. *American Journal of Mental Retardation, 100*(March), 468–480.

Umilta, C., & Stablum, F. (1998). Control processes explored by the study of closed-head-injury patients. In G. Mazzoni, & T. O. Nelson (Eds.), *Metacognition and Cognitive Neuropsychology: Monitoring and Control* (pp. 37–52). Mahwah, NJ: Lawrence Erlbaum Associates.

Underwood, B. J. (1966). Individual and group predictions of item difficulty for free learning. *Journal of Experimental Psychology, 70*, 673–679.

Urmson, J. O. (Ed.) (1960). *The Concise Encyclopedia of Western Philosophy and Philosophers* (1st ed.). New York: Hawthorn Books Inc.

van Overschelde, J. P. (2008). Metacognition: Knowing about knowing. In J. Dunlosky, & R. A. Bjork (Eds.), *Handbook of Metamemory and Memory* (pp. 46–71). New York and Hove: Psychology Press, Taylor and Francis.

Veenman, M. V. J., Van Hout-Wolters, B. H. A. M., & Afflerbach, P. (2006). Metacognition and learning: Conceptual and methodological considerations. *Metacognition and Learning, 1*(1), 3–14.

Vermunt, J. D. (1996). Metacognitive, cognitive and affective aspects of learning styles and strategies: A phenomenographic analysis. *Higher Education, 31*, 25–50.

Vockell, E., & van Deusen, R. M. (1989). *The Computer and Higher Order Thinking Skills*. Watsonville, CA: Mitchell Publishing.

Vojnovich, C. M. (1998). *Improving Student Motivation in the Secondary Classroom Through the Use of Critical Thinking Skills, Cooperative Learning Techniques, and Reflective Journal Writing*. Unpublished Master's Research Project, Saint Xavier University, Illinois (ERIC Document Reproduction Service No. ED 411334).

Vygotsky, L. S. (1978). *Mind in Society: The Development of Higher Psychological Processes*. Cambridge, MA: Harvard University Press.

Vygotsky, L. S. (1981). The genesis of higher mental functions. In J. V. Wertsch (Ed.), *The Concept of Activity in Soviet Psychology* (pp. 157). Armonk, NY: Sharpe.

Vygotsky, L. S. (1986). *Thought and Language*. Cambridge, MA: The MIT Press.

Vygotsky, L. S. (1987/1934). *The Collected Works of LS Vygotsky: Problems of General Psychology*. (Vol. 1). New York: Plenum Press.

Wagoner, S. A. (1983). Comprehension monitoring: What is it and what we know about it. *Reading Research Quarterly, 18*(3), 328–346.

Weed, K. A., Ryan, E. B., & Day, J. D. (1990). Metamemory and attributions as mediators of strategy use and recall. *Journal of Educational Psychology, 82*(Dec), 849–855.

Weinert, F. E. (1987). Introduction and overview: Metacognition and motivation as determinants of effective learning and understanding. In F. E. Weinert, & R. H. Kluwe (Eds.), *Metacognition, Motivation, and Understanding* (pp. 1–16). Hillsdale, NJ: Lawrence Erlbaum Associates.

Weinert, F. E. (1988). Epilogue. In F. E. Weinert, & M. Perlmutter (Eds.), *Memory Development: Universal Changes and Individual Differences* (pp. 381–395). Hillsdale, NJ: Lawrence Erlbaum Associates.

Wellman, H. M. (1977). Tip of the tongue and feeling of knowing experiences: A developmental study of memory monitoring. *Child Development, 48*(1), 13–21.

Wellman, H. M. (1978). Knowledge of the interaction of memory variables: A developmental study of metamemory. *Developmental Psychology, 14*, 24–29.

Wellman, H. M. (1983). Metamemory revisited. In M. Chi (Ed.), *Trends in Memory Development Research: Contributions to Human Development* (pp. 31–51). Basel: Karger.

Wellman, H. M. (1985a). A child's theory of the mind: The development of conceptions of cognition. In S. R. Yussen (Ed.), *The Growth of Reflection in Children* (pp. 169–206). Orlando, FL: Academic Press, Inc.

Wellman, H. M. (1985b). The origins of metacognition. In D. L. Forrest-Pressley, G. E. MacKinnon, & T. Gary Waller (Eds.), *Metacognition, Cognition, and Human Performance* (Vol. 1, Theoretical Perspectives, pp. 1–30). Orlando, FL: Academic Press, Inc.

Wellman, H. M. (1988a). The early development of memory strategies. In F. E. Weinert, & M. Perlmutter (Eds.), *Memory Development: Universal Changes and Individual Differences* (pp. 3–27). Hillsdale, NJ: Lawrence Erlbaum Associates.

Wellman, H. M. (1988b). First steps in the child's theorizing about the mind. In J. Astington, P. L. Harris, & D. Olson (Eds.), *Developing Theories of Mind* (pp. 64–92). Cambridge, UK: Cambridge University Press.

Wellman, H. M. (1990). *The Child's Theory of Mind.* Cambridge, MA: The MIT Press.

Wells, A. (2000). *Emotional Disorders and Metacognition.* Chichester: John Wiley & Sons Ltd.

Wertsch, J. V. (1985a). Adult–child interaction as a source of self-regulation in children. In S. R. Yussen (Ed.), *The Growth of Reflection in Children* (pp. 69–98). Orlando, FL: Academic Press, Inc.

Wertsch, J. V. (1985b). *Vygotsky and the Social Formation of Mind.* Cambridge, MA: Harvard University Press.

Wheeler, M. A., Stuss, D. T., & Tulving, E. (1997). Toward a theory of episodic memory: The frontal lobes and autonoetic consciousness. *Psychological Bulletin, 121*, 331–354.

Wilen, W. W., & Phillips, J. A. (1995). Teaching critical thinking: A metacognitive approach. *Social Education, 59*(March), 135–138.

Winne, P. H. (1995). Inherent details of self-regulated learning. *Educational Psychologist, 30*(4), 173–187.

Wolters, C. A. (1998). Self-regulated learning and college students' regulation of motivation. *Journal of Educational Psychology, 2*, 224–235.

Wolters, C. A. (2003). Regulation of motivation: Evaluating an underemphasized aspect of self-regulated learning. *Educational Psychologist, 38*(4), 189–205.

Wolters, C. A., & Pintrich, P. R. (2001). Contextual differences in student motivation and self-regulated learning in mathematics, English and social studies classrooms. In H. J. Hartman (Ed.), *Metacognition in Learning and Instruction: Theory, Research and Practice* (pp. 103–124). Dordrecht, Netherlands: Kluwer Academic Publishers.

Wood, D. J., Bruner, J., & Ross, G. (1976). The role of tutoring in problem solving. *Journal of Child Psychology and Psychiatry, 17*(2), 89–100.

Wood, P. K. (1997). Development of assessment measures of epistemic cognition: How do students think about real-world ill-structured problems? *Assessment Update, 9*(6), 11–16.

Yussen, S. R. (1985). The role of metacognition in contemporary theories of cognitive development. In D. L. Forrest-Pressley, G. E. MacKinnon, & T. Gary Waller (Eds.), *Metacognition, Cognition, and Human Performance* (Vol. 1, Theoretical Perspectives, pp. 253–283). Orlando, FL: Academic Press, Inc.

Yussen, S. R., & Berman, L. (1981). Memory predictions for recall and recognition in first-, third-, and fifth-grade children. *Developmental Psychology*, *17*(2), 224–229.

Yussen, S. R., & Bird, J. E. (1979). The development of metacognitive awareness in memory, communication, and attention. *Journal of Experimental Psychology*, *28*, 300–313.

Zajorc, R. (1980). Feeling and thinking. *American Psychologist*, *35*(2), 151–175.

Zajorc, R., & Markus, H. (1984). Affect and cognition: The hard interface. In C. Izard, J. Kagan, & R. Zajorc (Eds.), *Emotions, Cognition, and Behavior* (pp. 73–102). Cambridge: Cambridge University Press.

Zan, R. (2000). A metacognitive intervention in mathematics at university level. *International Journal of Mathematical Education in Science and Technology*, *31*(1), 143–150.

Zechmeister, E. B., & Nyberg, S. E. (1982). *Human Memory: An Introduction to Research and Theory*. Monterey, CA: Brooks/Cole Publishing Company.

Zimmerman, B. J. (1986). Becoming a self-regulated learner: Which are the key subprocesses? *Contemporary Educational Psychology*, *11*, 307–313.

Zimmerman, B. J. (1989a). Models of self-regulated learning and academic achievement. In B. J. Zimmerman, & D. H. Schunk (Eds.), *Self-Regulated Learning and Academic Achievement* (pp. 2–25). New York: Springer-Verlag.

Zimmerman, B. J. (1989b). A social cognitive view of self-regulated academic learning. *Journal of Educational Psychology*, *81*(3), 329–339.

Zimmerman, B. J. (1995). Self-regulation involves more than metacognition: A social cognitive perspective. *Educational Psychologist*, *30*(4), 217–221.

Zimmerman, B. J. (2000). Attaining self-regulation: A social cognitive perspective. In M. Boekarts, P. R. Pintrich, & M. Zeidner (Eds.), *Self-Regulation: Theory, Research, and Applications* (pp. 13–39). Orlando, FL: Academic Press, Inc.

Zimmerman, B. J., & Schunk, D. H. (2001). *Self-Regulated Learning and Academic Achievement*. New York: Springer-Verlag.

Author index

Abell, S., 4
Ach, N., 13
Ackerman, R., 72, 73
Afflerbach, P., 3, 4
Alexander, P. A., 3, 4, 5, 180, 181, 215
Amdur, L., 46, 51
Andersen, C., 150, 151, 155
Anderson, J. R., 157
Anderson, L. W., 7, 8, 193
Andreassen, C., 117
Antaki, C., 4
Antonietti, A., 180
Appel, L. P., 60
Armbruster, B. B., 13, 15, 138, 140, 181
Armon, C., 17, 18
Astington, J., 35, 68
Augustine, 14

Babbs, P., 4
Babkie, A. M., 4
Bacon, E., 107, 109
Bahrick, H. P., 76
Bailey, K. D., 7, 193
Baker, L., 1, 3, 13, 15, 77, 94, 95, 128, 136, 137, 138, 140, 141, 155, 181
Bakracevic Vukman, K., 19
Balcerak, L. J., 113
Baldwin, M. J., 13
Bandura, A., 113, 169
Barclay, C. R., 116
Baumeister, R. F., 168
Baumfield, V., 7, 187
Baxter, G. P., 95, 154, 156, 169
Beare, J. I., 59
Beauchamp, J., 15, 46, 50, 128
Bell, T., 1
Bellezza, F. S., 96

Belmont, J. M., 77, 78, 102
Bendixen, L. D., 152
Berliner, D. C., 17, 60
Berman, L., 68
Berry, J. M., 113
Best, J., 100
Betts, J., 4
Biggs, J. B., 1
Binet, A., 13
Bird, J. E., 61
Birenbaum, M., 46, 51
Bjork, R. A., 59, 65, 107
Bjorklund, D., 65, 95, 96, 103, 123
Black, J., 150, 151
Blasi, A., 17, 18, 44
Bloom, B. S., 7, 71, 193
Bobrow, D. G., 155
Boekaerts, M., 155, 166, 168, 169
Bogdan, R. J., 44, 46
Boraas, J., 33
Borkowski, J. G., 4, 5, 44, 45, 46, 65, 66, 67, 68, 73, 80, 83, 85, 95, 100, 101, 102, 115, 116, 117, 127, 142, 144, 145, 146, 152, 166, 180
Bouchard, M., 169
Boud, D., 15
Bouffard, T., 169
Bowne, B. P., 28, 69
Boylor, A. L., 4
Bransford, J. D., 1, 3, 4, 5, 6, 77, 91, 95, 136, 137, 140, 154, 169, 220
Braten, I., 23, 24
Bray, N. W., 117
Briggs, L. J., 8, 193
Brookfield, S., 6, 30, 31, 33, 34
Brown, A. L., 1, 2, 3, 4, 5, 6, 13, 15, 23, 24, 44, 46, 60, 61, 62, 64, 66, 68, 69, 71, 77, 78, 80, 82, 83, 84, 85, 86, 89, 91, 94, 95, 98, 100, 102, 105, 111, 115,

116, 118, 127, 128, 134, 136, 137, 138, 140, 141, 145, 152, 154, 155, 166, 169, 181, 220
Brown, C., 50, 52
Brown, R., 63, 64, 69, 71, 78, 87, 94, 111
Bruner, J., 23, 24, 61
Bruning, R. H., 33, 37
Bryson, M., 24
Butler, D. L., 168, 169
Butterfield, E. C., 1, 64, 77, 78, 79, 102
Buysse, A., 165, 180

Callison, D., 23
Campione, J. C., 1, 3, 4, 5, 6, 23, 68, 77, 85, 91, 95, 98, 100, 105, 115, 116, 134, 136, 137, 140, 141, 145, 152, 154, 155, 169, 220
Cantlon, D. J., 23
Carnap, R., 1
Carr, M., 101, 127, 142, 144, 145, 146, 180
Cary, M., 162
Cavanaugh, J. C., 2, 3, 4, 13, 46, 60, 65, 66, 67, 69, 71, 78, 79, 80, 83, 85, 91, 93, 94, 95, 111, 113, 115, 117, 155
Chambres, P., 71, 72, 162
Chan, L. K. S., 4, 101, 144, 145, 146, 166, 180
Cheng, P., 1, 154
Chi, M., 93, 95, 96, 98, 100, 160
Cho, K.-L., 24
Christensen, C. A., 51
Cicognani, A., 50
Commons, M. L., 17, 18
Cooper, R. G., 60
Corno, L., 168, 169
Cornoldi, C., 47, 48, 65, 155, 158
Corsini, D. A., 61, 64, 80
Courture, N., 169
Cowan, W., 65
Cullen, J. L., 180
Cunicelli, C., 23
Cunningham, D. J., 23
Cunningham, J. G., 78

Daley, B. J., 51
Danthiir, V., 74
Darling, S., 109, 162
Davidson, J. E., 154
Day, J. D., 154, 166, 180
Dean, D., 35, 150, 151
Della, Sala, S., 109, 162
DeLoache, J. S., 60, 89, 91, 138, 140, 166

Demetriou, A., 17, 19
Dennison, R. S., 44, 45, 46, 154
Denoncourt, I., 169
Descartes, R., 14
Deshler, D., 6
Desoete, A., 165, 180
Dewey, J., 13, 15, 16, 21, 33
Dienes, Z., 162
Digby, G., 116
Dinsmore, D. L., 3, 4, 5
Dixon, R. A., 65, 67, 80, 95, 96, 98, 102, 113, 114
Dominowksi, R. L., 24
Douglas, G., 168
Duffy, T., 23
Dunlosky, J., 4, 59, 65, 71, 72, 74, 76, 78, 107, 113

Efklides, A., 1, 2, 3, 4, 5, 17, 19, 74, 155, 166, 170, 172, 173, 174, 175
Elder, L., 30, 33, 35
Ellery, S., 23
Elliott, J., 7, 187
Ellis, D., 168
Emont, N. C., 180
Ennis, R. H., 30, 31, 32, 33
Ertmer, P. A., 47, 48
Estrada, M. T., 145
Eteläpelto, A., 158
Everson, H., 2, 4, 72

Ferrara, R. A., 1, 3, 4, 5, 6, 77, 91, 95, 136, 137, 140, 154, 169, 220
Ferry, B., 50, 52
Fischer, K. W., 34
Flavell, E. R., 44
Flavell, J. H., 1, 2, 3, 4, 5, 8, 17, 18, 19, 44, 45, 47, 51, 60, 61, 64, 65, 66, 67, 68, 74, 80, 82, 83, 85, 86, 87, 88, 89, 90, 93, 94, 95, 96, 97, 98, 100, 101, 102, 105, 111, 120, 127, 128, 129, 130, 131, 132, 135, 152, 155, 158, 159, 169, 170, 172, 173, 180, 183
Fletcher, K. L., 117
Fletcher, P. C., 109
Fox, E., 4, 44
Freire, P., 44
Friebert, S. E., 67, 144
Friedrichs, A. G., 60, 61, 65, 66, 87, 111
Friedrichsen, G., 2, 154, 166
Funnell, M., 71, 72

Gage, N. L., 17, 60
Gagné, R. M., 7

Galbraith, P., 23
Garcia-Mila, M., 150, 151, 155
Garner, R., 4, 156, 160, 165, 166, 170, 172, 180, 181
Gaskins, I. W., 23
Gathercole, S. E., 95, 102
Gensemer, E., 23
Georghiades, P., 4
Ghatala, E. S., 102, 117, 144
Gobbo, C., 65
Goldsmith, M., 102, 105, 107
Goos, M., 23
Gould, O. N., 113
Goulet, G., 169
Gourgey, A. F., 168, 176, 181
Gray, C., 109, 162
Green, F. L., 44
Greene, M., 24
Greene, M. J., 72
Gregg, M., 29, 46
Gregson, M., 7, 187
Grimes, P. W., 4

Habermas, J., 24, 44
Hacker, D. J., 3, 4, 19, 60, 72, 73, 75, 77, 78, 129, 154, 166
Hagen, J. W., 64, 77, 78, 79, 89
Hale, C., 65, 68, 85, 101, 142, 144, 145, 146, 180
Hall, L. K., 76
Hanley, G. L., 39, 47
Hannafin, M. J., 45, 60, 100, 117, 145, 181
Harper, B., 50
Harris, P. L., 68
Hart, J. T., 63, 64, 69, 71, 77, 78, 81, 87, 95, 111
Hartley, K., 152
Hartman, H. J., 35, 38, 46, 95, 155, 156, 160, 165, 169, 176, 180
Hattie, J., 168
Hatton, N., 51
Hauenstein, A. D., 193
Healy, A., 100
Hedberg, J., 50
Henson, R. N. A., 109
Hertzog, C., 65, 67, 72, 80, 95, 96, 98, 102, 113, 114
Higgins, S., 7, 187
Hilbert, D., 1
Hine, A., 39, 50, 51, 52
Hirst, W., 109, 111
Hmelo, C., 50
Hoeffel, E. C., 17, 18, 44

Hofer, B. K., 37
Howard-Rose, D., 169
Howe, M. L., 96, 113
Hoyt, J. D., 60, 61, 65, 66, 87, 111
Huberman, A. M., 5, 6
Huet, N., 117
Huffman, L. F., 117
Hultsch, D. F., 113

Ignazi, S., 180
Inhelder, B., 17, 18, 19
Iran-Nejad, A., 29, 46
Izaute, M., 71, 72, 162

Jacob, E., 24
Jacobs, J. E., 154, 155, 156, 157, 160, 162, 165, 166
Jacoby, L. L., 3
James, W., 16, 44, 59, 63, 69, 70, 77, 94
Jameson, K. A., 71, 72, 73, 74, 76
Janowsky, J. S., 71, 72, 109, 111
Jausovec, N., 75, 81
Johnson, J. W., 65, 68
Johnston, M. B., 144
Jonassen, D. H., 7, 8, 24, 44, 45, 50, 52, 156, 193
Joyner, M. H., 65, 66, 67, 68, 95, 96, 111, 113

Kail, R. V., 89, 102, 117
Kant, I., 21
Kaplan, D., 150, 151
Keeler, M. L., 116
Keleman, W. L., 72, 73
Kelley, C. M., 3
Kelly, M., 65, 68
Kemmis, S., 16, 24, 28, 46
Keogh, R., 15
Keselman, A., 150, 151
Kidder, D. P., 72
King, P. M., 15, 25, 33, 34
Kingsley, P. R., 64, 77, 78, 79
Kinzer, C. K., 50
Kitchener, K. S., 3, 15, 25, 33, 34
Klausmeier, H. J., 5
Kleitman, S., 74
Kluwe, R. H., 2, 4, 60, 85, 102, 154, 155, 156, 160, 166
Knopf, M., 96
Kobasigawa, A., 79
Koriat, A., 68, 71, 72, 73, 74, 76, 78, 102, 105, 107, 162
Körkel, J., 96
Kornell, N., 73

Kozminsky, E., 51
Krathwohl, D. R., 7, 8, 193
Kreutzer, M. A., 60, 61, 66, 89
Kuhlmann, F., 13
Kuhn, D., 1, 24, 33, 35, 37, 128, 147, 150, 151, 155, 160
Kuiper, R., 40
Kurtz-Costes, B., 65, 66, 67, 68, 95, 96, 111, 113

Lajoie, S. P., 50
Langford, G., 1, 4
Langrehr, D., 4, 15, 24, 44, 154
Larochelle, S., 71, 72
Lawson, M. J., 154
Lawton, S. C., 66, 69, 77, 78, 118
Leal, L., 66
Lee, V. A., 71, 72, 73, 74, 76
Leonard, C., 60, 61, 66, 89
Leonesio, R. J., 71, 72, 73, 94, 95, 102, 103
Levin, J. R., 102, 117, 144
Levy-Sadot, R., 68, 72
Lewis, C., 4, 116
Light, L. L., 113
Lin, X., 50
Lindauer, B. K., 79, 89, 101, 166
Lindsay, P. H., 66
Linn, M. C., 19
Lipman, M., 15, 30, 33, 34, 35, 38, 193, 216
Lipson, M., 155, 160, 165
Locke, E. A., 169
Locke, J., 13
Lockl, K., 3, 65, 66, 67, 85, 93, 95, 96, 120, 123, 156, 165
Lockyer, L., 50
Lodico, M. G., 117
Loughlin, S. M., 3, 4, 5
Lyons, W., 14, 43

Ma'ayan, H., 74
McAlpine, L., 15, 46, 50, 128
McCarrell, N., 60
McCombs, B. L., 168, 169
McCracken, D. J., 13
McCrindle, A. R., 51
McDonald-Miszczak, L., 113
McNeil, D., 63, 64, 69, 71, 78, 87, 95, 111
Madigan, S. A., 60
Marescaux, P.-J., 162
Marine, C., 117
Markman, E. M., 66, 77

Markus, H., 180
Marra, R. M., 50
Martin, B. L., 8, 193
Marzano, R. J., 166
Mathews, R., 162
Maule, R. J., 4
Mayer, R. E., 169
Mazzoni, G., 65
Meacham, J. A., 180
Meichenbaum, D., 154
Metallidou, Y., 17, 19, 172
Metcalfe, J., 4, 13, 65, 69, 71, 72, 73, 74, 75, 76, 78, 81, 109
Mezirow, J., 15, 28, 29, 33, 34, 35, 46
Miles, M. B., 5, 6
Miller, J., 7, 169, 187
Miller, P. H., 1, 3, 8, 17, 18, 19, 60, 95, 180
Miller, S. A., 1, 3, 8, 17, 18, 19, 60, 95, 180
Milstead, M., 65, 68, 85, 101, 142, 144, 145, 146
Miner, A. C., 71, 72, 76, 78
Moe, A., 4
Moely, B. E., 79
Moon, J. A., 15, 24, 25
Moran, D., 14
Moseley, D., 7, 187
Moshman, D., 2, 3, 7, 17, 18, 19, 21, 22, 25, 27, 95, 154, 155, 156, 160, 165, 166, 216
Muthukrishna, N., 4, 101, 144, 145, 146, 166, 180

Narens, L., 1, 3, 71, 72, 73, 74, 75, 76, 80, 103, 105, 106, 107, 108, 154, 173
Neisser, U., 166
Nelson, T. O., 1, 3, 4, 64, 71, 72, 73, 75, 78, 79, 80, 94, 95, 103, 105, 106, 107, 108, 154, 173
Newby, T. J., 47, 48
Newman, H., 39, 50, 52
Newton, D., 7, 187
Newton, E. V., 51
Nhouyvanisvong, A., 71
Niemivirta, M., 173
Nisbet, J., 48, 154, 166
Nisbett, R. E., 46
Norman, D. A., 66
Novak, J., 7, 50
Nyberg, S. E., 1, 72, 73

O'Hara, C., 23
Olson, D., 35, 68

Osman, M. E., 45, 60, 100, 117, 145, 181
O'Sullivan, J. T., 65, 66, 67, 73, 80, 85,
  95, 96, 100, 101, 102, 113, 116, 142,
  144, 145, 146

Pak, P. G., 14
Palincsar, A. S., 3, 23, 24, 77, 95, 100,
  116, 134, 136, 137, 138, 140, 152,
  155
Pallier, G., 74
Palmer, B. C., 4, 15, 24, 44, 154
Paris, A. H., 168, 169
Paris, S. G., 4, 46, 79, 89, 95, 101, 154,
  155, 156, 157, 160, 162, 165, 166, 168,
  169, 172, 180
Parkin, A. J., 109
Paul, R., 30, 33, 35
Peacock, L., 39, 50, 52
Pearsall, S., 150, 151
Pearson, M., 25, 28
Peck, V., 64, 78, 79
Perego, P., 180
Perfect, T. J., 74, 78
Perkins, D., 35
Perlmutter, M., 2, 3, 4, 13, 59, 60, 65,
  66, 69, 71, 78, 79, 80, 91, 93, 94, 95,
  111, 155
Perner, J., 162
Perry, W. G., 37
Phillips, J. A., 35
Phillips, L. J., 4
Piaget, J., 17, 18, 19, 20
Pintrich, P. R., 37, 44, 45, 95, 154, 155,
  156, 158, 160, 165, 166, 169
Pithers, R. J., 33, 35
Plato, 13
Plucker, J., 17
Plude, D. J. 107
Polanyi, M., 128
Pressley, M., 65, 66, 67, 68, 73, 80, 85,
  95, 96, 100, 101, 102, 116, 117, 127,
  142, 144, 145, 146, 180, 218
Provost, M. C., 4
Pruyne, E., 34
Pugalee, D. K., 52
Purdie, N., 168

Rauch, S., 23
Rebok, G. W., 113
Reder, L., 71, 72, 76, 78, 103, 105, 111,
  162
Reeve, R. A., 44, 137, 140, 141
Reeves, T. C., 50
Reid, M. K., 144

Rellinger, E., 101, 142, 144, 145, 146,
  180
Renshaw, P., 23
Resnick, L. B., 38, 216
Reynolds, C. R., 109
Richards, F. A., 17, 18
Richards, L., 6
Richards, T. J., 6
Riconscente, M., 4, 44
Riefer, D., 72
Rimor, R., 51
Robinson, A. E., 72
Roebers, C. M., 74
Roehler, L. R., 23
Roeyers, H., 165, 180
Rogoff, B., 23
Romine, C., 109
Ronning, R. R., 33, 37
Rosenthal, D. M., 43, 44, 45
Ross, G., 23
Ryan, E. B., 154, 166, 180
Ryle, G., 5, 43, 44, 155

Salatas, H., 65, 68
Salomon, G., 35
Samuels, M., 4
Scardamalia, M., 24
Schatschneider, C. W., 67, 144
Schneider, W., 3, 65, 66, 67, 68, 71, 72,
  73, 76, 85, 93, 95, 96, 102, 103, 116,
  120, 123, 144, 145, 156, 165
Schoenfeld, A. H., 3, 4, 155, 166, 176,
  180
Scholnick, E. K., 65, 68, 107
Schraw, G., 1, 2, 3, 4, 5, 44, 45, 46, 48,
  75, 95, 154, 155, 156, 160, 165, 166,
  180
Schraw, G. J., 33, 37
Schunk, D. H., 3, 4, 5, 168, 169, 218
Schunn, C. D., 103, 105, 111
Schwartz, B. L., 69, 71, 72, 76, 78, 95,
  107, 109
Schwebel, M., 1, 24
Scott, T., 23
Secules, T. J., 50
Sheffer, L., 74
Shimamura, A. P., 71, 72, 105, 109, 111
Short, E. J., 67, 144
Shucksmith, J., 48, 154, 166
Shuell, T. J., 157
Siegel, H., 19, 30, 33, 37
Simons, P. R. J., 180
Simpson, G. G., 7
Sims-Knight, J., 60

Sinclair, G. P., 100
Sinkavich, F. J., 71, 74, 180
Sinnott, J. D., 17, 18, 19, 180
Sitko, B., 46
Six, L., 23
Slife, B. D., 1
Slusarz, R., 160
Smiley, S. S., 77, 80, 134, 155
Smith, D., 25, 28, 51
Smith, S, M., 71
Soden, R., 33, 35
Son, L. K., 72, 73, 76
Sorabji, R., 13
Spearman, C., 13, 102
Spinoza, B., 14
Squire, L. R., 71, 72, 109, 111
Stablum, F., 103, 105, 109
Stanovich, K. G., 79
Sternberg, R. J., 1, 18, 19, 38, 154, 162, 176, 180
Stuss, D. T., 44, 109
Sun, R., 160, 162
Suzuki Slakter, N. S., 117
Swanson, H. L., 116
Swindal, J., 25, 28

Tama, M. C., 35
Tan, S. C., 24
Tessmer, M., 7, 8, 44, 45, 156, 193
Tobias, S., 2, 4, 72
Travers, S. H. 65, 68
Trepanier, M. L., 115
Trivelli, C., 109, 162
Tsai, C., 24, 34, 35, 180
Tsapkini, K., 71, 72
Tsiora, A., 172, 173, 174, 175
Tulving, E., 44, 60, 109
Turgeon, A. J., 24
Turner, L. A., 100, 101, 144, 145, 146, 180
Tychynski, D., 113

Udell, W., 150, 151, 155
Umilta, C., 103, 105, 109
Underwood, B. J., 73
Urmson, J. O., 14, 44

van Deusen, R. M., 38, 216
Van Hout-Wolters, B. H. A. M., 3, 4
van Overschelde, J. P., 107
Vauras, M., 170, 172, 173

Veenman, M. V. J., 3, 4
Vermunt, J. D., 166, 180
Vianello, R., 47
Vockell, E., 38, 216
Vohs, K. D., 168
Vojnovich, C. M., 39
Volet, E. E., 172
Vygotsky, L. S., 23, 24, 169

Wagoner, S. A., 181
Walker, D., 15
Wambold, C., 102
Wang, S., 50
Waters, H. S., 117
Weaver, S. L., 78
Weed, K. A., 154, 166, 180
Weinert, F. E., 1, 3, 46, 67, 80, 93, 95, 96, 103
Weiss, J., 1
Wellman, H. M., 2, 3, 4, 5, 47, 60, 61, 64, 65, 66, 67, 68, 69, 78, 79, 80, 81, 82, 85, 86, 87, 88, 89, 90, 93, 94, 95, 96, 97, 98, 100, 101, 103, 105, 111, 115, 118, 120, 127, 128, 154, 155, 166, 170
Wells, A., 180
Wertsch, J. V., 23, 24
Weston, C. B., 15, 46, 50, 128
Wheeler, M. A., 44, 109
Wiebe, D., 75, 81
Wilen, W. W., 35
Wilkinson, R., 74
Wilson, T., 46
Winne, P. H., 168, 169
Winograd, P., 4, 46, 95, 154, 155, 156, 166, 172, 180
Wixson, K., 155, 160, 165
Wolters, C. A., 95, 154, 156, 168, 169
Wood, D. J., 23
Wood, P. K., 30, 34
Wright, R., 50

Yamauchi, H., 173
Yussen, S. R., 3, 4, 46, 60, 61, 68

Zajonc, R., 169, 180
Zan, R., 180
Zechmeister, E. B., 1, 72, 73
Zimmerman, B. J., 166, 168, 169
Zohar, A., 150, 151, 155
Zouzounis, J. A., 109, 111

Subject index

Page numbers in *italic* indicate figures and tables.

Ability, 95, 129
Academic self-concept, 173, 176
Accessibility model, 72
Act of knowing, 44
Affective beliefs, 176, 180
Agency, 72, 169
Aids, 14
Amplification diagrams, 6
Argumentation, 19, 23, 24, 26, 27
Aristotle, 13, 16, 59
Associationism, 59
Attributional beliefs, 144, 145, 155
Augustine, 14
Auto criticism, 13
Automatic processes, 160, 162
Autonoetic awareness, 13, 44
Awareness, 15, *see also* Self-awareness
Axiomatisation, 20–21, 27

BACEIS model, 38
Beliefs
    about motivations, 158, 159
    affective beliefs, 176, 180
    critical reflection, 28
    critical thinking, 30–31, 32
    knowledge of memory, 95
    memory, 67, 69, 83, 96–97, 113–118,
        119
    person metacognitive knowledge,
        129–130
    personal beliefs about knowing
        abilities, 155
    problem solving, 180
    reflection, 15, 16
    self-competence, 168
    strategy use, 144, 145, 146, 147

Categories of metamemory, 93–121
Children
    feeling-of-knowing phenomena,
        78–79
    metamemory, 66, 116–117
    problem-solving processes, 34
'Cogito, ergo sum', 14
Cognition, 1
Cognitive actions, 128, 129, 133
Cognitive development
    memory development, 89, 91
    Piaget's theory, 17–20
Cognitive goals, 128–129, 131, 133, 183
Cognitive knowledge, 157
Cognitive monitoring, 2, 127, 128–134,
    135
Cognitive operative system, 61, *62*
Cognitive problem, 131–132
Cognitive strategies, 128, 129, 133
Cognitive subgoals, 128–129, 133
Cognitive subtasks, 128–129, 133
Cognitive tasks, 128–129, 133
Cognitive tools, 50
Collaboration, 23, 29, 32
Commission error, 72
Complex learning situations and
    domains, 144
Complex problem solving, 24, 129, 140,
    159, 160, 169, 216
Complex thinking, 35, 37, 38, 42
Comprehension monitoring, 180–181
Concept mapping, 40, 50–51
Conceptual framework of
    metacognition, 6–7, 187, *188*, *189*,
    190, *191*, *192*
Conditional knowledge, 155, 156,
    165–166, *167*

Conditional metacognitive knowledge, *195, 206*
Confidence judgments, 74
Connotative knowledge, 158
Conscious processes, 162
Consciousness, reflection and introspection, 43–46, 53
Constitutive memory, 61
Construct development, 5–6
Content of knowledge, 44
Context
  metacognitive experiences, 172
  metacognitive knowledge, 129
  strategy knowledge, 144, 146
  strategy use, 165–166
Contextual conditions, 166
Contextual knowledge, 155, 165
Control
  control processes as metacognition, 2
  memory development, 63
  metacognitive experiences, 173
  problem solving, 16
  regulation of cognition, 186
  regulation of memory, 91, 102–103, 105–113, 119–120
Cooperation, 23, 32
Creative judgment, 34
Criteria, 30
Critical ability, 33
Critical consciousness, 44
Critical knowing, 28–29, 30
Critical problematisation, 44
Critical reflection, 28–30, *31*, 41, 42, 215
Critical self-reflection, 34
Critical thinking
  abilities, 32
  beliefs, 30–31, 32
  components and facilitators, 32
  metacognition, 35, 37–41, 42, 215
  reflective judgment, 33–34, 37
  self-reflection, 37
  skilful thinking, 30–41
Critical thinking journals, 39

Decision making, 15
Declarative knowing, 147, 150,
Declarative knowledge, 136, 137–138, 155, 156–160, *161*
Declarative metacognitive knowledge, 129, *194, 198–202*
Declarative metamemory, 83, 84, 91, 95, 96–99, *104*, 118–119, 183
Declarative person metamemory, 97, 119

Declarative strategy knowledge, 145, 147
Declarative strategy metamemory, 97, 119
Declarative task metamemory, 97, 119
Deliberate memorization, 64
Deliberate memory, 64
Deliberate remembering, 64, 83
Descartes, R., 14
Dewey, J., 15–16
Dialectic reflection, 22, 23–24, 27, 28
Dialectical thinking, 32, 33
Dialogical thinking, 32
Dialogue, 23
Direct-access, 68, 71–72
Direct-link approach, 68
Domain knowledge, 157
Doubt, 15, 16, 169

Ease-of-learning judgments, 72, 73
Educational taxonomies, 7–8
Emancipatory learning, 32
Emotions, 169, 180
Epistemic assumptions, 34
Epistemic cognition, 151
Epistemic knowledge, 66–67
Epistemic understanding, 151, 152
Epistemological knowing, 37
Epistemological meta-knowing, 150, 151, 152
Epistemological understanding, 151, 152
Estimate of solution correctness, 174–175
Evaluation, 37
Exam preparation, 73
Executive functioning, 2, 102, 109, 111, *112*, 120, 121, 138, 140–142, 145, 147, 166, *196, 208–210*
Executive processes, 3, 145, 147
Experience, 61, 71, 130, 172
Expert learners, 47
Explicit control, 105
Explicit knowledge, 162
Explicit metacognitive experiences, 173
Eyewitness testimony, 74

Facets of metamemory, 86–88
Fallible knowledge, 136
Far transfer, 45
Feedback, 173
Feeling and knowing phenomena, 63–64, 69–79, 80–81, 107
Feeling of confidence, 174, 176
Feeling of difficulty, 74, 174, 176

Feeling of familiarity, 74, 174, 176
Feeling of satisfaction, 74, 174, 176
Feeling-of-warmth judgments, 75
Feelings, *see* Metacognitive feelings
Formal operations stage, 17–19
Formalisation, 20–21, 27
Frontal lobe, 109, 111, 120, 121
Fuzzy concepts, 3, 5

General and abstract knowledge, 150
General strategy knowledge, 144, 146
Goal setting, 145
Goal specification, 166
Goals, 50, *see also* Cognitive goals
Good Information Processing Model,
    101, 127, 142, 144–147, *148, 149*
Good Strategy User Model, *see* Good
    Information Processing Model

Habermas' theory of self-reflection,
    24–25
Higher-order reasoning, 17–20, 21, 26
Higher-order thinking, 38, 42, 145–146,
    216
Hot cognitions, 169
Hypotheses, 19
Hypothetico-deductive reasoning, 19

'I think, therefore I am', 14
Impersonal knowledge, 150
Implicit control, 105
Implicit metacognitive experiences, 173
Implicit processes, 160, 162
Inefficacious thinking, 169
Inference, 21–23, 27
Inferential reasoning, 137
Inferential view, 72
Informed strategy knowledge, 144, 146
Inner perception, 44
Inner speech, 23–24, 26
Insight, 75
Inter-individual differences, 130, 133,
    158
Internal verbalisation, 23–24, 26, 27, 28,
    169
Interpsychological functioning, 24, 26
Intra-individual differences, 129–130,
    133, 158
Intrapsychological functioning, 24, 26
Intrinsic context, 172
Introspection 14, 27, 43–44, 53
Introspective knowledge, 83
Intuitions, 129–130
Involuntary remembering, 83

Journal keeping, 39, 40, 50, 51–52
Judgment
    creative judgment, 34
    criteria, 30
    knowledge of memory, 95
    metacognitive experiences, 172
    metamemory, 67, 69
    problem solving, 15, 16
    prospective judgment, 75
    reflective judgment, 15, 33–34
    reflective judgment model, 15, 25
    self-judgments, 169
    see also Metacognitive judgments
Judgment of agency, 72
Judgment of confidence, 74
Judgment of knowing, 72, 73
Judgment of learning, 72, 73, 174
Judgment of performance, 72
Judgment of prose, 73
Judgment of solution correctness, 74,
    174–175, 176
Judgment of uncertainty, 72, 73
Justifications, 31

'Know thyself', 14
Knowing, 82, *85*, 91
Knowing about knowing, 82, 83, 84, 91,
    96–99, *194, 198–202*
Knowing how, 128, 147, 150, 160
Knowing how to know, 82, 83–84,
    91–92, 100–102, *195, 203–205*
Knowing process, 147
Knowing strategy effectiveness, 137,
    138
Knowing that, 136, 147
Knowing what, 136
Knowing what you know and do not
    know, 137
Knowing what you need to know,
    137
Knowing when, where and why, *195,
    206*
Knowing when you know and when you
    do not know, 137
Knowledge
    action and, 68
    critical thinking, 37
    memory retrieval, 71, 81
    regulatory processes, 136
    self-reflection, 25
Knowledge about cognition, 134
Knowledge of cognition, 134, 136–138,
    139, 155–166, *167,* 184–186, *194–195,*
    197

Knowledge of memory, 60, 63–64, *65*, 83, 93, 94–102, 118–119, 120, 183–184
Knowledge of others, 158–159, 162–163, 185
Knowledge of self, *see* Self-knowledge
Knowledge of strategies, 150–151, 152, 186
Knowledge of strategy attributes, 144, 146
Knowledge of task context including sensitivity, 159, 185
Knowledge of task objectives, 150, 151, 152
Korsakoff's syndrome, 109, 111

Language, 95
Late-developing knowledge, 136
Learning
    critical reflection, 29
    expert learners, 47
    internal verbalisation, 23–24
    judgment of, 72, 73, 174
    move from social cognitive to metacognitive process, 24, 26
    self-knowledge, 14
    thinking and reflection, 15
Learning disabilities, 78, 116–117
Logic, 19

Mathematical disability, 116
Meaningful goals, 145
Meaningful situations, 83–84
Memorisation strategies, 60, 61–63, 83
Memory and memory monitoring
    awareness, 95
    beliefs, 67, 69, 83, 96–97, 113–118, 119
    Brown's taxonomy, 82–85, *86*
    categories, 85–86
    constitutive memory, 61
    deliberate memory, 64
    development, 60, 61–63, 89, 91
    early views on, 59
    experience, 71
    feeling and knowing phenomena, 69–79, 81
    foundation of metamemory, 63–65
    knowledge and, 71, 81
    knowledge of memory, 60, 63–64, *65*, 83, 93, 94–102, 118–119, 120, 183–184
    performance and metamemory, 67
    reconstruction, 83–84

reflection, 13–14, 81
regulation, 91, 93–94, 102–103, 105–113, 119, 120
relationship to metamemory, 65–69, *70*
schemas, 96
self-efficacy, 98, 113–118, 119
short-term memory, 78
strategy training, 116–117
see also Metamemory
Mental imagery, 13–14
Mental reflexivity, 46
Meta, use of term, 1
Meta-knowing, 37, 128, 147, 150–152, *153*, *194–195*, *197*
Meta-level, 106–107
Metaattention, 46
Metacognition
    conceptual foundation, 3–4
    conceptual framework, 6–7, 187, *188*, *189*, *190*, *191*, *192*
    critical thinking, 35, 37–41, 42, 215
    difficulties in defining, 4
    difficulty of the construct, 3
    distinction between cognition and metacognition, 1
    distinction between meta and cognition, 1
    first operational definition, 1–3
    fuzziness, 3, 5
    major conceptual contributions, 48, *49*
    models, 127–154
    obscurity, 3
    problems with the term, 2
    research possibilities, 217–218
    self-knowledge, 44–45
    self-regulation, 168, 169
    simplistic descriptions, 4
    taxonomy, 7–8, 187, 193, *194–214*
    theoretical framework, 4–5
Metacognitive acquisition procedures, 145, 147
Metacognitive attitude, 47–48
Metacognitive beliefs, 180
Metacognitive competence, 150
Metacognitive conceptualisation, 47–48
Metacognitive control, 47, 180
Metacognitive experiences, 74, 128, 129, 130–131, 134, 170, 172–176, *177*, *178*, *179*, 187, *196*, *211–213*
Metacognitive feelings, 74, 172, 173, 174–175, 176, *178*, 187, *211–212*

Metacognitive judgments, 74, 174–175, 176, *179*, 187, *212–213*
Metacognitive knowing, 37, 147, 150, 151
Metacognitive knowledge, 47–48, 128, 129–131, 133, 155–166, *167*, 172–173, 180, 184–186, *194–195*, *197*
Metacognitive knowledge about specific strategies, 144, 146
Metacognitive knowledge of strategies, 159
Metacognitive monitoring, 180
Metacognitive operations, 150
Metacognitive reflection, 47–48
Metacognitive regulation, 166, 168–170, *171*
Metacognitive skills, 138, 140, 142, 166, 168–170, *171*, *196*
Metacognitive strategies, 131, 168
Metacognitive tool for students' reflections, 51
Metacomprehension, 46, 134, 180–181
Metamemorial knowledge, 83
Metamemory, 3, 46, 59–81, 183–184
  beliefs, 114
  categories, 93–121
  children, 66, 116–117
  facets, 86–88
  foundation of, 82–92
  influences on, 113–118
  judgments, 67, 69
  memory monitoring, 63–65
  memory performance, 67
  memory self-efficacy, 113–114, *115*
  regulation processes, 93–94
  relationship to memory, 65–69, *70*
  research possibilities, 216–217
  strategy training, 116–117
  taxonomy, 85–89, *90*
Metamemory about strategies (MAS), 101, 142
Metamemory acquisition procedures (MAPs), 101, 142
Metamentation, 46
Metaprocedural reorganisation, 6
Metastrategic competence, 150
Metastrategic knowing, 150, 151, 152, 160
Metastrategic knowledge, 150–151, 152
Metastrategic operations, 150
Metastrategic skill, 37
Metastrategic understanding, 150–151, 152
Metatask, 150, 152

Methods, 14
Mind mapping, 50
Mind tools, 50
Mnemonic mediation, 60
Mnemonic strategies, 83–84
Mnemonic training, 68
Models of metacognition, 127–154
Monitoring
  accuracy, 166
  clarity, 166
  memory development, 63
  metacognitive experiences, 131, 172, 173
  online, 172
  problem solving, 15, 16
  prospective, 75, 107
  regulation of cognition, 186
  regulation of memory, 91, 102–103, 105–113, 119–120
  retrospective, 107
  strategy application, 144
Motivation
  beliefs about, 158, 159
  critical thinking, 32
  metacognitive experiences, 173
  self-regulation, 169
  strategy use, 144, 162
Multimedia journals, 52

Near transfer, 45
Need for attainment, 168
New knowledge, 28
Node-link networks, 96

Object-level, 106–107
Omission error, 72
Online awareness, 172
Online metacognition, 172
Online monitoring of cognition, 172

Performance judgments, 72
Person declarative knowledge, 158–159, 185
Person declarative metamemory, 97, 119
Person knowledge, 155, 158–159, 162–163
Person metacognitive knowledge, 129–130, 133, 158–159, 185
Person variable, 86, *87*, 88, 89, 95, 96–99, 114–118, 120
Personal agency, 169
Personal expectations of achievement, 168–169, 170

Personal knowledge, 150
Personal-motivational states, 146
Personal theories about knowing
 abilities, 155
Piaget's theories
 axiomatisation and formalisation,
  20–21, 27
 cognitive development, 17–20
Plans, 61
Plato, 59
Postformal stage, 19
Prefrontal cortex, 109, 111
Prior knowledge, 28
Problem setting, 131–132
Problem solving
 beliefs, 180
 complex problems, 24, 129, 140, 159,
  160, 169, 216
 critical reflection, 29–30
 differences between adults and
  children, 34
 executive functioning, 140–142
 knowledge of memory, 95
 reflection, 15–16
 self-knowledge, 45
Problematisation, 44
Procedural knowing, 147, 150
Procedural knowledge, 137, 138, 155,
 156, 160, 162–163, *164*
Procedural metacognitive knowledge,
 129, *195*, *203–205*
Procedural metamemory, 84, 91–92, 95,
 100–102, *103, 104*, 118–119, 183
Procedural strategy knowledge, 129,
 133, 145, 147
Procedural task knowledge, 163
Process monitoring, 166
Processes, 14
Processing rules, 100
Production rules, 100
Propositional knowledge, 157
Propositional manner, 157
Propositional reasoning, 19, 21, 26
Prospective judgment, 75
Prospective monitoring, 75, 107
Psychological space, 8

Reactions, 172
Reasoning
 critical thinking, 37
 higher-order reasoning, 17–20, 21,
  26
 inference, 21–23, 27
 reflection and, 14, 16–17, 26–27

Recall-judgment-recognition paradigm,
 78
Reconstruction, 83–84
Reflection, 13–27, 182–183
 awareness, 15
 beliefs, 15, 16
 consciousness, 43–46
 critical reflection, 28–30, *31*, 41, 42,
  215
 critical thinking, 33–34, 37
 dialectic, 22, 23–24, 27, 28
 formal operations, 17–19
 higher-order reasoning, 17–20, 21, 26
 historical foundations, 13–15
 inference, 21–23, 27
 introspection, 43–44, 53
 knowledge of cognition, 136–137
 learning, 15
 major conceptual contributions, 48,
  49
 memory, 13–14, 81
 metacognitive knowledge, 129, 133
 metacognitive reflection, 47–48
 metacognitive skills, 140, 142
 monitoring, 15
 problem solving, 15–16
 reasoning, 14, 16–17, 26–27
 regulation, 15
 regulation of cognition, 140
 research possibilities, 215–216
 self-awareness, 13, 16
 self-knowledge, 14, 16, 17, 21, 44–45
 self-regulation, 13, 27
 task knowledge and sensitivity, 159
 three senses of, 17–18
 tools, 50
 see also Self-reflection
Reflective abstraction, 20–21
Reflective awareness, 147
Reflective interpretation, 29
Reflective journals, 39, 40, 50, 51–52
Reflective judgment, 15, 33–34
Reflective judgment model, 15, 25
Reflexion, 44
Regulation
 problem solving, 15, 16
 strategy knowledge, 160
 see also Self-regulation
Regulation of cognition, 134, 136, 138,
 140–142, *143*, 166, 168–170, *171*,
 186–187, *196, 207–210*
Regulation of memory, 91, 93–94,
 102–103, 105–113, 119, 120
Regulation of skills, 138, 140, 141

Relational strategy knowledge, 145
Remembering, 13, 83, 94
Report writing, 50
Representational abilities, 61
Retrospection, 20–21
Retrospective metacognitive feelings, 174
Retrospective monitoring, 107
Rich structural knowledge, 137
Rules, 14, 100

Scaffolding, 23, 24, 35, 50
Schematic knowledge, 96
Schematic propositional networks, 96
Schemes, 61
Scientific theory building, 5–6
Second-degree operations, 19
Second-order cognitions, 1
Self-appraisal, 46, 155, 166
Self-awareness
    consciousness, 44
    executive functioning, 109, 111, *112*
    knowing about knowing, 83
    metacognitive knowledge, 155, 158
    motivation, 158
    reflection, 13, 16
    self-regulation, 169
Self-competence beliefs, 168
Self-concept
    metacognitive experiences, 173
    self-regulation, 169
    strategy use, 162
Self-consciousness, 44
Self-control, 17, 21
Self-correction, 17, 21, 33
Self-doubt, 169
Self-efficacy
    knowledge of cognition, 155
    memory, 98, 113–118, 119
    self-regulation, 169
    strategy use, 144, 162
Self-esteem, 144, 155
Self-imposed rationality, 22
Self-judgments, 169
Self-knowledge, 26, 43–54, 146
    consciousness, 44
    critical knowing and critical reflection, 28–29, 41
    introspection, 44
    knowledge of cognition, 136, 158–159, 162–163, 185
    knowledge of memory, 95
    learning, 14

link between reflection and introspection, 15
    metacognition, 44–45
    motivation, 158
    problem-solving, 45
    reflection, 14, 16, 17, 21, 44–45
Self-management of cognition, 166
Self-monitoring, 16, 102–103
Self-reflection
    critical self-reflection, 34
    critical thinking, 37
    Habermas' theory, 24–25
    knowledge of cognition, 155
    metacognitive experiences, 173
Self-regulated learners, 168–169, 170
Self-regulation
    metacognitive acquisition procedures, 145
    metacognitive experiences, 173
    problem solving, 16
    reflection, 13, 27
    regulation of cognition, 168–170, 186
    strategy use, 144
Self-reports of strategy use, 117
Self-system
    knowledge of cognition, 155, 162–163
    knowledge of memory, 95
    specific and general strategy knowledge, 144, 146–147
    strategy use, 162–163
Semantic knowledge, 137
Semantic networks, 50
Sensitivity, 86, *87*, 88, 89, 92, 95, 117–118, 120, 130, 133, 159, 163, 165–166, 172
Short-term memory, 78
Situational element, 144, 146
Skilful thinking, 30–41
Skill development and learning, 160
Social cognitive processes, 23
Social interaction, 23, 24
Social problem solving, 24
Socrates, 13
Specific and situational knowledge, 150
Specific metacognitive knowledge, 47–48
Specific strategy knowledge, 144, 146
Spinoza, B., 14
Stable knowledge, 136
Statable knowledge, 136
Stored metamemory, 96
Strategic processes, 37

Strategies, 14
Strategy application, 100–102, 144, 145, 147, 150, 163
Strategy attribute knowledge, 144, 146
Strategy declarative metamemory, 97, 119
Strategy knowledge, 67, 134, 144, 146, 155, 159–160, 165–166
Strategy metacognitive knowledge, 130, 186
Strategy monitoring, 144
Strategy selection, 144, 145, 146, 147, 150
Strategy training, 116–117, 145
Strategy transfer, 100
Strategy variable, 86, 88, 89, 95, 96–99, 100–101, 114–118, 120
Structured questioning, 40
Study time, 73
Subclasses, 7
Subtaxa, 7
Subtypes, 7
Suppositional thinking, 32

Task complexity, 80, 91
Task declarative metamemory, 97, 119
Task demands, 130, 133, 159
Task information, 130, 133, 159
Task interest, 129
Task knowledge, 150, 155, 159, 163, 165
Task metacognitive knowledge, 130, 133, 159, 185
Task objectives, 150, 151, 152
Task sensitivity, 163, 165, 172
Task variable, 86, *87*, 88, 89, 95, 96–99, 100–101, 114–118, 120

Taxonomies, 7
  memory, 82–85, *86*
  metacognition, 7–8, 187, 193, *194–214*
  metamemory, 85–89, *90*
Teacher education and training, 218
Theory building, 5–6
Theory of mind, 68
Thinking, 14, 15, 16
  higher-order thinking, 38, 42, 145–146, 216
  see also Critical thinking
Third-order reasoning, 19
Tip-of-the-tongue phenomenon, 69, 71, 72, 76, 77, 78, 94–95
Tool use, 50
Trace-access, 68, 71–72
Training
  mnemonics, 68
  strategy use, 116–117, 145
  teachers, 218
Trans-situational metacognitive skill, 138, 140, 141
Transfer, 45
Transferability, 145

Uncertainty judgments, 72, 73
Unconscious processes, 160, 162
Universal cognitions, 130, 133, 158

Verbal reports, strategy use, 117
Verbalisation, 23–24, *25*, 26, 27, 28, 169
Volitional control, 169
Vygotsky, L. S., 23

Zone of proximal development, 23